P9-DDV-579

Three Studies in the Renaissance:

Sidney, Jonson, Milton

ENGLISH PETRARKE: A STUDY OF SIDNEY'S
ASTROPHEL AND STELLA

RICHARD B. YOUNG

BEN JONSON'S MASQUES

W. TODD FURNISS

THE IDEA OF NATURE IN MILTON'S POETRY

WILLIAM G. MADSEN

ARCHON BOOKS 1969

©Copyright, 1958, by Yale University Press
Reprinted 1969 with permission of Yale University Press
in an unaltered and unabridged edition

[*Yale Studies in English, Vol. 138*]

SBN: 208 00780 6
Library of Congress Catalog Card Number: 69-15695
Printed in the United States of America

Contents

ENGLISH PETRARKE:

A STUDY OF SIDNEY'S *ASTROPHEL AND STELLA*

by Richard B. Young

Preface

This study was originally submitted as a dissertation to the Faculty of the Yale Graduate School in candidacy for the Ph. D. degree. Its original condition is betrayed in more ways than I could wish, or alter. Among other difficulties, I hardly know any more how much of it is really mine and how much I owe to the people who had been or who were my teachers at the time it was undertaken. But I am conscious of, and anxious to acknowledge, a particular debt, and a great one, to Mr. Louis Martz, who first interested me in Sidney and in the poetic traditions of the Renaissance, who guided my reading, and who suffered my writing, however gladly only he can say.

To the editors of Yale Studies in English, whose assistance and generosity has made possible the publication of this study, I express my gratitude. And to my wife I would like to make what public restitution I can, for she listened to it all, more than once, and late at night.

R. B. Y.

Florence, May 29, 1957

Part 1

I

But truly many of such writings, as come under the banner of
unresistable love, if I were a mistress, would never perswade mee
they were in love: so coldly they applie firie speeches, as men that
had rather redde lovers writings, and so caught up certaine swelling Phrases, which hang togither like a man that once tolde me
the winde was at Northwest, and by South, because he would be
sure to name winds inough, then that in truth they feele those
passions, which easily as I thinke, may be bewraied by that same
forciblenesse or *Energia*, (as the Greeks call it of the writer).
. . . . so is it that hony-flowing Matrone *Eloquence*, apparrelled,
or rather disguised, in a Courtisanlike painted affectation. One
time with so farre fet words, that many seeme monsters, but must
seeme straungers to anie poore Englishman: an other time with
coursing of a letter, as if they were bound to follow the method
of a Dictionary: an other time with figures and flowers, extreemlie
winter-starved.

The Defence of Poesie [1]

You that do search for everie purling spring,
  Which from the ribs of old *Parnassus* flowes,
  And everie floure, not sweet perhaps, which growes
  Neare therabouts, into your Poesie wring.

You that do Dictionaries methode bring
  Into your rimes, running in ratling rowes:
  You that poore *Petrarchs* long deceased woes,
  With new-borne sighes and denisend wit do sing.

You take wrong waies: those far-fet helpes be such,
  As do bewray a want of inward tuch:
  And sure at length stolne goods do come to light.

---

1. *The Complete Works of Sir Philip Sidney*, ed. Albert Feuillerat (Cambridge, England, 1912-26), *3*, 41-2. Hereafter cited as *Works*.

But if (both for your love and skill) your name
    You seeke to nurse at fullest breasts of Fame,
    Stella behold, and then begin to endite.

                                    Astrophel and Stella, Sonnet 15 [2]

THE relation of form and content or, in Sidney's phrase, "manner and matter," which is the subject of the passages above, is a central issue in Sidney's criticism and in his poetry. As a critic he is writing in the Aristotelian tradition, elaborating a theory of imitation in which the relation of manner and matter is an aspect of the fundamental relation of Art—the imitation—and Nature, or Truth, or Reality—that which is imitated. As a poet he is writing within a fully articulated literary convention which is, at least in part, a "manner" supplied from the outside, related to the "matter" in question by the sanctions of tradition and the rules of the genre.

It is the conventional relation of manner and matter in contemporary love poetry that is criticized in both of the passages above. The passage from the *Defence* asserts that the conventional manner is farfetched; it departs from the matter, "those passions" of love that the poetry is supposed to be about.

The sonnet from *Astrophel and Stella* makes the same criticism, even adducing some of the same evidence. But the difference in context makes a radical difference in the status of the criticism, for the speaker here is a poet rather than a critic, and he raises the critical problem for rhetorical purposes. He is distinguishing his own from the conventional manner in order to assert his sincerity. Consequently, the critical problem, which is the subject matter of the *Defence*, becomes part of the rhetorical manner of *Astrophel and Stella.* As a matter of fact, it is a thoroughly Petrarchan manner, with all the authority of the master behind it.

                E certo ogni mio studio in quel tempo era
                    Pur di sfogare il doloroso core
                    In qualche modo, non d'acquistar fama.[3]

---

2. All quotations of Sidney's sonnets are from *The Countesse of Pembrokes Arcadia,* London, 1598. In a few cases the readings of the 1591 Quartos have been preferred, and in adopting them I have followed the edition of Alfred W. Pollard, *Sir Philip Sidney's Astrophel and Stella, Wherein the Excellence of Sweet Poesy is Concluded* (London, 1888). I have retained the punctuation of the 1598 text where possible, and where I have amended it I have tried to retain the effect of the original, which is extremely light and predominantly rhetorical.

3. Francesco Petrarca, Sonetto CCXCIII ("S' io avesse pensato"), *Le "Rime sparse,"* commentate da Ezio Chiorboli (Milano, 1924), p. 670. Hereafter cited as Petrarch.

And it is a mild paradox that, by the time of the Pléiade, to deny any Petrarchan affiliations is an established gambit of the Petrarchan poet.[4]

The sincerity, furthermore, that is being asserted is not just that of the poet but of the lover, Astrophel, a character in a love story. As a result, the problem of relation between manner and matter is placed at still another remove from the literary criticism of the *Defence*. It becomes part of the dramatic situation.

> I never dranke of *Aganippe* well,
>> Nor ever did in shade of *Tempe* sit:
>> And Muses scorne with vulgar braines to dwell,
>> Poore Layman I, for sacred rites unfit.
>
> Some do I heare of Poets furie tell,
>> But (God wot) wot not what they meane by it:
>> And this I sweare by blackest brooke of hell,
>> I am no pick-purse of anothers wit.
>
> How falles it then, that with so smooth an ease
>> My thoughts I speake, and what I speake doth flow
>> In verse, and that my verse best wits doth please?
>
> Guesse we the cause, what is it thus? fie, no:
>> Or so? much lesse: how then? sure thus it is:
>> My lips are sweet, inspired with *Stellas* kisse.

Sonnet 74

This poem follows the Second Song, in which Astrophel describes a kiss stolen from the sleeping Stella, and it deals with the difference between writing poems and stealing kisses, the one an artificial, the other an essential manner of loving. As Janet Scott has pointed out,[5] the poem has a most impressive ancestry ranging from Persius to the Pléiade, and that is precisely the point: the vehement denial of literary pretension in a poem so thoroughly literary is a joke in which the poet-lover, assuming the pose of ingenuousness and simplicity he finds in his models, makes fun of it by protesting too much; he insists on his homeliness ("Poore Layman I"), is clumsy in a studied and witty way ("[God wot] wot not what they meane by it"), swears his grim alliterative oath, and ends with a rhetorical guessing game. Astrophel is distinguishing himself from the conventional manner of his models (or of a sonnet like the one above) by means of parody, and the parody

---

4. See Robert J. Clement, "Anti-Petrarchism of the Pléiade," *MP*, *39* (1941-42), 15-21.
5. Janet G. Scott, *Les Sonnets Élisabéthains* (Paris, 1929), pp. 44-5.

itself constitutes a manner which enables him to demonstrate, even dramatize, the difference between writing and kissing, a difference expressed finally in the gaiety and exuberance which in this particular case make up the matter of love.

In this poem, then, the literary manner seems to stand not for an aspect of poetry but for poetry itself, and the literary relation of manner and matter for a larger, dramatic relationship. Both poems, as a matter of fact, illustrate a process, running throughout the sequence, of defining the speaker's individual attitudes by antithetical reference to the manners of the world about him. In this process all manners, all conventions, have the same status, whether specifically literary or not, as they threaten to obscure or impede the material interests of the lover. Thus, the preoccupations of the court society, the precepts of morality, the advice of friends, all are treated, like the conventional poetry, as artificial or irrelevant, representing manners that have little or nothing to do with the essential matter.

The literary manner, however, as it is also the manner of love, identifying the world of the poet-lover as the social manner identifies the world of the courtier, is the dominant one. And the lover's chief adversary in relation to the literary manner is not the poets but the lady—his *douce adversaire.* His assertion of sincerity is made to persuade her he is in love.

> *Stella* oft sees the verie face of wo
>   Painted in my beclowded stormie face:
>   But cannot skill to pitie my disgrace,
>   Not though thereof the cause herself she know:
>
> Yet hearing late a fable, which did show
>   Of Lovers never knowne, a grievous case,
>   Pitie thereof gate in her breast such place,
>   That from that sea deriv'd, teares spring did flow.
>
> Alas, if Fancy drawne by imag'd things,
>   Though false, yet with free scope, more grace doth breed
>   Then servants' wracke, where new doubts honor brings;
>
> Then thinke my deare, that you in me do reed
>   Of Lovers ruine some sad Tragedie:
>   I am not I, pitie the tale of me.
>
> Sonnet 45

Stella, like the conventional poets, is accused of indulging a passion that is purely literary, a fiction. Her sentimental susceptibility to love in fiction as opposed to Astrophel, love in fact, is a version of the typical schizophrenia—the Venus and Diana—of the conventional Petrarchan mistress. Astrophel's response to this phenomenon is to extend the parody of Sonnet 74 beyond the manner to the mimetic principle itself. If Art ("imag'd things/Though false") is more persuasive than Nature, then let Nature imitate Art: "I am not I, pitie the tale of me."

By going beyond the question of the particular illusion, the conventional manner, to illusion itself, this sonnet makes explicit an issue implicit in the others. As Levin has suggested, when literature is criticized as diverging from life some definition of life is necessarily involved.[6] For Astrophel the definition is easy. One of the functions of this sonnet is to define "life" in terms of his own individual experience; he can pretend to relinquish it only because he is so confident of it.

For his readers, however, it has not been so easy. What is the status of the actor calling attention to the stage he stands upon ("Nay then, God buy you an you talk in blank verse")? Is Astrophel "real" or really a tale? Critical evaluation of the sonnets seems more often than not to have been dictated by the answer to this question, and Sidney's critics have divided widely upon it. Those, like Lee, who emphasize the literary provenance of the sequence conclude that it is simply an exercise in the Petrarchan manner, with no real matter at all; those who emphasize the allusions to Sidney's own life and times conclude that it is the material record of biographical fact, which the manner serves less to express than to disguise.

Both points of view are not only allowed but invited by the sequence itself. They are, indeed, represented by the attitudes opposing each other in the poems we have been examining. But in the sequence they are presented as extreme limits of a continuous scale, poles between which the lover moves, the "life" he so confidently expresses generated by a dynamic relation to both. The development of *Astrophel and Stella* as a sequence is determined by the way in which the two extremes modify one another.

What I have been trying to show is that there is an analogy between the technical problems presented by the literary convention and the dramatic problems presented by the love story, and that it is not an accidental one. Sidney has exploited the technical problem, the poetic relation of manner and matter, as the chief means of presenting the dramatic problem, the relation of lady and lover. Midway between the two areas is the Janus-figure of the poet-lover looking in both directions: within the dramatic context toward the lady and beyond it toward the reader. The effect, finally, is to establish a unity of action incorpo-

6. Harry Levin, "Notes on Convention," *Perspectives in Criticism*, by Walter Jackson Bate and others (Harvard, 1950), p. 59.

rating the lover, the poet, and the reader, all engaged in the process of discovering and defining the relation of surface and essential, manner and matter, Art and Nature, in which lie both the dramatic vitality and the poetic merit of *Astrophel and Stella*.[7]

II

All Petrarchan poetry seems to share a fixed relation of lover to lady: the lady is always unobtainable—at least unobtained—the lover hopeless, or at least hapless; it is a permanent impasse. Petrarchan love is the attitude of the lover in this static situation, and it has really only two characteristics: first that it is frustrated, unfulfilled—the aubade is not a Petrarchan type of poem—and second, that it sets an extremely high value on the unobtainable lady, idealizing her either physically or spiritually, or most often both physically and spiritually, as in Petrarch. These two characteristics define the dominant Petrarchan forms, the idealizing description of the lady, the " blason,"

> Li occhi sereni e le stellanti ciglia,
>   La bella bocca, angelica, di perle
>   Piena e di rose e di dolci parole,
>
> Che fanno altrui tremar di meraviglia,
>   E la fronte, e le chiome, ch' a vederle
>   Di state, a mezzo dí, vincono il sole.[8]

and the introspective meditation, the Petrarchan definition of love.

> Pace non trovo, en non ò da far guerra;
>   E temo, e spero; et ardo, e son un ghiaccio;
>   E volo sopra 'l cielo, e giaccio in terra;
>   E nulla stringo, e tutto 'l mondo abbraccio.[9]

The defining features of these two forms, the elaborate lady in the blason, the elaboration of rhetorical pattern in the meditation, have the same status and perform the same function in the strategy of the Petrarchan poem. In the meditation, the attitude of the lover is treated directly and made available for contemplation by the rhetorical pattern;

7. This relation is approached from a different point of view by Hallet Smith, *Elizabethan Poetry*, Cambridge, Mass., 1952; see especially his discussion of " the problem of two audiences," pp. 147 ff. See also the remarks on " persona " and convention by Theodore Spencer, " The Poetry of Sidney," *ELH, 12* (1945), 251-78.
    8. Petrarch, CC (" Non pur quell' una bella ignuda mano "), p. 474.
    9. Petrarch, CXXXIV (" Pace non trovo "), p. 343.

in the blason, it is projected in the description of the lady who represents it. But in both cases the subject is love, the attitude of the speaker, as it is in all love poems; to assume that it is the lady is to mistake the beloved for love, the object for the subject, the manner for the matter.

" Most arts," says Pound, " attain their effects by the use of a fixed element and a variable."[1] Conventional poetry tends to suffer from hypertrophy of the fixed element and atrophy of the variable. And the reason is that it follows a genre theory of poetic, a shortcut in the Aristotelian process of mimesis: the place of the Nature to be imitated is taken by approved models, and the imitation itself is prescribed by rules of decorum. Thus, in a blason like Sonnet 9 of *Astrophel and Stella*, the attitude is as fixed as the situation; it is not generated by the particular structure but accepted by hypothesis and simply celebrated.

> Queene *Vertues* Court, which some call *Stellas* face,
>   Prepar'd by Natures choisest furniture,
>   Hath his front built of Alabaster pure;
> Gold is the covering of that stately place.

> The doore, by which sometimes comes forth her Grace,
>   Red Porphir is, which locke of pearle makes sure,
>   Whose porches rich (which name of cheekes endure)
> Marble mixt red and white do enterlace.

The decorum of the poem demands that we understand in terms of an abstract and general value, variously suggested by alabaster, gold, porphyry, and pearl, and not in terms of the monstrous, mineral idolatry the concrete details might suggest. Furthermore, the abstractness and impersonality leave a gap where the speaker ought to be, and it is signalized by tonelessness, or at least a monotone; it is public poetry, employing an editorial " I." The meditation differs only in that there is no object involved, just the rhetorical details that identify the attitude.

> Now that of absence the most irksome night
>   With darkest shade doth overcome my day;
>   Since *Stellas* eyes, wont to give me my day,
> Leaving my Hemisphere, leave me in night;

> Each day seemes long, and longs for long-staid night,
>   The night as tedious, wooes th' approach of day.
>   · · · · ·
> That living thus in blackest winter night,
> I feele the flames of hottest sommer day.
>   Sonnet 89

1. Ezra Pound, *ABC of Reading* (New Haven, 1934), p. 191.

The point of such a poem lies just in the iteration of the defining terms as a means of illustrating and rehearsing the conventional frustration.

Repetition without development is an adequate symbol, perhaps a definition, of the Petrarchan data as such. But the limitation of structure that corresponds to the restriction of situation leads to a ritualistic poetry, static rather than active; the rhetorical balance, the regular rhythms, the stylized ornament of the Petrarchan sonnet constitute a decorum that is the sign of formal orthodoxy. Among the rude mechanicals of the tradition, of whom Thomas Watson is the best example in English, it marks a poetry of stock response, one in which both the stimuli and the responses are organized into a formal rite.

Ritual seems to be involved in the function of most love conventions. In the background of the Petrarchan convention is the *Frauendienst* of courtly love, with more or less feudal formulae ("midons"), and of Neo-platonic love, with more or less Christian formulae. The distinctive formulae of the Petrarchan ritual are neither social nor metaphysical but verbal, the formulae of oxymoron, "dolce nemica," "viva morte . . . dilettoso male."

As in ritual, the subject matter of the convention is anterior to the actual performance. The function of the form is to generalize and universalize it, which in part explains the impersonal tone. Convention relies, as Levin observes, "on prior awareness and widespread acceptance." [2] It is therefore highly vulnerable to skeptical or heretical points of view and needs to insulate itself by various kinds of exorcism, which can be performed in part by the setting. The garden is the archetype of this kind of setting. In the Petrarchan poem, however, exorcism is frequently assumed as part of the conventional hypothesis, more a process of omission than of exclusion. In some cases the omissions are sweeping, and mean that there is no setting at all; Petrarchan love to this extent is like pastoral, in Greg's phrase, "love in vacuo" [3]—a vacuum that abhors nature, in the sense of finite natural forces or processes that have conclusions.

When there is one, the Petrarchan setting serves primarily to identify the symbols as belonging to the convention and therefore to be understood by its terms, and to isolate them as absolute, relative neither to the standards of the practical world nor to any actual achievement. In this respect it is similar to the settings of other love conventions—for example, the dream world of the medieval love complaint—and like them is strongly ritualistic in character. It corresponds, furthermore, to the two basic Petrarchan activities, idealization and lament,

2. Levin, "Notes on Convention," p. 59.
3. W. W. Greg, *Pastoral Poetry and Pastoral Drama* (London, 1906), p. 411.

and tends to be incorporated into the respective forms, the blason and the meditation. In the first, the ritualistic detail is simply transferred from the lady to the world around her; the attitude is identified by reference to a Nature saturated in the appropriate values, and purified of anything else.

> Clear Anker, on whose silver-sanded shore
> My soul-shrined saint, my fair Idea lies,
> O blessed brook, whose milk-white swans adore
> Thy crystal stream, refined by her eyes,
> Where sweet myrrh-breathing Zephyr in the spring
> Gently distils his nectar-dropping showers,
> Where nightingales in Arden sit and sing
> Amongst the dainty dew-empearled flowers.[4]

In the second, the process is reversed; the attitude is identified by alienation from an abstract, occasionally allegorized, harmony of Nature.

> Zefiro torna, e 'l bel tempo rimena,
> E i fiori e l'erbe, sua dolce famiglia,
> E garrir Progne, e pianger Filomena,
> E primavera candida e vermiglia.
> . . . . .
> E cantar augelletti, e fiorir piagge,
> E 'n belle donne oneste atti soavi
> Sono un deserto, e fere aspre e selvagge.[5]

The setting is used here to generalize the condition rehearsed elsewhere by the formula of oxymoron ("Pace non trovo") and by the extended conceit, say, of the shipwreck.

> Passa la nave mia colma d'oblio
> Per aspro mare, a mezza notte il verno,
> Enfra Scilla e Caribdi; et al governo
> Siede 'l signore, anzi 'l nimico mio,;[6] . . .

The condition is made absolute: the lover alienated from the lady is alienated from everything; his world, it has been suggested, is a Heracleitan world, in which "antagonism lies at the very heart of reality

4. Michael Drayton, "Idea," from Poems (1619), in *Poetry of the English Renaissance* 1509-1660, ed. J. William Hebel and Hoyt H. Hudson (New York, 1947), p. 289.
5. Petrarch CCCX, p. 702.
6. Petrarch, CLXXXIX, p. 450.

. . . 'Est in amore odium, et in pace bellum, et in consensione dis-
sensio.' "[7]

The need for a more effective exorcism than the convention itself
supplies is attested historically by the concurrent development with the
convention of satire of it, written in a good many cases by Petrarchan
poets. The principal target of such satire is the characteristic hyperbole, particularly the ritualism of the lady *in excelsis,* and occurs frequently as parody. Thus, Sidney's counter-blason of the bucolic Mopsa
in the *Arcadia* focuses on exactly the sort of procedure we have observed in Sonnet 9 of *Astrophel and Stella.*

> Her forhead jacinth like, her cheekes of opall hue,
> Her twinkling eies bedeckt with pearle, her lips as Saphire blew:
> Her haire like Crapal-stone; her mouth O heavenly wyde;
> Her skin like burnisht gold, her hands like silver ure untryde.[8]

Inversion of the ritual was the basis for a widely imitated burlesque by
Berni, to which Sidney, at many removes, is no doubt indebted.

Sometimes the satire itself supplies a kind of insulation, at least
against the dangers of *hybris;* this may be in part the effect of the
paired blasons made popular by Marot's *Le blason du beau tétin* and
Le blason du laid tétin (1536). Or it may serve as a kind of exorcism,
as in Donne's Elegie VIII,

> Leave her, and I will leave comparing thus,
> She, and comparisons are odious.[9]

Shakespeare's use of the satirical tradition in his Sonnet 130 ("My
mistress' eyes are nothing like the sun") makes clear that the inversion
of the Petrarchan ritual is related to the assertion of sincerity, which
is itself a Petrarchan theme.

> And yet, by heaven, I think my love as rare
> As any she belied by false compare.[1]

Like the parody of naïveté in Sidney's Sonnet 74, it suggests an awareness of alternative possibilities, expressed by a complex attitude, implying a context in which the lover's claims must justify themselves.

It is precisely the lack of specific context that makes the conventional

---

7. Marcel Francon, "Petrarch, Disciple of Heraclitis," *Speculum* 11 (1936),
265-71, citing the *De remediis utriusque fortunae.*

8. *Works I,* 21.

9. John Donne, Elegie VIII, *The Poems of John Donne,* ed. Sir Herbert
Grierson (Oxford, 1933), p. 82.

1. *Shakespeare's Sonnets,* ed. Edward Bliss Reed (New Haven, 1923), p. 65.

hyperbole distasteful and so vulnerable to parody. For examples of successful hyperbole one would look first to the drama, where there is a context to permit, perhaps demand, highly charged language. Warren has pointed out such a context in the garden scene of *Romeo and Juliet*, where the "purity" of the poetry within the garden depends upon the "impurity" of the conjuring Mercutio, walled out of it.[2] The "purity," it might be added, is Petrarchan; the play moves from ritual to ritual, not only the literal ceremonies of feasting, marriage, and funeral, but the Petrarchan rituals: the formulae by which Romeo celebrates his love for the shadowy Rosalind—"O brawling love, O loving hate"—the *innamoramento* expressed in the antiphonal sonnet, and the exorcism of the archetypal garden. But the play puts the Petrarchan data in motion, as the sentimental lover stumbles into a situation where the loving hate is an actual fact, where the sweet enemy is a mortal danger, and where the stylized Petrarchan conceit is spoken by a lover on the point of death.

> Come bitter conduct, come unsav'ry guide,
> Thou desp'rate pilot, now at once run on
> The dashing rocks thy seasick weary bark.[3]

The ritual of the convention is propelled by the context and becomes transformed into dramatic act.

III

Lyric, of course, even a sequence of lyrics, cannot have the fullness of context or the completeness of action that is provided by drama. Nevertheless, the lyric attitudes of *Astrophel and Stella* are expressed in a context that is remarkably concrete.

> Having this day my horse, my hand, my launce
> Guided so well, that I obtain'd the prize,
> Both by the judgment of the English eyes,
> And of some sent from that sweet enemie *Fraunce*;
>
> Horsemen my skill in horsmanship advaunce:
> Towne-folkes my strength, a daintier judge applies
> His praise to sleight, which from good use doth rise:
> Some luckie wits impute it but to chaunce:

2. Robert Penn Warren, "Pure and Impure Poetry," in *Critiques and Essays in Criticism*, ed. Robert W. Stallman (New York, 1949), pp. 87-8.

3. *The Tragedy of Romeo and Juliet*, ed. Richard Hosley (New Haven, 1954), v.3.116-8, p. 121.

> Others, because of both sides I do take
>> My bloud from them, who did excell in this,
>> Thinke Nature me a man of armes did make.
>
> How farre they shot awrie? the true cause is,
>> *Stella* lookt on, and from her hav'nly face
>> Sent forth the beames, which made so faire my race.   (41)

In method this sonnet resembles some of the attacks on conventional poetry (see p. 5). The conceit at the end, on which the poem turns, gives another version of Stella's inspirational powers. The manners of the poets are replaced by the manners of the contemporary society, its members busy with their opinions, each opinion faithfully reflecting the type, all wrong. The detail of the poem creates a powerful sense of audience, the presence of a concrete, emphatically solid background. Some of the solidity, however, seems to be more than dramatic. Astrophel talks almost as if he were Philip Sidney. The fourth line seems to refer to the French envoys who were in England during the spring and summer of 1581 to arrange a marriage between Elizabeth and the Duke of Anjou. Sidney we know was involved in the various tournaments arranged for their entertainment. He was also involved in the actual question of the marriage and earned the Queen's displeasure by vigorously opposing it.[4] The Petrarchan phrase, "that sweet enemie *Fraunce*," seems to be a witty and ironic allusion to the purpose of the French mission.

The possibility of a real as well as a dramatic context seems to be extended in other sonnets.

> Whether the Turkish new-moone minded be
>> To fill his hornes this yeare on Christian coast:
>> How *Poles* right king meanes without leave of hoast,
>> To warme with ill-made fire cold *Moscovy*.
>
> If French can yet three parts in one agree,
>> What now the Dutch in their full diets boast,
>> How *Holland* hearts, now so good townes be lost,
>> Trust in the shade of pleasing *Orange* tree?
>
> How *Ulster* likes of that same golden bit,
>> Wherewith my father once made it halfe tame?
>> If in the *Scotch* Court be no weltring yet.

---

4. See "A Discourse of Sir Ph. S. to the Queenes Majesty Touching Hir Mariage with Monsieur," *Works*, *3*, 51-60.

> These questions busie wits to me do frame:
> I cumbred with good maners, answer do,
> But know not how, for still I thinke of you. (30)

The rhetorical subject of this poem is the rejection of the busy wits. Astrophel, like all Petrarchan lovers, must exclude from his experience irrelevant or unsympathetic attitudes and interests, but he is not allowed simply to ignore them; they exert a palpable pressure that must be resisted. The topical allusion sharpens this effect, for the world rejected for love seems to be a real world, and a world in which the lover has been deeply involved. The involvement, furthermore, corresponds to Sidney's own. His correspondence with Languet, with Leicester, Burghley, and Walsingham, as well as his three tracts,[5] demonstrate how closely the interests mentioned here parallel his actual interests and activities.

The accumulation of highly specific detail raises two problems which, as far as the critical tradition is concerned, have probably received more attention than any others. They are the problems of biography and sincerity, and they have been closely related in studies of Petrarchan poetry. The sincerity of the poetry has been felt to depend on whatever biographical material, interpreted according to a variety of standards of propriety as well as probability, may appear in it. But this relation of sincerity and biography is reliable only if sincerity is defined in the literal sense: if the poems are regarded as an account of an actual love affair and judged as true or false. To establish such a relation is the task of the historian and biographer, not the literary critic, and when the evidence is purely literary (Sidney, unlike Petrarch,[6] left no evidence of an affair other than the sonnets) it is an extremely difficult one. "A man may write of Love and not be in love; as well as of husbandry and not go to the plough; or of witches and be none; or of holiness and be flat profane."[7]

From a critical point of view, sincerity in the literal sense can be applied only to the dramatic character of the lover, within the framework of the poems. Needless to say, all Petrarchan lovers are unequivocal on this point. As I have remarked above, by the time of Sidney to

---

5. In addition to the "Discourse" mentioned above, "A Discourse on Irish Affairs" (1577?) and "Defence of the Earl of Leicester" (1582). *Works, 3*, 46-50, 61-71.

6. Petrarch, in the autograph note in his Virgil and in the prose dialogue called the *Secretum*, explicitly avowed the reality of Laura and the sincerity of his love for her.

7. Giles Fletcher, epistle dedicatory to *Licia* (1593), in *English Sonnet Cycles*, ed. Martha Foote Crowe, London, 1896.

deny the insincerity associated with the Petrarchan manner had become
a conventional theme.

To talk of the poems themselves as insincere (that is, to say that the
lovers, "if I were a mistresse, would never perswade mee they were in
love") involves a different definition, insincerity in the sense Richards
defines. "The flaw that insinuates itself when a writer cannot himself
distinguish his own genuine promptings from those which he hopes
will make a good poem. Such failures on his part to achieve complete
imaginative integrity may show themselves in exaggeration, in strained
expression, in false simplicity, or perhaps in the manner of his indebtedness to other poetry." [8] The emphasis on formal characteristics here
corresponds closely to the criticism Sidney makes both in the *Defence*
and in *Astrophel and Stella*: the labored figures of hyperbole and
oxymoron, "living deaths, deare wounds, faire stormes, and freesing
fires" (Sonnet 6); strained, or rather "strange similies" (Sonnet 3);
the false simplicity parodied in Sonnet 74,

> Some do I heare of Poets furie tell,
> But (God wot) wot not what they meane by it;

and the conventional imitation in Sonnet 15,

> You that poore *Petrarchs* long deceased woes,
> With new-borne signes and denisend wit do sing.

Sincerity in the literary, as opposed to the literal, sense must be
controlled by formal literary considerations; the poetry itself must
govern the degree to which biography is relevant. It is clear from a
number of the sonnets that the relation between Astrophel, the *dramatis
persona*, and Sidney, *in propria persona,* is relevant to our understanding of the sequence. The critical task is to see what this relation is.

I have tried to show the rhetorical and dramatic function of Sonnets
like 30, where through topical allusions the emphasis falls on the
"reality" of the lover's world. Sonnets in which the emphasis is on
his identity have a similar function. As Pollard and others have pointed
out, the last line of Sonnet 65 is a reference to the Sidney coat of arms,
Or a Pheon Azure. [9]

> Love by sure proofe I may call thee unkind,
> That giv'st no better eare to my just cries:
> Thou whom to me such my good turnes should bind,
> As I may well recount, but none can prize:

8. I. A. Richards, *Practical Criticism* (New York, 1949), p. 95.

9. Pollard gives the Sidney arms as *argent a pheon azure,* and Mona Wilson
(ed. *Astrophel and Stella*, London, 1931) apparently accepts his authority.
Burke's General Armory gives *or a pheon azure.*

For when nak'd boy thou couldst no harbour find
    In this old world, growne now so too too wise;
    I lodg'd thee in my heart, and being blind
    By Nature borne, I gave to thee mine eyes.

Mine eyes, my light, my heart, my life, alas,
    If so great services may scorned be,
    Yet let this thought thy Tygrish courage passe:

That I perhaps am somewhat kinne to thee;
    Since in thine armes, if learnd fame truth hath spread,
    Thou bear'st the arrow, I the arrow head.

The context in which the identification occurs is the ordinary stuff of conventional complaint. There is an allegorical history, the occasion for which is kept conventionally vague; the allegory merely stands for the usual conflict between Love and the lover, with the lover's "good turnes" representing his initial attitude, his willingness to love, and Love's ingratitude the standard slings and arrows of the Petrarchan experience.

In these terms the heraldic conceit which resolves the conflict is a witty way of describing Sidney as Petrarchan lover; he bears the arrowhead in the sense of being wounded by it, an emblem of the bleeding heart. But the claim of kinship makes firmer an association suggested in the second quatrain. Love, the "nak'd boy," is described in relation to an alien world, "growne now so too too wise," a world in which the speaker's heart is the only "harbour" to be found. The implication is that Love and the lover are alone together in a world that has no place for love, and that the real conflict is between them and such a world. When the kinship is asserted in terms of the Sidney arms, it not only draws them into closer association, it introduces another basis for distinguishing them from the "wise" world. That is, it invokes another standard by referring to another area of being, the reality of a real man. On the one hand, then, are "real" or true love (Love itself) and the lover as a real person, and on the other a world too wise: a world, apparently, that is artificial and without genuine feeling. And finally, because the lady is necessarily involved in the basic conflict, implicit at the center of the wise world to which the genuine lover is opposed, the poem lodges its main complaint against her, not the conventional one that she is "more chaste than kind," but simply that she is conventional. It is the conventional standard of pretense and artificiality that causes grief between lovers, Astrophel-Sidney argues, and by subscribing to it, he seems to imply, the lady relinquishes part of her own reality.

The function of the identification, then, is not autobiographical revelation. Rather, the identification is a means by which Sidney, the real
historical figure, in a sense lends his reality to Astrophel, the dramatic
character, as a kind of concrete "existential" value. The poem deals
with contrasting modes of existence, and the identification, in this context, has a rhetorical function. It identifies Astrophel *with* Sidney, not
as Sidney.[1]

There are three sonnets punning on the name "Rich" which have
traditionally been accepted as identifying Stella as Lady Rich: 24,
which begins, "Rich fooles there be"; 35, which has the line,

> and now long-needy Fame
> Doth even grow rich, naming my *Stellas* name;

and 37, which tells a "riddle" of a "Nymph" who "Hath no mis-
fortune, but that Rich she is." The various, rather perverse objections
to understanding the pun have by now been effectively overruled.[2]
There is still another sonnet, however, so far overlooked by plaintiffs
and defendants alike, which seems to reaffirm the traditional identification, and if it does so, illustrates more clearly than Sonnet 65 the
function of identification in the sequence. It is Sonnet 13.

> *Phoebus* was Judge betweene *Jove, Mars,* and *Love,*
>   Of those three gods, whose armes the fairest were:
>   *Joves* golden shield did Eagle sables beare,
>   Whose talents held young *Ganimed* above:
>
> But in Vert field Mars bare a golden speare,
>   Which through a bleeding heart his point did shove:
>   Each had his creast, *Mars* caried *Venus* glove,
>   *Jove* on his helme the thunderbolt did reare.
>
> *Cupid* then smiles, for on his crest there lies
>   *Stellas* faire haire, her face he makes his shield,
>   Where roses gueuls are borne in silver field.

---

1. Miss Wilson has no doubt that Sidney wrote *Astrophil* (lover of a star)
instead of the meaningless "Astrophel," and points out that Harvey and Royden
wrote "Astrophil"; the anonymous author of *Zepheria* (1594) also wrote
"Astrophil." The suggestion is an attractive one, particularly when one compares the anagramatic "Philisides" of the *Arcadia.* The quartos and the folio,
however, have "Astrophel."

2. Hoyt H. Hudson, "Penelope Devereux as Sidney's Stella," *The Huntington Library Bulletin, 7* (1935), 87-129. Hudson presents a convenient summary
of the arguments and evidence. See also L. C. John, *The Elizabethan Sonnet
Sequences,* New York 1938.

Phoebus drew wide the curtaines of the skies,
    To blaze these last, and sware devoutly then,
    The first, thus matcht, were scantly Gentlemen.

Ostensibly this is the same kind of poem as 65, an allegory of the most conventional sort. The chief difference is that here the allegory is a compliment instead of a complaint, and Cupid is allied with the lady, not at odds with her. The conceit is a familiar one (see Sonnets 11, 12, 17, 20, 29, 43), asserting that Stella's beauty, her power to compel love, is that of the god, the universal. The use of "silver" in describing her face, however, seems unnecessarily malapropos; the figure does not require it. One would expect something more like Constable's heraldic description of Lady Rich, "A field of lilies, roses proper bare."[3] Explanation of this anomaly, and a more pointed meaning for the line, may lie in an allusion to the Devereux arms, which were *argent a fesse gules in chief three torteaux*. A *torteau* is a roundel or sphere painted red; thus, in the upper part of the shield (above the *fesse*, or bar) were three red spheres on a silver background; an exercise of poetic license no more than normal might translate them as "roses." Such an allusion cannot be proven, but its obvious appropriateness in the context makes it credible. The point of it is to assert that Stella's essential superiority lies in the fact that she is real. Whatever ironies there may be about the solemnity or enormity of the conventional mythological allusion, the primary argument is that Jove and Mars, Venus and Ganymede, are scantly anything, they do not exist. It might be added that this sonnet comes early in the sequence, before any suggestion of Stella's marriage. She is Penelope Devereux at this stage, not Lady Rich.

If the allusion can be accepted, it will be seen to be parallel to the Sidney allusion in Sonnet 65. The function of the identification in both poems is the same. It is an inversion of the allusive procedure of the conventional poem. That procedure, whether mythological,

    In life she is Diana chast,
    In truth, Penelope,[4]

or specifically Petrarchan, "Though thou, a Laura, hast no Petra[r]ch found,"[5] is a generalizing one; the identification points in a direction opposite to Sidney's. The names are used not as types of a particular

3. Henry Constable, *Diana* (1592), First Decade, Sonnet X, in *Elizabethan Sonnets*, ed. Sidney Lee (New York, n. d.), *2*, 83.
4. Heywood, "A praise of his lady," in Hebel and Hudson, p. 11.
5. Samuel Daniel, "Delia," Sonnet XL, *The Whole Workes of Samuel Daniel Esquire in Poetrie* (London, 1623), p. 168.

value—beauty, chastity, fidelity—so much as types of the traditional literary value which has consecrated them. Sidney emphasizes this literary characteristic as the salient vice of the convention by opposing to it, as the essential value of his lovers, the assertion that they are real.

In these two sonnets the lover identifies himself with the real world as a means of asserting his superiority to the mannered artifice of the convention. In the Rich sonnets, however, the point of view is reversed; the lover identifies himself with the convention as a world of love threatened by an inimical reality beyond it.

> My mouth doth water, and my breast doth swell,
> My tongue doth itch, my thoughts in labour be.
> Listen then Lordings with good eare to me,
> For of my life I must a riddle tell.

> Towards *Auroras* Court a Nymph doth dwell,
> Rich in all beauties which mans eye can see:
> Beauties so farre from reach of words, that we
> Abase her praise, saying she doth excell:

> Rich in the treasure of deserv'd renowne,
> Rich in the riches of a royall hart,
> Rich in those gifts which give th' eternall crowne;

> Who, though most rich in these and everie part,
> Which make the patents of true worldly blisse,
> Hath no misfortune, but that Rich she is.

This is the sonnet *à clef* omitted from the sequence until the folio of 1598. It is on a theme that fascinates the Petrarchan poet, the paradox of love ("O dilettoso male") expressed in the conventional form of a blason of the lady as "dolce nemica."

Sidney follows the conventional pattern to the extent that he describes Stella as a kind of secular divinity—"Rich in those gifts which give th'eternal crowne" and ". . . the patents of true worldly blisse"; her "flaw," however, is not that she is proud or hard of heart, but "that Rich she is." There is no question here of a "dolce nemica"; it is more than a way of putting it, in a worn-out poetical fashion: the enemy is the husband, in itself a rarity in Petrarchan poetry, and he is therefore "real," in the sense that he has an objective dramatic existence independent of the lover. But even more, he is a proper name, Lord Rich; the purged and circumscribed isolation of the Petrarchan lovers opens on what, in this poem, is the dark world of actual fact.

The fact is powerful, however, because it is dramatic, not because it is confessional. This seems to be true of all the biographical detail in the sequence. The allusions and identifications are consistently wrought into the poetic structure wherever they occur, carefully and significantly balanced against the characteristic methods and procedures of the convention, always contributing to a total effect that is poetic. The emphasis is on the substantial character, the material fact of the personality, emerging from the impersonal, verbal manners of the convention.

IV

It is possible, I think, to distinguish in Sidney's sonnets some of the qualities Eliot distinguishes in Elizabethan drama: between the rhetoric " which was only the trick of its age " or " monotonous, inflexible to the alterations of emotion," and the rhetoric which " occurs in a situation where a character . . . *sees himself* in a dramatic light " (Eliot's emphasis).[6] The biographical allusion is a special kind of self- awareness and of self-assertion on the part of the lover, a way of seeing himself in an order of being outside the convention that for the most part defines his particular experience and controls his central relationships. But his " life " comes from a dramatic awareness of the sort Eliot describes; it is produced by his ability to see himself, not as a historical figure, but as an actor in a variety of situations to which his thought, his feeling, and his manner of expression are adapted.

> What, have I thus betrayed my libertie?
>> Can those blacke beames such burning markes engrave
>> In my free side? or am I borne a slave,
>> Whose necke becomes such yoke of tyranny?
>
> Or want I sense to feele my miserie?
>> Or sprite, disdaine of such disdaine to have?
>> Who for long faith, tho dayly helpe I crave,
>> May get no almes but scorne of beggerie.
>
> Vertue awake, Beautie but beautie is,
>> I may, I must, I can, I will, I do
>> Leave following that, which it is gaine to misse.
>
> Let her go:[7] soft, but here she comes, go to,
>> Unkind, I love you not: O me, that eye
>> Doth make my heart give to my tongue the lie. (47)

This is a Petrarchan meditation in which Astrophel contemplates him-

6. T. S. Eliot, *Selective Essays* (New York, 1950), p. 27.
7. The Folio reading is " do ".

self in the wretched condition of the conventional lover and vows to cast off his chains. And it is a contemplation in the grand manner— "Can those blacke beames such burning markes engrave/ In my free side? or am I borne a slave . . . ?" The exaggeration of the diction seems to be calculated and suggests that the speaker is aware of the rebel as of the slave, and that the rebel is even more the subject of the incredulous rhetoric.

As Eliot observes, "when any one is conscious of himself as acting, something like a sense of humour is present."[8] The verve with which Astrophel plays his role is amusing because he is so thoroughly aware that it is a role. The point is that he is not a rebel at all, but a most willing lover: one who, far from suffering his condition, enjoys the contemplation of it. The shift from monologue to dialogue as he bursts out, "Go to, Unkind, I love you not," and the sudden wrench in the last line, are managed with a dramatic effect that is surprising within the formal limits of a sonnet. It is almost a virtuoso demonstration of the lyric attitude as gesture, as posture, as incipient act.[9] The persuasive factor of the poem is not Stella's power, for that is entirely the lover's dramatic creation. It is rather this quality of attitude.

At the opposite extreme from the frank and exuberant theatrics of this sonnet is the direct sincerity of Sonnet 64.

> No more, my deare, no more these counsels trie,
>> O give my passions leave to run their race:
>> Let Fortune lay on me her worst disgrace,
>> Let folke orecharg'd with braine against me crie.
>
> Let clouds bedimme my face, breake in mine eye,
>> Let me no steps but of lost labour trace:
>> Let all the earth with scorne recount my case,
>> But do not will me from my *Love* to flie.
>
> I do not envie *Aristotles* wit,
>> Nor do aspire to *Caesars* bleeding fame;
>> Nor ought do care, though some above me sit:
>
> Nor hope, nor wish another course to frame,
>> But that which once may win thy cruell hart:
>> Thou art my Wit, and thou my Vertue art.

The effectiveness of the contrast with a sonnet like 47 (though the effect is the product of its own structure, the sonnet benefits by the

---

8. Eliot, *Essays*, p. 29.

9. See Kenneth Burke, "Three Definitions," *Kenyon Review, 13* (1951), **173-92.**

contrast) is precisely in the omission of the role, the sense of the speaker in propria persona. This artlessness is an aspect of both manner and matter, of technique and theme, for Astrophel's problem is to persuade Stella that he is as devoted as he claims; here if ever the character of the speaker is important, but there must be no suggestion of a part played.

His "proof" is to repudiate worldly ambition, to deliver a general indictment of the world in terms of *vanitas vanitatis*. Logically, Stella's influence would be more fully demonstrated if the world, or whatever area of experience is specified as competing with her, exerted a claim as powerful as hers, or more nearly so. This is the procedure in some of the other sonnets (for example, 18, 19, 21). From the standpoint of persuasion, however, the indictment is highly relevant, for by showing what he scorns it shows what kind of man he is: a man of principle, unpretentious, utterly sincere, utterly devoted, the honest man in a world of error.

In Sonnet 90 we hear the same voice, speaking now of the poet, for whom worldly ambition is represented by literary renown.

> *Stella,* thinke not that I by verse seeke fame,
>   Who seeke, who hope, who love, who live but thee;
>   Thine eyes my pride, thy lips mine history;

The repudiation is made in the same measured rhythms, the same simple, almost monosyllabic diction, and with the same restraint of tone as in 64.

>   nothing from my wit or will doth flow,
>   Since all my words thy beauty doth endite,
>   And love doth hold my hand, and makes me write.

The directness and simplicity of these two poems are characteristics frequently associated with Sidney's poetic norm; simplicity, furthermore, a "plain sensibleness," is the stylistic standard recommended in the *Defence*. There may be some warrant, then, for feeling that this is the voice of the poet himself. But the effort to achieve simplicity is a dramatic theme in *Astrophel and Stella*, closely associated with the theme of sincerity, and the lover in the role of the simple, forthright man speaks in a variety of accents. Thus, in Sonnet 28, though the theme, stated in the last three lines,

>   know that I in pure simplicitie,
>   Breathe out the flames which burne within my heart,
>   Love onely reading unto me this arte.

is exactly the same as in 64 and 90, it is arrived at by a different process. Astrophel does not simply assert that he is sincerely in love, he defends himself against the imputation that he is not. The result is simplicity in a somewhat different form.

> You that with allegories curious frame,
>> Of others children changelings use to make,
>> With me those paines for Gods sake do not take:
>> I list not dig so deepe for brasen fame.

> When I say, *Stella*, I do meane the same
>> Princesse of Beautie, for whose only sake,
>> The raines of *Love* I love, though never slake,
>> And joy therein, though Nations count it shame.

> I beg no subject to use eloquence,
>> Nor in hid wayes do guide Philosophie:
>> Looke at my hands for no such quintessence . . .

The singleness of mind and heart affirmed on psychological and ethical grounds in the other sonnets is given here a metaphysical value; Astrophel's " pure simplicitie " is played off ironically against the " quintessence " of the philosophers. But the effectiveness of the witty metaphysics depends upon the brusque and impatient tone that makes the character of the speaker concrete and immediately apprehensible; he is too forceful, too frank, too plain-spoken a man to mean anything but what he says. The firm sense of the personality is supported by racy, colloquial rhythms in marked contrast to the movement characteristic of the other sonnets, suggesting not a restrained but an energetic simplicity.

In Sonnet 54 the character proper to the lover is the explicit subject. Because he lacks the conventional manners of love—he does not " use set colours for to weare, / Nor nourish speciall lockes of vowed haire " —the court coquettes are convinced that Astrophel is no lover.

> What he? say they of me, now I dare sweare,
> He cannot love: no, no, let him alone.

His response is to distinguish the matter from the manner.

> Professe in deed I do not *Cupids* art;
> But you faire maides, at length this true shall find,

> That his right badge is but worne in the hart:
>> Dumbe Swannes, not chatring Pies, do Lovers prove,
>> They love indeed, who quake to say they love.

The gnomic last line is Petrarchan—" Chi pò dir com' egli arde, e 'n picciol foco ";[1] that it appears in the midst of considerable body of verse devoted to saying how he loves is neither ironic nor absurd; it is a means of identifying, in an almost official way, the *persona* that the other sonnets present.

In a number of sonnets this persona is parodied, and when it is, Astrophel usually appears in the role of the *naïf*, or *ingénu*. We have already had occasion to look at his performance in this role (see Sonnets 45, 47 and 74); Sonnet 59 is another example, with somewhat broader effects.

> Deare, why make you more of a dog then me?
>> If he do love, I burne, I burne in love:
>> If he waite well, I never thence would move:
>> If he be faire, yet but a dog can be.
>
> Litle he is, so litle worth is he;
>> He barks, my songs thine owne voyce oft doth prove:
>> Bid'n perhaps he fetcheth thee a glove,
>> But I unbid, fetch even my soule to thee.
>
> Yet while I languish, him that bosome clips,
>> That lap doth lap, nay lets in spite of spite,
>> This sowre-breath'd mate tast of those sugred lips.
>
> Alas, if you graunt only such delight
>> To witlesse things, then *Love*, I hope (since wit
>> Becomes a clog) will soone ease me of it.

Simplicity here is simple-mindedness, expressed in the abject humility and earnestness with which Astrophel looks upon the dog as a serious rival. It is this quality, the result of accepting and sustaining the role, that distinguishes Sidney's treatment from that in such analogues as Ronsard's sonnet, "Petit barbet," where the irony is more studied, less dramatic.

The offer to relinquish his wits—like the offer to relinquish his reality in Sonnet 45 ("I am not I, pitie the tale of me")—is a way of protesting against Stella's own behavior: the love of a dog is witless; she is witless to prefer the dog, and her perversity is making the lover witless by making him assume the posture and perform the service of the conventional lover. There may be a further suggestion that her innocent fondling of the dog is calculated, that she too is playing a role—that of a teasing coquette. Part of the humor is that, though he solemnly contrasts himself to the dog as spirit to sense, it is the sensual advantages of the dog that he resents.

1. Petrarch, CLXX ("Piú volte già dal bel sembiante umano"), p. 416.

This preposterous performance is designed to laugh the lady into reason and thence into love. It continues in the three sonnets that follow in the sequence. In Sonnet 60 Astrophel professes utter bewilderment at Stella's behavior—cruel when he is with her, kind when he is not.

> Now I wit-beaten long by hardest Fate,
>> So dull am, that I cannot looke into
>> The ground of this fierce *Love* and lovely hate:
>
> Then some good body tell me how I do,
>> Whose presence, absence, absence presence is;
>> Blist in my curse, and cursed in my blisse.

The sign of perplexity here is the Petrarchan jargon. It relates both the lover and the phenomenon that perplexes him to the artifice of the convention. Use of this jargon in parody, like the studied clumsiness in Sonnet 74 (" [God wot] wot not what they meane "), is characteristic of Astrophel's language in the role of the naïf, as the sudden prostration of the rebel in Sonnet 47 is characteristic of his posture.

The method in Sonnets 61 and 62 is the same, the chief difference a change in the form of Stella's perversity from that of the coquette to that of the Petrarchan *platonique*, whose ingenious logic and subtle semantics threaten to turn the lover's language against him. His response in each case is to call for help.

> O Doctor *Cupid*, thou for me reply,
>> Driv'n else to graunt by Angels sophistrie,
>> That I love not, without I leave to love.   (61)
>
> Deare, love me not, that ye may love me more.   (62)

In Sonnet 46, though the treatment of Stella has much the same irony, the use of persona appears in a somewhat more complicated form.

> I curst thee oft, I pitie now thy case,
>> Blind-hitting boy, since she that thee and me
>> Rules with a becke, so tyrannizeth thee,
>> That thou must want or food, or dwelling-place,
>
> For she protests to banish thee her face,
>> Her face? O *Love*, a Rogue thou then shouldst be!
>> If *Love* learne not alone to love and see,
>> Without desire to feed of further grace.
>
> Alas poore wag, that now a scholler art
>> To such a schoole-mistresse, whose lessons new
>> Thou needs must misse, and so thou needs must smart.

Yet **Deare**, let me his pardon get of you,
    So long (though he from book myche to desire)
    Till without fewell you can make hot fire.

The complication is produced by the presence of the Anacreontic Cupid between the lover and the lady. Cupid represents her beauty; and therefore her attempts to be tyrannical, to banish him, are delightfully futile. But he is also a projection of the lover's own desire; as he is characterized—"poore wag, that now a scholler art/ To such a schoole-mistresse"—he is a kind of surrogate persona, who performs the conventional role, smarting under the rod, while the speaker looks on sympathetically—"I pitie now thy case." The essential irony of the poem lies just in this urbane detachment, in the role of the observer, interested but not involved.

V

When the lover is presented with a threat to his central values that must be taken seriously, and he cannot pretend detachment, we see him in another role, the opposite of the naïf, and we hear a new voice.

Rich fooles there be, whose base and filthy hart
    Lies hatching still the goods wherein they flow:
    And damning their owne selves to *Tantals* smart,
    Wealth breeding want, more rich,[2] more wretched grow.

Yet to those fooles heav'n such wit doth impart,
    As what their hands do hold, their heads do know,
    And knowing *Love*, and loving lay apart,
    As sacred things, far from all daungers show.

But that rich foole who by blind Fortunes lot,
    The richest gemme of Love and life enjoyes,
    And can with foule abuse such beauties blot;

Let him deprived of sweet but unfelt joyes,
    (Exil'd for ay from those high treasures, which
    He knowes not) grow in only follie rich. (24)

Dominating this sonnet, with the obvious play on the name, is the metaphor of the miser. Considered solely from the point of view of Stella's lover, the purpose is to distinguish between misers who know the value of their treasure and so hide it, and the particular miser, Lord Rich, abysmally ignorant of the value of his treasure which Astrophel

2. The Folio reading is "blist".

covets and hopes will not be hoarded. On the other hand, the role here does not seem to be simply that of the jealous lover waiting for opportunity to knock. The tone implies something graver, to be justified not by the particular miser but by the general theme of miserliness that the name Rich has suggested.

Implicit in the metaphor, and translating the pun, is the parable of the rich man—the " Dives "—tormented in Hell like Tantalus, " Exil'd for ay " from Heaven, a " rich foole " to whom knowledge comes too late. The Christian symbol extends and defines the general terms of moral judgment. But Astrophel converts the symbol, like everything else, into the terms of his own passion. The specific viewpoint from which the miser is judged comes from the philosophy of love—" amator divitias . . . contemnit,"[3] says Ficino (and Plato); this Dives, then, loving money, contemptuous of love, who " can with foule abuse such beauties blot," is virtually Anti-Love incarnate. The particular adversary, Stella's husband, is seen in terms of the lover's philosophy as the universal.

This symbolic structure, a kind of parody, perhaps, of both the Christian and the Platonic symbol, is responsible for a tone like that of Petrarch denouncing Avignon,

> Fontana di dolore, albergo d'ira,
>   Scola d'errori, e templo d'eresia,
>   Già Roma, or Babilonia falsa e ria,
>   Per cui tanto si piange e si sospira;[4]

It is a tone which has, in Maynard Mack's phrase, the accents of the hero, the public defender.[5] And that is the role Astrophel has assumed. He is the champion of good, fulfilling his responsibility to identify and combat evil—good and evil always understood, however, from the single point of view of the dramatic character.

Astrophel appears in the same role of hero and defender in Sonnet 14. The danger there comes not from vice but from error, not from evil itself but from a failure to perceive the good. The procedure, therefore, is more affirmative than in 24; it is to anatomize good instead of evil.

> Alas have I not paine enough my friend,
>   Upon whose breast a fiercer Gripe doth tire

---

3. Ficino, *Commentary on Plato's ' Symposium,'* text and trans. by S. R. Jayne, Univ. of Missouri Stud. 19 (Columbia, 1944), p. 48.

4. Petrarch, CXXXVIII, p. 355.

5. Maynard Mack, " The Muse of Satire," *Studies in the Literature of the Augustan Age*, ed. Richard C. Boys (Ann Arbor, 1952), p. 228. My indebtedness to Mr. Mack's article is a general one.

Then did on him who first stale downe the fire,
While *Love* on me doth all his quiver spend,

But with your Rubarb words ye must contend
To grieve me worse, in saying that Desire
Doth plunge my wel-form'd soule even in the mire
Of sinfull thoughts, which do in ruine end?

If that be sinne which doth the maners frame,
Well staid with truth in word and faith of deed,
Readie of wit and fearing nought but shame:

If that be sinne which in fixt hearts doth breed
A loathing of all loose unchastitie,
Then Love is sinne, and let me sinfull be.

Astrophel in this poem is the hero as martyr, with all the symbolic suggestion, pagan and Christian, that the Promethean image bears. The accent we hear in this case is to a remarkable extent a function of sheer technical mastery of the two-part Petrarchan sonnet. It is expressed by the vehemence of the violently enjambed lines, running on without pause to make the octave a single outburst, dramatically contrasted to the stopped lines and balanced phrasing of the sestet, in which the lover defines the love his friend has condemned.

The mutual reflections of speaker and adversary in sonnets like these constitute a decorum and identify a persona that seem closer to satire than to Petrarchan love poetry. Satire, however, belongs to the rhetorical category of *laus et vituperatio*, praise and blame, and so does the Petrarchan sonnet; they represent the two extremes of it. Sidney as Petrarchan sonneteer shifts the balance, gives a turn and emphasis to the *vituperatio* that justifies, indeed invites, comparison of his sequence, in some of its procedures, to the structure of formal verse satire.

Lord Rich represents one end of a scale of antagonism, of blame, at the other end of which is Stella, the "douce adversaire," and between them at different distances are the adversaries of most of the poems we have been discussing. And the roles Astrophel adopts in response to them tend to group around the other two personae Mack suggests as comprising the ethos of the satirist: thus, the *vir*—or *amator—bonus* of Sonnet 54, the genuine, unaffected lover, who proves that true love "is but worne in the hart"; and the naïf of Sonnet 59, "Deare, why make you more of a dog then me?"

In some places there are indications of the actual satiric form. For example, the exordium of Sonnet 37, which identifies Rich, suggests the apologia of the satirist.

My mouth doth water, and my breast doth swel!,
>   My tongue doth itch, my thoughts in labour be.

"Difficile est saturam non scribere." The parody of the conventional
poetry (Sonnets 3, 6, 15, 74) is perhaps another part of the apologia:
it is part of the lover's persona, as it is Martial's and Juvenal's, to abjure
the grandiloquent and to expose the spurious. Even the blason, which
seems so characteristically Petrarchan a device, is used for blame as well
as praise, to describe a paragon or a miser, and may provide a formal
link with the "character-portraiture" which, according to Mary Claire
Randolph, "is ever a forerunner or concomitant of satire." [6]

The "minimum essentials" of formal verse satire, writes Miss
Randolph, are: "two actors or participants, a Satirist and his Adversa-
rius; a setting of sorts; and a thesis to be argued." [7] These essentials
are prominent in *Astrophel and Stella*; Astrophel has a variety of adversaries, including Stella, and the story is set in a definite society, with
a cast composed of its members. But it is chiefly in terms of the thesis
and the way it is argued that the satirical elements are significant.

The end of satire is "the correction of folly and vice by persuasion
to rational behavior," and the persuasive technique is one of "dialectical
argument." [8] In Astrophel's dialectic the "wrong waies" and "stolne
goods" of the conventional poets represent irrational behavior, so he
argues with them about the sources of true inspiration. Similarly, he
argues with courtiers and coquettes about the outward, social manifestations of love, and with his friend about its inward, moral consequences. All are guilty of folly in that they mistake manner for matter,
surface for essential; they are, in one way or another, conventional.

The courtiers are conventional in that they represent the mass attitudes and motives of the court society, and specifically, in that they
ascribe the same attitudes and motives to Astrophel, simply as a matter
of course. A striking example occurs in Sonnet 51, where the archetypal butt of social satire, False-Wit, Osric, the pretentious bore, in-
trudes on the lover's world.

>   Pardon mine eares, both I and they do pray,
>   So may your tongue still fluently proceed
>   To them that do such entertainment need,
>   So may you still have somewhat new to say.

Astrophel ironically renounces the heroic role so formidable an adversary requires, and declares himself the naïf.

---

6. Mary Claire Randolph, "The Structural Design of the Formal Verse
Satire," *PQ*, *21* (1942), 370, n. 7.

7. Ibid., p. 372.   8. Ibid., p. 373.

On silly me do not the burden lay,
  Of all the grave conceits your braine doth breed;
  But find some *Hercules* to beare, insteed
  Of *Atlas* tyr'd, your wisedomes heav'nly sway.

The moral standard that exerts its pressure on Astrophel is considered conventional—though not with the same consistency as the social standard—in the sense that it is institutionalized, academic, out of touch with realities. Sonnet 4 is the moral counterpart of Sonnet 51.

Vertue alas, now let me take some rest,
  Thou setst a bate betweene my will and wit:
  If vaine love have my simple soule opprest,
  Leave what thou likest not, deale not thou with it.

Thy scepter use in some olde *Catoes* brest;
  Churches or schooles are for thy seate more fit:
  I do confesse, pardon a fault confest:
  My mouth too tender is for thy hard bit.

But if that needs thou wilt usurping be,
  The little reason that is left in me,
  And still th' effect of thy perswasions prove:

I sweare, my heart such one shall shew to thee,
  That shrines in flesh so true a Deitie,
  That *Vertue*, thou thy selfe shalt be in love.

The dramatic situation is the same, "Vertue" intruding between the lover and his love, and there is the same sardonic acknowledgment of the intruder's powers via an ironic use of persona. Here, however, it is not the naïf, but the vir bonus, frank and forthright to the point of bluntness.

I do confesse, pardon a fault confest:
  My mouth too tender is for thy hard bit.

This is apparently a parody of the sacrament of confession. The boldness—perhaps even the unpleasantness—of it expresses the intensity of the motivation, and is justified by the characterization of "Vertue" as a cold, institutionalized ideal, fit only for old Catos, schools, and churches. That characterization is also the justification of the more serious parody of incarnation in the next to the last line. To oppose the exaggerated austerity of the moral ideal, the lover feels he can insist on an exaggerated ideality for his love; conventional "Vertue" personified is opposed by the conventional lady personified, that is, by Stella, as goddess. To this extent the dialectic of the sestet is sophistic and satirical. But in another sense it is seriously intended, for the essential conflict in the poem is between the "flesh" that enshrines Stella and the bits, seats, and scepters of the abstraction. The satirist's thesis here is Stella's triumphant reality.

It is recognition of this reality which constitutes the "rational behavior" to which the satire persuades, and this reality—the reality, that is to say, of the lover's experience, with Stella as its symbol—is the ultimate "truth" to which the dialectic leads.

VI

Both the characterization of "Vertue," in Sonnet 46, and the satirical persona through which Astrophel rejects it, suggest the description of moral philosophers in *The Defence of Poesie*, "sophistically speaking against subtiltie. . . . These men casting larges as they go of definitions, divitions, and distinctions, with a scornful interrogative, do soberly aske, whether it be possible to find any path so ready to lead a man to vertue, as that which teacheth what vertue is." [9] The argument in the *Defence* is the Aristotelian distinction between philosophy and history on one hand and poetry on the other: philosophy teaches by precept; history, lacking the precept, is tied to the particular example; but poetry combines precept and example, and has the superior power of "mooving. . . . And that mooving is of a higher degree then teaching, it may by this appeare, that it is well nigh both the cause and effect of teaching." [1]

The civil war of Love and Virtue, which is the subject of Sonnet 46, and one of the "topoi" of the convention, is based upon this distinction; the precepts of moral virtue, like the teaching of the philosopher, lack the power of "mooving" the lover. It is also the basis for the treatment of the social "virtues" he rejects; the "busie wits" of Sonnet 30, full of affairs of state, the "curious wits" of Sonnet 23, completely misjudging the affairs of the lover, and the pretentious bore of Sonnet 51, suggest the characterization of the historian in the *Defence*: "better knowing how this world goes, then how his owne wit runnes, . . . inquisitive of Novelties, a wonder to yoong folkes, and a Tyrant in table talke." [2] Like the historian, the wits are tied to their own particular examples. And so, of course, are the conventional poets, slaves to "poore *Petrarchs* long deceased woes," whom Astrophel admonishes, "*Stella* behold, and then begin to endite."

9. *Works*, 3, 12.
1. Ibid., 19.
2. Ibid., 12.

Love, with Stella as its symbol, has the power to move the lover; the various precepts and examples that compete with it can only teach him. The distinction is made again and again, whether the context is moral, social, or literary, by means of a structural device highly characteristic of Sidney's technique as sonneteer—the reversal or inversion of the movement of a sonnet in the last line. Thus, in Sonnet 5, for thirteen lines the lover gives a catalogue of Christianized Platonism: "It is most true, that eyes are form'd to serve/ The inward light. . . . True, that true Beautie Vertue is indeed . . . True, that on earth we are but pilgrims made . . ." but in the fourteenth line turns away: "True, and yet true that I must Stella love." In Sonnet 30 ("Whether the Turkish new-moone minded be"; see p. 16 above) the catalogue is of international politics, supplied by the "busie wits"; the conclusion is just as abrupt,

> I cumbred with good maners, answer do,
> But know not how, for still I thinke of you.

In Sonnet 1, the poet-lover makes inventory of his literary efforts, "Studying inventions fine . . . Oft turning others leaves . . . ," but the last line pulls him away from his study to the source of true poetic power, "Foole, said my Muse to me, looke in thy heart and write."

The distinction between teaching and "mooving" is also involved in the treatment of Stella. In Sonnet 68, for example, her efforts to teach Astrophel the moral virtue that will make him leave love are subverted by the powers of charm and beauty that move him to love. She defeats her own purpose.

> *Stella*, the onely Planet of my light,
>   Light of my life, and life of my desire,
>   Chiefe good, whereto my hope doth only aspire,
>   World of my wealth, and heav'n of my delight.
>
> Why doest thou spend the treasures of thy sprite,
>   With voice more fit to wed *Amphions* lyre,
>   Seeking to quench in me the noble fire,
>   Fed by thy worth, and blinded by thy sight?
>
> And all in vaine, for while thy breath most sweet,
>   With choisest words, thy words with reasons rare,
>   Thy reasons firmly set on *Vertues* feet,
>
> Labour to kill in me this killing care:
>   O thinke I then, what paradise of joy
>   It is, so faire a Vertue to enjoy.

The civil war of Love and Virtue is located within the lady instead of
the lover, and represents the division of her powers between Venus
and Diana, Beauty and Chastity, her power to attract and her power
to resist. Both aspects are contained in the single term " Vertue," the
ambiguities of which are exploited as a vehicle for the conventional
conflict. The point of the poem lies in the difference between the moral
" Vertue" that Stella would like Astrophel to possess and the " Vertue"
that Astrophel himself would like to possess—namely, Stella, by virtue
of whom he feels the "noble fire" whose virtues, in the sense of essential qualities and moving power, he has celebrated in the first quatrain.

The sonnets that celebrate Stella's particular qualities or " virtues "—
her eyes, her lips, her voice, her hair, and so forth—all demonstrate
her "virtue" in this second sense, her power to move the lover, as the
Star who guides him, the Muse who inspires him, the Beauty who
inflames him. And this virtue is constantly played off against the other
kinds of virtue represented by the world he rejects for love, urged on
him by the lady or considered by the lover himself in meditation.

In Sonnet 25 the ambiguous virtues are represented by the structure
of the Platonic Idea as the good and the beautiful, *to agathon* and
to kalon.

> The wisest scholler of the wight most wise,
>> By *Phoebus* doome, with sugred sentence sayes,
>> That Vertue if it once met with our eyes,
>> Strange flames of *Love* it in our soules would raise.
>
> But for that man with paine this truth descries,
>> Whiles he each thing in senses ballance wayes,
>> And so nor will, nor can behold those skies,
>> Which inward sunne to *Heroicke* mind displaies,
>
> Vertue of late with vertuous care to ster
>> *Love* of her selfe, tooke *Stellas* shape, that she
>> To mortall eyes might sweetly shine in her.
>
> It is most true, for since I her did see,
>> Vertues great beautie in that face I prove,
>> And find th' effect, for I do burne in love.

The specific reference is to the beatific vision in the *Phaedrus.*[3] But
the witty, mannered, and elaborately alliterative way in which Astrophel
" Platonizes " (the Platonic lover as ingénu) suggests that the reference
is not made very seriously. The archness of tone is a playful criticism
of the extravagant behavior it is the " virtue " of love to produce—the

---

3. Plato, *Phaedrus,* p. 251.

apotheosis of the lady—and a skeptical smile at the treatment of it as
a mystical experience.

The criticism, however, is aimed at the metaphysical theory, not at
the rhetorical principle it supports. Rhetoric in Plato is virtually dialectic; to know the best means of persuasion is to know the Truth. It is
rhetoric that makes the Platonism appropriate here. Astrophel distinguishes, as in Sonnet 68, between the respective " virtues " of goodness and beauty; his syllogism proves the Platonic theorem by the
Petrarchan fire—" I do burne in love." He has changed the philosopher's *virtutis amor* to the lover's *virtus amoris*.

The lover's rhetoric, furthermore, like the philosopher's, is dialectic.
The " virtue " of love for Astrophel is that it is true, a material fact
and not a conventional manner. Stella is its symbol, and therefore the
ultimate persuasion—"now she is nam'd, need more be said?" The
difference lies in the nature of the truth he knows. She is his Idea,
the formal and the efficient cause, the producing agent and the form
or essence of his experience, but that experience is passionate, not
philosophical.

In Sonnet 58 the lover's rhetoric is presented in Aristotelian rather
than Platonic terms, with an allusion to a traditional rhetorical problem,
whether the speech or the speaker is the more persuasive factor.

> Doubt there hath bene when with his golden chaine,
>   The Oratour so farre mens harts doth bind,
>   That no pace else their guided steps can find,
>   But as he them more short or slacke doth raine.
>
> Whether with words this soveraignty he gaine,
>   Cloth'd with fine tropes, with strongest reasons lin'd,
>   Or else pronouncing grace, wherewith his mind
>   Prints his owne lively forme in rudest braine.
>
> Now judge by this; in piercing phrases late,
>   The anatomy of all my woes I wrate,
>   *Stellas* sweete breath the same to me did reed.
>
> O voice, O face, maugre my speeches might,
>   Which wooed wo, most ravishing delight,
>   Even those sad words, even in sad me did breed.

The exemplum which answers the question involves Stella's " virtue "
in still another form, a continuation and mutation of the theme of the
sonnets on poetry. The mistress as muse is the source of good poems;
as orator, or *rhetor*, she transcends poetry. The rhetorical problem is
obviously grist from which to grind a standard type of compliment, but

it nevertheless serves .to emphasize an important aspect of Sidney's own rhetorical practice in the sequence.

The principle involved is what in Aristotle's *Rhetoric* is the first of the three "proofs" furnished by a speech (as opposed to actual evidence), the ethos of the speaker: "moral character constitutes the most effective means of proof."[4] Mona Wilson thinks that the sonnet alludes to the discussion of Antonius and Crassus in Cicero's *De oratore*; perhaps Sidney had in mind such a passage as this, "Such influence, indeed, is produced by a certain feeling and art in speaking, that the speech seems to represent, as it were, the character of the speaker."[5] A reference to Cicero seems the more probable if we recall Sidney's remark in the *Defence* on precisely the same point. "For my part, I doo not doubt, when *Antonius* and *Crassus*, the great forefathers of *Cicero* in eloquence, the one (as *Cicero* testifieth of them) pretended not to knowe Art, the other not to set by it, (because with a plaine sensiblenesse, they might winne credit of popular eares, which credit, is the nearest steppe to perswasion, which perswasion, is the chiefe marke of Oratorie)."[6]

These are the characteristics ("not to knowe Art—not to set by it—plaine sensiblenesse") emphasized again and again as Astrophel's. The rhetorical value of his character is the principle behind the various aspects of Sidney's technique that I have been discussing: the use of biographical allusion to give it solidity, the use of the persona to give it dramatic life. But the character is finally the creation and the expression of attitude. The precision with which the attitude is presented in a poem is a measure of the poem's power to be persuasive, within the dramatic framework, vis-à-vis the lady, and beyond it, vis-à-vis the reader. Astrophel persuades us of his character as a lover by what he shows us that he feels. And that is love. Subject and technique, matter and manner coalesce.

4. Aristotle, *The Art of Rhetoric*, I.2.4-5, trans. J. H. Freese (London, 1926), p. 17.

5. Cicero, *De oratore*, II.xlii, trans. J. S. Watson (New York, 1890), p. 131.

6. *Works*, 3, 43.

Part 2

I

THE two observations about *Astrophel and Stella* most frequently cited are probably those of Nash and Lamb. In the preface to the first edition Nash describes it as "the tragicommody of love—performed by starlight. . . . The argument cruell chastitie, the Prologue hope, the Epilogue dispaire. . . ." Lamb, in the *Last Essays of Elia*, describes it as "full, material, and circumstantiated." The interesting thing about both comments is that they seem to refer rather to the condition of the sequence as a whole than to the excellence of individual poems, and it is the organization of the sequence that perhaps more strikingly than anything else distinguishes *Astrophel and Stella* from the usual Petrarchan collection of "amours," in which the primary structural device is an over-all uniformity of tone or, as often as not, the name of the lady involved—Idea, Delie, Diella, Delia, and so forth.

Consideration of the order of the sonnets, however, raises a special problem that must be acknowledged, if at present it cannot be solved. That is the problem of textual authority. Although manuscript copies of *Astrophel and Stella* were circulating in Sidney's lifetime, no printed version appeared until 1591, five years after his death. The three editions that appeared in that year, two printed by Newman and one by Lownes, are all "bad quartos," and it was not until 1598, when the folio edition of Sidney's works was printed by Ponsonby with the sanction and presumably the supervision of Sidney's sister, the Countess of Pembroke, that there was a published text substantially free from error.

In all of the editions the order of the sonnets is exactly the same, but in the 1598 text they are numbered for the first time, and several important additions are made: Sonnet 37, the riddle on the name of Rich; eight stanzas of the Eighth Song, containing Stella's reply; three stanzas of the Tenth Song; and all of the Eleventh Song. Furthermore, all of the songs, which in the quartos had been placed together at the end, in the folio are placed with dramatic effect in the body of the sequence. Pollard's judgment of the arrangement in this text seems to me both temperate and persuasive:

> . . . the general sequence of the Sonnets is justified against its attackers by the consensus of all the manuscripts, by the failure

of commentators to find any single group which has been broken
up and can be reconstructed, and by the readiness with which the
present order yields itself to a connected narrative. As regards
the position of the songs the case is not equally clear. Here the
folio and the quartos are at variance, but the obvious correctness
of the placing of the more important songs, and the gap which the
omission of these leaves in what may be called the narrative of the
sonnets, is a strong argument in favour of following the order of
the best edition.[1]

Whatever authority there may have been for this text, it provides us
with a whole poetic structure which is of a high order. It is in reference
to the arrangement of the poems in this structure that the relation of
manner and matter is most significant.

    Though they comprise a continuous sequence with no interruption
of the movement, the sonnets of *Astrophel and Stella* seem to fall into
three major groups or sections marked by various formal devices and
involving definite shifts of tone. That there is some principle of order
is suggested at once by the disposition of the various manners adopted
by Sidney's poet-lover. The majority of the most dramatic sonnets
seem to be clustered toward the center of the sequence; the most conventional, the most " mannered " sonnets are by and large confined to
the beginning and the end. There is, furthermore, a notable difference
in the type of conventional sonnet prominent in these two places. Characteristic of the beginning, for example, is the allegorical conceit of
Cupid, as in Sonnet 8.

> At length he perch'd himself in *Stellas* joyfull face,

> Whose faire skin, beamy eyes, like morning sun on snow,
>   Deceiv'd the quaking boy, who thought from so pure light,
>   Effects of lively heat must needs in nature grow.

Sonnets 11, 12, 17, 20, and 43 are of the same type. At the end of
the sequence such allegory is conspicuously absent, and the ritualistic
meditation predominates, as in Sonnet 89,

> Now that of absence the most irksome night
>   With darkest shade doth overcome my day;

and in Sonnets 94, 95, 96, 98, 99, and 108.
    The first section of the sequence, which I will consider as including
the first forty-three sonnets, is devoted to a process of analysis in which
the lover attempts to define and establish—in a sense to discover—the

    1. Pollard, ed., p. xxxviii. See also Mona Wilson, ed. *Astrophel and Stella*.

values essential to his experience. The development is managed chiefly through a series of sonnets presenting an active conflict between love and competing aspects of experience or standards of value. There is a simultaneous expansion and contraction, as Astrophel moves from an isolated and detached position through successive stages of involvement in the moral and social world, an involvement which at the same time forces him deeper into introspective activity, into a new and more meaningful isolation.

The opening sonnets have been felt by a number of readers to be inferior to the standard set by the rest of the sequence, and to represent an earlier stage in Sidney's poetic development. There is some warrant for such a criticism. The conjunction of sonnets such as 3 ("Let daintie wits crie on the Sisters nine") and 6 ("Some lovers speake when they their Muses entertaine"), in which the conventional manner is satirized and rejected, with sonnets in which it is fully exemplified, such as 9 ("Queene *Vertues* Court, which some call *Stellas* face") seems to be a serious inconsistency. As Pollard remarks in a note on Sonnet 6, Sidney's "strictures" on the conventional poetry of other lovers "apply with equal force to many among the first twenty of these sonnets, notably the ninth, which it is hardly possible to believe that he composed after his poetic vision reached this clearness." But the criticism has been anticipated within the dramatic framework of the sequence itself. In the first sonnet Astrophel is introduced as poet, describing the slow and painful process by which the source of sincere poetry is discovered: "Studying inventions fine . . . Oft turning others leaves,"

> words came halting forth, wanting Inventions stay,
> Invention, Natures child, fled step-dame Studies blowes,
> And others feete still seem'd but strangers in my way.

The process is one of imitating the conventional manner until, in the last line, the discovery is made: "Foole, said my Muse to me, looke in thy heart and write." In the second sonnet he is introduced as lover, describing the gradual development of sincere passion.

> Not at the first sight, nor with a dribbed shot
> *Love* gave the wound, which while I breathe will bleed:

That is, there was no instantaneous innamoramento, as in Petrarch,

> Mille trecento ventisette, a punto
> Su l'ora prima, il dí sesto d'aprile
> Nel laberinto intrai; né veggio ond' esca.[2]

---

2. Petrarch, CCXI ("Voglia mi sprona, Amor mi guida e scorge"), p. 504.

The discovery of love and of inspiration are both described by the same rhetorical figure, *reduplicatio* or *gradatio*, the linking of clauses by repetition of the end word of one at the start of the next.

> I saw and liked, I liked but loved not,
>> I loved, but straight did not what *Love* decreed;
>> At length, to *Loves* decrees, I forc'd, agreed,
>> Yet with repining at so partiall lot.

The figure is exploited logically and metaphorically to suggest that the two processes are essentially one, and although they are presented as already completed—we are beginning *in medias res*—they are in fact anticipatory. What the two sonnets describe is actually taking place in the first part of the sequence.

This double process is represented dramatically by Astrophel's effort to resolve or eliminate a fundamental conflict that appears in all of these poems, cutting across individual differences of treatment and linking them together in a significant way. All of these poems deal with the same basic distinction between surfaces and essentials, appearance and reality. The distinction between the literary manner and matter in the anti-Petrarchan poems is only one expression of it. Its dominant form in this part of the sequence—at least the form it takes in the most powerful poems here—is in the conflict of love and "Vertue" (Sonnet 4) or Christianized Platonism (Sonnet 5), or Reason (Sonnet 10); the distinction, that is, between an abstract, generalized value and the personal symbol of value in the heart,

> That shrines in flesh so true a Deitie,
> That *Vertue*, thou thy selfe shalt be in love.

And the same basic distinction is involved in the conventional blasons and allegories (Sonnets 7, 8, 9, 11, and 12), all of which are concerned with the difference between Stella's beauty ("most faire, most cold") and her inaccessible heart; Cupid is content with

> Playing and shining in each outward part;
> But, foole, seekst not to get into her hart.
>> (Sonnet 11)

The difficulty is that Astrophel must share Cupid's failure. In most of these poems he treats Stella in a thoroughly conventional way; she exists only as the goddess of the Petrarchan ritual. The weakness of the poems as a group is largely, I think, in the abstractness and formality of the conventional decorum. That very formality, however, serves as a dramatic device, keeping the real issues Astrophel faces at a distance. He does not look steadily in his heart, as in Sonnets 1 and

4, but turns from it to the alabaster, gold, porphyry, and pearl of Stella's face, " Queene *Vertues* Court."

If the suggestion made earlier can be accepted, that there is a reference to the Devereux arms in Sonnet 13 (see above, p. 21), then it may be considered a witty acknowledgment of the impersonal and artificial qualities of the preceding sonnets. The poem is related to the conventional celebrations of her beauty by the conceit of the beauty contest, and perhaps to the anti-Petrarchan poems by the ironic emphasis on the literary aspect of the convention, as Stella triumphs over the classical deities. The identification itself adds another dimension to the basic contrast of the apparent and the real, one that puts the earlier poems in a new perspective, criticizing them as conventional. The irony within the poem also operates outside of it, in the sequence, as Penelope Devereux triumphs over the conventional goddess.

If the poem can be read in these terms, the sequence begins to turn on it, away from the conventional mode of the first sonnets in the direction of realism, of a world where Astrophel can delight in the knowledge of Stella's substantiality. But it is also a world in which there are real adversaries, considerably more substantial than the abstractions and personifications with which he has been dealing.

> Alas have I not paine enough my friend,
>   Upon whose breast a fiercer Gripe doth tire
>   Then did on him who first stale downe the fire,
>   While *Love* on me doth all his quiver spend,
>
> But with your Rubarb words ye must contend
>   To grieve me worse, in saying that Desire
>   Doth plunge my wel-form'd soule even in the mire
>   Of sinfull thoughts, which do in ruine end?
>
>   (Sonnet 14)

What is involved here is a shift from the conventionally insulated point of view of the lover to one that is more objective, that represents to some extent the collective interests of the world of nonlovers, and that is expressed not by a personified abstraction but by a dramatic character who is independent of Astrophel. Consequently, Astrophel's defense must be more than an invocation of the ritual deity; Stella, as goddess or woman, is not mentioned at all. Instead there is the effort to define love in such a way that it is in fact reconciled with a virtue conceived in social rather than in spiritual terms (suggesting the *virtus* of the courtly tradition), produced, not impeded, by love.

The emphasis, however, falls on the character of the speaker. The intrusion of the friend comes with a shock and elicits an entirely new

tone; the tone, as we noted earlier, of Astrophel as hero. The sudden
expansion of the context exposes the perilous vulnerability of the conventional situation and provokes a violent assertion of personality. The
intensity with which it is asserted persuades us of the real presence of
the lover and of a level of seriousness in his love which was not apparent
before.

The new perspective supplied by the friend seems to force Astrophel
into a re-examination of the conflict between his reason and his love,
and in Sonnets 18 and 19 he is again withdrawn, isolated, as at the
beginning.

> With what sharpe checkes I in my selfe am shent,
>   When into Reasons audite I do go:
>   And by just counts my selfe a banckrout know
>   Of all those goods which heav'n to me hath lent;
>
> Unable quite to pay even Natures rent,
>   Which unto it by birthright I do ow;
>   And which is worse, no good excuse can show,
>   But that my wealth I have most idly spent.
>
> My youth doth waste, my knowledge brings forth toyes,
>   My wit doth strive those passions to defend,
>   Which for reward spoile it with vaine annoyes.
>
> I see my course to loose my selfe doth bend:
>   I see and yet no greater sorow take,
>   Then that I loose no more for *Stellas* sake.
>
>   (Sonnet 18)
>
> On *Cupids* bow how are my heart-strings bent,
>   That see my wracke, and yet embrace the same?
>   When most I glorie, then I feele most shame;
>   I willing run, yet while I run repent.
>
> My best wits still their owne disgrace invent:
>   My verie inke turnes straight to *Stellas* name;
>   And yet my words, as them my pen doth frame,
>   Avise themselves that they are vainly spent.
>
> For though she passe all things, yet what is all
>   That unto me, who fare like him that both
>   Lookes to the skies, and in a ditch doth fall?
>
> O let me prop my mind, yet in his growth,
>   And not in Nature for best fruits unfit:
>   Scholler, saith *Love*, bend hitherward your wit.
>
>   (Sonnet 19)

Both of these poems resemble Sonnet 5, the Platonic catalogue: they have the same theme and the same form, the reversal in the last line. But the tone is utterly different. In place of the abstract concept of the earlier poem, the lover seems to be facing an ideal of personal behavior, violated by love; the division of his nature between mind and heart is not a philosophical problem so much as a private, intensely felt experience. Seeing himself, perhaps, with the eyes of the friend, he cannot reconcile the conflict and seems to repudiate the claim of virtuous love made in Sonnet 14. Consequently, the effect of the reversal in the final lines, which in Sonnet 5 is subdued, in these two poems is an almost physical wrench.

The operation of the sequence itself at this point demonstrates his dilemma, for Sonnets 18 and 19 are framed by two allegories of a thoroughly conventional sort: in Sonnet 17, Stella's eyes are the weapons with which Cupid wounds the lover, in 20 the ambush from which he shoots. These are the "toyes" Astrophel's knowledge brings forth, and they make a dramatically effective contrast with his condemnation of them. The contrast is expressed in part by the radical difference in tone, but it is also expressed formally by the radically different manners appropriate to the two kinds of poem involved. The ritualistic treatment of Stella is continued from the earlier sonnets into a context where it is no longer an adequate symbol, and it serves therefore to emphasize and dramatize the lover's psychological struggle.

In Sonnet 21 the moral issue is again raised by the friend, and again in the same form, with a reversal in the last line. But compared to the preceding sonnets on this theme, the facility and confidence with which it is handled here seem to imply that the conflict is at an end. The tension is gone; love has conquered reason.

> Sure you say well, your wisdomes golden mine
> Dig deep with learnings spade. Now tell me this,
> Hath this world ought so faire as *Stella* is?

The sententious, heavyhanded idiom of the friend suggests that Astrophel has recovered so far from the pain of Sonnets 14, 18, and 19 that he can treat the moral agent as he does the conventional poets, in parody.

Sonnet 23 is one of the sonnets responsible for the sense of audience I referred to earlier (see above, p. 16). Astrophel is placed in a solid and populous social context, fending off "curious wits" who, like the friend of Sonnets 14 and 21, are intruders in his personal world, and like him mistaken in their opinions of it.

> Some that know how my spring I did addresse,
> Deeme that my Muse some fruit of knowledge plies:

> Others, because the Prince my service tries,
> Thinke that I thinke state errours to redresse.
>
> But harder Judges judge ambitions rage,
> Scourge of it selfe, still climing slipprie place,
> Holds my young braine captiv'd in golden cage.

In this poem, however, the error is more complicated. The sententious idiom that characterized the moral friend of Sonnet 21 is even more obtrusive in the wits, with their talk of "ambitions rage, / Scourge of it selfe, still climing slipprie place." In one sense the inflated diction is simply the symptom of irrelevance. Utterly deceived by the lover's behavior, the wits make judgments that seem to have nothing to do with the real situation.

> O fooles, or over-wise, alas, the race
> Of all my thoughts hath neither stop nor start,
> But only *Stellas* eyes and *Stellas* hart.

But in another sense their accusations are more relevant than they know. They attribute to him the very ambition, and concern for achievement, the lack of which disturbs the friend of Sonnet 21 and Astrophel himself in Sonnets 18 and 19. Part of the irony, then, is directed wryly at his own condition, which the wits unwittingly have touched upon. The emphasis, nonetheless, is on their obtuseness— "fooles, or over-wise"—and through them on the inversion of the ethical theme that has taken place. The wits have replaced the friend as moral agent, and morality, consequently, has degenerated for the lover to mere sententiousness, an aspect of social convention.

The process by which the moral terms are inverted suggests, it seems to me, a possible account of Sonnet 24, the invective against Lord Rich as miser (see above, p. 29), which may make the placing of that poem less of an anomaly than it has seemed to most commentators. The expansion of the setting, as Astrophel moves out of his original isolation into the social context implied by his friend, and then into the public world of the court, has been accompanied by an increase in the force of the lover's exclusively personal standards; that is, the exposure to more and more external, general criteria has had the effect of intensifying the internal, individual values. This twofold process is carried on by the repeated demonstrations of the superiority of Stella's "virtue" to the virtuous precepts that attempt to compete with her, and it is expressed by the repeated use of the reversal technique.

Sonnet 24 extends the process in both respects. The proper name, on one hand, adds further particularity to the social context, and on

the other, through the metaphor of the miser, it represents, as I tried
to show earlier, what in the doctrine of love is absolute evil.   The
violence of the tone is the same as in Sonnet 14, and identifies Astrophel
as hero.   But in 14 he is attempting to define love in terms of moral
virtue; here the logic is reversed and he defines virtue—or more precisely, vice—in terms of love.   The relationship to the preceding poem,
then, is quite pointed: the ordinary standards of the court society,
expressed by the wits, are irrelevant to the lover, a mere convention, and
therefore false; Rich as evil is " real," an actual character who is part
of a " real " world.   The violent tone, as a means of emphasizing a
" real " distinction, is perhaps justified by this contrast.[3]

The point is that Astrophel, like all lovers, especially Petrarchan
lovers, is creating his own metaphysics.   Stella is his supreme value,
and therefore good and evil must be defined in terms of her.   Sonnet 25
is thus the logical sequel to 24, celebrating her precisely as the *summum
bonum*, the Platonic Idea, by means of a witty manipulation of the term
" virtue " (see above, p. 36).

> The wisest scholler of the wight most wise,
>> By *Phoebus* doome, with sugred sentence sayes,
>> That Vertue if it once met with our eyes,
>> Strange flames of *Love* it in our soules would raise.
>
>>   . . . . .
>
> It is most true, for since I her did see,
>> Vertues great beautie in that face I prove,
>> And find th' effect, for I do burne in love.

Although compared to the intensity and violence of Sonnet 24 there
is a striking shift of tone, both poems nevertheless involve the same
activity.   The playful, sophistic treatment in Sonnet 25 suggests an
acknowledgment that that activity is a commonplace; Astrophel seems
to be announcing his awareness of what he is doing and admitting the
possible absurdities.   That does not mean an abdication or repudiation
of any sort, but it does serve to keep the whole process in place.   The
two sonnets together produce a complex attitude in which the conventional hyperbole is modified on the one hand by the speaker's ironic
self-contemplation and on the other by the practical facts of the situation, where there is a real husband, and an extraordinarily unpleasant
one.

Sonnet 25 introduces a series of sonnets which in a witty way assert

---

3. I do not mean to suggest that the placing of the sonnet is inevitable; I am
simply trying to show the kind of relation that, placed in this position, it bears
to the sonnets around it.

the " virtue " of love and claim a status for it that is more than personal, the status of a " precept," metaphysical or otherwise.   In Sonnet 26 Astrophel contradicts the " dustie wits," the " fooles " who dare to scorn astrology, and think the stars

> To have for no cause birthright in the skie
>> But for to spangle the blacke weeds of night;
>> Or for some brawle, which in that chamber hie,
>> They should still daunce to please a gazers sight.

He knows " great causes great effects procure,"

>> Who oft fore-judge my after-following race,
>> By only those two starres in *Stellas* face.

He is exploiting a " virtue " implicit in Stella's name, virtue as one of the orders of the celestial hierarchy.   In Sonnet 28 he counters the charge of allegorizing that the hyperbole of 25 and 26 might suggest by insisting on the " pure simplicitie " of his attitude and his symbol.

> When I say, *Stella,* I do meane the same
>> Princesse of Beautie, for whose only sake,
>> The raines of *Love* I love, though never slake,

and by opposing it to the " quintessence " of the philosophers (see above, p. 26).

Still another celebration occurs in Sonnet 29, and in this case there seems to be a reversion to the technique of the earlier sonnets.   It is an allegory, with the distinction between Stella's beauty and her inaccessible heart that is made in Sonnets 8, 11, and 12, and it uses the blason form of 9, with a similar catalogue of charms.

> Like some weake Lords, neighbord by mighty kings,
>> To keepe themselves and their chiefe cities free,
>> Do easly yeeld, that all their coasts may be
>> Ready to store their campes of needful things:

> So *Stellas* heart, finding what power *Love* brings,
>> To keep it selfe in life and liberty,
>> Doth willing graunt, that in the frontiers he
>> Use all to helpe his other conquerings:

> And thus her heart escapes, but thus her eyes
>> Serve him with shot, her lips his heralds arre,
>> Her breasts his tents, legs his triumphall carre,

> Her flesh his food, her skin his armour brave,
>> And I, but for because my prospect lies
>> Upon that coast, am giv'n up for a slave.

It is more effective than the earlier sonnets because of the operation of the sequence. This elaborate image of Stella as a country, with coasts and frontiers, developed by the conventional military conceit, constitutes a kind of microcosm which is immediately contrasted, in Sonnet 30, to the macrocosm of the real world, with all its wars located and identified item by item (see p. 16).

> Whether the Turkish new-moone minded be
> > To fill his hornes this yeare on Christian coast;
> > How *Poles* right king meanes without leave of hoast,
> > To warme with ill-made fire cold *Moscovy*.

The extraliterary values of the world of Sir Philip Sidney are invoked for the sake of dramatic intensity. Because the two sonnets are paired, the biographical particularity of the one modifies and qualifies the conventional generality of the other. The expansion of the setting is now complete; the lover is placed firmly at the center of a real and a whole world, which he scorns for love.

> > I cumbred with good maners, answer do,
> > But know not how, for still I thinke of you.

This is the first direct address to Stella, and it marks a transition. In the preceding sonnet Astrophel is constructing the ritual image he opposes to the world. The following sonnet introduces a new movement dealing with the consequences of rejecting the world.

> With how sad steps, O Moone, thou climb'st the skies,
> > How silently, and with how wanne a face,
> > What, may it be, that even in heav'nly place
> > That busie archer his sharpe arrowes tries?

> Sure if that long with *Love* acquainted eyes
> > Can judge of *Love*, thou feel'st a *Lovers* case;
> > I reade it in thy lookes, thy languisht grace
> > To me that feele the like, thy state descries.

> Then ev'n of fellowship, O Moone, tell me
> > Is constant *Love* deem'd there but want of wit?
> > Are Beauties there as proud as here they be?

> Do they above love to be lov'd, and yet
> > Those Lovers scorne whom that *Love* doth possesse?
> > Do they call *Vertue* there ungratefulnesse?

This is deservedly one of Sidney's best-known sonnets. It is an impressive performance, all the more impressive in view of the conventional nature of the materials: a nocturnal meditation—the sleepless

lover making his complaint—with the generalizing tendency characteristic of the convention. In the first two lines Astrophel is performing
the familiar ritual, seeing analogues of his condition everywhere; it is
a kind of hyperbole, a means of emphasizing the extent of his melancholy, that appears at first to be the basic theme of the poem. In the
next two lines this idea is treated as a discovery, a surprising one—
"What, may it be . . ." !—but the surprise, of course, is feigned, and
the wry, faintly ironical tone involved in the pretense seems to be a
recognition of the fact that it is he who is melancholy, not the moon.
Though the pretense is sustained—"Then ev'n of fellowship, O Moone
. . ."—the real discovery is dealt with in the sestet, the discovery, that
is, of the speaker's own personal position as not only wretched but
ridiculous, forced into making appeals to the moon. The point seems
to be that Astrophel is deliberately trying to universalize his experience,
to relate himself to the symbol provided by the Endymion myth, as a
means of organizing his lover's world and transcending the limitations
of his personal despair.

The effect of the poem depends upon the skill with which the conventional form is maintained while the personal impulse works against
it. It is an effect of poise, of control, which can be felt in the movement
of the verse and particularly in the handling of the tone. The melancholy which the poem has for its subject is both concrete and universal,
a product of the generalizing effect of the conventional mode and the
individual modulations of tone.

This sonnet suggests the situation with which the sequence began.
Astrophel is again in isolation, writing in the conventional mode. The
most obvious difference is that we have seen his withdrawal actually
performed; he is isolated now within a context whose pressures are
remembered if they are not present.

The effect of the context is most important in regard to the position
and treatment of Stella. The remarkably detailed elimination of competing values has been the means of establishing love as the central and
single value, with Stella as its symbol. Consequently, now that the
exorcism has been performed she is magnified beyond anything in the
earlier sonnets. But to establish her in this transcendent position means
that the lover is utterly dependent on her; he must face the facts of his
situation, isolated not only from the world but from Stella too. As a
result, in this group of sonnets (31 through 40) there is a new attitude
of melancholy and of reproach, even bitterness—"Do they call *Vertue*
there ungratefulnesse?"—and of supplication,

> Since then thou hast so farre subdued me,
> That in my heart I offer still to thee,
> O do not let thy Temple be destroyd.
>   (Sonnet 40)

The sequence is focusing now on the central conflict, not Love and moral Virtue, or Passion and Reason, or Astrophel and the curious, dusty, busy wits of the court, but Astrophel and Stella: that is to say, the central conflict of the Petrarchan convention. Discovery of this, the realization of Stella's importance to him and of the distance that separates them, is the subject of these poems as a group. It is expressed most strikingly in Sonnet 33.

> I might, unhappie word, O me, I might,
>> And then would not, or could not see my blisse:
>> Till now wrapt in a most infernall night,
>> I find how heav'nly day wretch I did misse.
>
> Hart rent thy selfe, thou doest thy selfe but right,
>> No lovely *Paris* made thy *Hellen* his:
>> No force, no fraud, robd thee of thy delight,
>> Nor Fortune of thy fortune author is:
>
> But to my selfe my selfe did give the blow,
>> While too much wit (forsooth) so troubled me,
>> That I respects for both our sakes must show:
>
> And yet could not by rising Morne foresee
>> How faire a day was neare, O punisht eyes,
>> That I had bene more foolish, or more wise.

This is an inversion of the conventional innamoramento, a restatement of the account given in Sonnets 2 ("I saw and liked, I liked but loved not") and 16 ("Love, I thought that I was full of thee"). Though it is difficult to read as a reference to anything but Stella's marriage ("No lovely *Paris* made thy *Hellen* his"), that does not mean that Astrophel has just learned of it. On the contrary, it seems more satisfactory to read it as a response not to an immediate event but rather to a situation that is made immediate by the lover's sudden and overwhelming realization of his total involvement, with the bitterness of a backward glance at his folly, his failure not just to take advantage of his opportunities before the marriage but to anticipate seriously the present situation.

> O punisht eyes,
> That I had bene more foolish, or more wise.

He has been as blind as the curious wits he mocked for thinking him ambitious.

The consequences for the poet of the lover's discovery are presented in terms that suggest a reprise of Sonnet 1. But the linked clauses that expressed the laborious study in the first sonnet are replaced by a technique of question and answer, expressing a sense of crippled purpose.

> Come let me write, and to what end? to ease
>   A burthned hart; how can words ease, which are
>   The glasses of thy dayly vexing care?
>
>   . . . . .
>
> What idler thing, then speake and not be hard?
>   What harder thing then smart, and not to speake?
>   Peace foolish wit, with wit my wit is mard.
>
> Thus write I while I doubt to write, and wreake
>   My harmes on Inks poore losse; perhaps some find
>   *Stellas* great powrs, that so confuse my mind.
>
>   (Sonnet 34)

The dramatic sequel of the discovery in Sonnet 33 is the riddle sonnet, 37. It comes as the third in a series of blasons celebrating Stella's transcendent powers, but it breaks the blason form with the identification of Rich in the last line (see above, p. 22).

> Towards *Auroras* Court a Nymph doth dwell,
>   Rich in all beauties which mans eye can see:
>   Beauties so farre from reach of words, that we
>   Abase her praise, saying she doth excell:
>
> Rich in the treasure of deserv'd renowne,
>   Rich in the riches of a royall hart,
>   Rich in those gifts which give th' eternall crowne;
>
> Who, though most rich in these and everie part,
>   Which make the patents of true worldly blisse,
>   Hath no misfortune, but that Rich she is.

The thoroughly conventional theme implicit in the allegories, the paradox of love, is here an actual and inescapable fact. The riddle, which was suppressed from the sequence until 1598, is a riddle for Astrophel as well as the reader, for the contrast of superficial appearance and essential reality characteristic of the early sonnets has developed into a permanent ambiguity that cannot be resolved by an act of will.

The conventional form and the personal feeling in this poem provide the defining terms of the lover's experience and are responsible for the pattern of the sonnets that follow 31, which seem to alternate between them. Astrophel's discovery of the extent of his involvement leads to a recognition of the convention as the only objective order to which he can refer the facts of his personal experience; it provides the only

" precepts " or examples to which to relate the " mooving " power of his love. The technical control of a Sonnet like 31, then, has a dramatic value, as it represents Astrophel's effort to control his relation to the conventional norms. Sonnet 39, like 31 an anthology piece, provides a further illustration.

> Come sleepe, O sleepe, the certaine knot of peace,
> > The baiting place of it, the balme of woe,
> > The poore mans wealth, the prisoners release,
> > Th' indifferent Judge betweene the high and low;
>
> With shield of proofe shield me from out the prease
> > Of those fierce darts dispaire at me doth throw.
> > O make in me those civill warres to cease;
> > I will good tribute pay, if thou do so.
>
> Take thou of me smooth pillowes, sweetest bed,
> > A chamber deafe of noise and blind of light,[4]
> > A rosie garland, and a wearie hed:
>
> And if these things, as being thine by right,
> > Move not thy heavy grace, thou shalt in me
> > Livelier than elsewhere *Stellas* image see.

Like Sonnet 31 this is a highly successful treatment of thoroughly conventional material; and as before, the lover first universalizes his situation—associating himself with all of suffering mankind, longing for release—then makes the particular application, here by means of the personal appeal. The success of the poem is to a large extent the result of sheer technical skill, not just in the various phonetic devices but in the way the whole structure is arranged, moving from the slow, repetitive definition, the incantatory invocation, of the octave to the sudden, intensely sensory evocation of the sestet.

The effect of this sonnet is heightened by its context in the sequence, for Sonnet 38, which begins, "This night," and Sonnet 40, which begins, "As good to write as for to lie and grone," seem to refer to the same night. After the comparative timelessness of the early part of the sequence, the effect here is of a sudden arresting of the movement, giving an emphasis that is not part of the nocturnal ritual itself. As a matter of fact, seven of the ten poems from 31 to 40 are nocturnal meditations, so that as a group they seem to be more tightly organized than the preceding sonnets. Their intensity is in part the product of this greater concentration, in part the product of the tension set up between the conventional mode of the blason and meditation and the

4. The Folio reading is " deafe to noise and blind to light."

curiously personal, even private references. But it is the personal tone
in these sonnets, produced by the sense of discovery, that most clearly
distinguishes the pain they deal with from the allegorical wounds of
the earlier sonnets—" I have my death wound, fly."

Of course, the most important difference between these and the earlier
sonnets is simply that these are better. Astrophel is no longer consciously poetizing, for language, he feels, has become inadequate, or at
the best a kind of therapy, " to ease a burthned hart." He is instead
looking in his heart, while with a feeling skill he paints his hell. But
he no longer has to identify his attitude by assertion, for the poems
themselves create it. This is the culmination, the fulfillment of the
process anticipated in the first two sonnets.

After the intensity of Sonnets 31 through 40 there is a diminuendo
as Astrophel seems to recover sufficiently from his melancholy to return
to the world. In Sonnet 41,

> Having this day my horse, my hand, my launce
> Guided so well, that I obtain'd the prize . . .

(see above, p. 15)

the dark night seems to be over; action replaces the stasis of the preceding poems, and the audience of horsemen, townfolk, wits, and so
forth ends the lover's isolation.

Sonnet 43, which it seems to me appropriate to consider as concluding the first section of the sequence, summarizes the dramatic development to this point.

> Faire eyes, sweet lips, deare heart, that foolish I
>   Could hope by *Cupids* helpe on you to pray;
>   Since to himselfe he doth your gifts apply,
>   As his maine force, choise sport, and easefull stay.
>
> For when he will see who dare him gainesay,
>   Then with those eyes he lookes, lo, by and by
>   Each soule doth at *Loves* feet his weapons lay,
>   Glad if for her he give them leave to die.
>
> When he will play, then in her lips he is,
>   Where blushing red, that *Loves* selfe them doth love,
>   With either lip he doth the other kisse:
>
> But when he will for quiets sake remove
>   From all the world, her heart is then his rome,
>   Where well he knowes, no man to him can come.

This is an allegory of the sort with which the sequence began, but

Cupid has changed sides; the heart that was impregnable to him is now his refuge. Astrophel, like Cupid, has removed from all the world, but that refuge is denied him, and the consequence is to experience "poore *Petrarchs* long deceased woes." The melancholy of Sonnets 31-40 lingers here, then, but it is qualified by a kind of wry acceptance, an acknowledgment of the ironies of the lover's situation. He is looking back on his earlier attitude, recalling his performance in such allegorical sonnets as 11 and 12. The propriety of the allegorical form here is that it suggests the comparison, expressing, perhaps, Astrophel's rueful awareness of the difference between performing the conventional exercise and feeling the conventional situation as a reality.

II

Sonnet 44, like 34, in a number of ways resembles Sonnet 1. It is an appraisal of the lover's poetical activities and employs as an analytical technique the same rhetorical figure of gradatio.

> My words I know do well set forth my mind,
>   My mind bemones his sense of inward smart;
>   Such smart may pitie claime of any hart,
>   Her heart, sweete heart, is of no Tygres kind:
>
> And yet she heares, and yet no pitie I find;
>   But more I crie, lesse grace she doth impart,
>   Alas, what cause is there so overthwart,
>   That Nobleness it selfe makes thus un kind?
>
> I much do guesse, yet find no truth save this,
>   That when the breath of my complaints doth tuch
>   Those daintie dores unto the Court of blisse,
>
> The heav'nly nature of that place is such,
>   That once come there, the sobs of mine annoyes
>   Are metamorphosed straight to tunes of joyes.

The process presented through the figure, however, is not the same. In Sonnet 1 Astrophel describes himself and his intentions,

> faine in verse my love to show,
> That she (deare She) might take some pleasure of my paine,
> Pleasure might cause her reade, reading might make her know,
> Knowledge might pitie winne, and pitie grace obtaine,
>
> I sought fit words to paint the blackest face of woe . . .

and the rest of the poem dealt with the problem of finding the fit words.

Now he feels that he has found them but is still faced with the problem of winning pity and obtaining grace. The emphasis, that is to say, has shifted from the poet-lover to the lady, and the poem ends on a new note, the "tunes of joyes."

This sonnet, then, marks a considerable recovery from the condition indicated in Sonnet 34 and 40, where despair had robbed the poet of his purpose—"As good to write as for to lie and grone." It seems to announce a shift in the direction of the sequence, the beginning of a new movement in which the lady's "virtue," her metamorphic power to transform the lover, is felt in a new way. The metamorphosis produces a new persona for him, and consequently a new position for her.

The shift is immediately apparent in the sonnets that follow. Sonnet 45 continues the theme of 44,

> Stella oft sees the verie face of wo
>   Painted in my beclowded stormie face:
>   But cannot skill to pitie my disgrace,

and like it ends with a metamorphosis; since she is not moved by Astrophel, but can weep over a "fable . . . Of Lovers never knowne,"

> Then thinke my deare, that you in me do reed
>   Of Lovers ruine some sad Tragedie:
>   I am not I, pitie the tale of me.

The actual transformation is from the despair of the earlier sonnets to the amusement of this one, from the prostrate victim pleading for mercy—"O do not let thy Temple be destroyd"—to the parodist, playing the role of ingénu. The difference between fact and fiction he offers to forgo is another manifestation of the fundamental distinction between appearance and reality, manner and matter. In the earlier sonnets it was Stella as the Petrarchan symbol who had necessitated the distinction; now it is she, not the lover, who confuses it.

The original terms, then, have been turned around, and the experience of the preceding sonnets is put in the perspective of a new point of view, expressed by the persona. It is in part Astrophel's previous behavior that is being parodied here: his "grievous case" now seems no more than a tale.

The new perspective involves a reduction of the scale on which Stella has been treated. Sonnet 46 ("I curst thee oft, I pitie now thy case"; see p. 28), is an allegory in which her beauty is celebrated by the presence of Cupid, her coldness deplored by having him banished. But to Astrophel contemplating her from a new point of view, the douce adversaire the allegory usually involves is a source of urbane amusement; she can no more banish her beauty than she can banish his love.

With ironic detachment he points out the impossibility and makes frank acknowledgment of desire for the first time in the sequence.

> Yet Deare, let me his pardon get of you,
>> So long (though he from book myche to desire)
>> Till without fewell you can make hot fire.

Astrophel is not distinguishing here between beauty and a cold, cold heart, but between what he considers a pose, an affectation of the coy and conventional mistress, and the nature of the real woman. The pose he mocks; the woman he appeals to on the basis of good sense and good humor. His detachment is for the benefit of the coy mistress, but there is an effect of familiarity, perhaps intimacy, with the woman, suggesting that he feels (as conventional lovers never do) that her intractability is not permanent; it is subject to will, and he expects it to be changed. Such an attitude obviously implies a confidence that is new in the sequence.

The impulse to parody carries over into Sonnet 47, where the subject is the conflict of Love and Virtue that was so painful in some of the earlier sonnets. The specific reference seems to be the Platonic context of Sonnet 5, "true Beautie Vertue is indeed." Here Astrophel purports to be in rebellion; "Vertue awake!" he cries, "Beautie but beautie is,"

> I may, I must, I can, I will, I do
> Leave following that, which it is gaine to misse.

> Let her go: soft, but here she comes, go to,
> Unkind, I love you not.

and then makes a profound obeisance, demonstrating the true "virtue" of beauty, and involving them both in the parody.

> O me, that eye
> Doth make my heart give to my tongue the lie.

The performance is continued in Sonnet 48, which presents the consequence of rebellion. The lover now is in utter slavery, appealing to his mistress for mercy: "Soules joy, bend not those morning starres from me"; he pays homage to the "virtue" of those stars,

> Where Vertue is made strong by Beauties might,
> Where *Love* is chastnesse, Paine doth learne delight,
> And Humblenesse growes one with Majestie;

and then makes the victim's ultimate plea, for swift execution.

> Deare Killer, spare not thy sweet cruell shot:
> A kind of grace it is to slay with speed.

This sonnet is almost the exact counterpart of Sonnet 42, which has the same blason of Stella's eyes,

> O eyes, which do the spheares of beautie move,
>> Whose beames be joyes, whose joyes all vertues be,
>> Who, while they make *Love* conquer, conquer *Love*,
>> The schooles where *Venus* hath learn'd chastitie.

and ends with the same appeal,

> Yet still on me, O eyes, dart downe your rayes:

> And if from Majestie of sacred lights,
>> Oppressing mortall sense, my death proceed,
>> Wrackes Triumphs be, which *Love* (high set) doth breed.

Comparison of the two sonnets provides a good illustration of the way Sidney exploits the force of context. Sonnet 42, while not a particularly solemn poem, is more or less conventional in effect; Sonnet 48, though the same type of poem, has almost the effect of burlesque. The difference results primarily from the function of the context, the fact that Sonnet 48 follows and seems to be a continuation of the mock ritual in 47.

The significance of the parody in these four poems is that the relation to the convention he had learned to accept and tried to control in the previous sonnets has now been replaced by the relation to Stella. His attitude has finally been unified and his personality released, battle by battle, not only from the competing claims of society and morality but from the limits of the Petrarchan impasse. Stella's coyness and perversity are now the manner he must master, and his effort is expressed through the pressure of his personality, the fact of his energy, the confidence and enthusiasm with which he counters fiction.

I noted above that desire is acknowledged for the first time in Sonnet 46; the fact that it is no longer denied, as it was so vehemently in Sonnet 14, makes possible the delight and the enthusiasm of the sonnets in this section. It is acknowledged again in Sonnet 52 with considerably more force and quite a different effect.

> A strife is growne between *Vertue* and *Love*,
>> While each pretends that *Stella* must be his.

Love claims Stella's "eyes, her lips, her all . . . Since they do weare his badge," while "Vertue" claims "that vertuous soule." Stella, so divided, seems very like the recondite symbol at the beginning of the sequence, and the distinction here between her "faire outside" and Stella's "selfe" recalls the distinctions in the earlier allegories. The

lover's choice, however, is quite different. It is expressed in the last
three lines with the blunt and dramatic intrusion of his personality into
the "strife."

> Well *Love*, since this demurre our sute doth stay,
>   Let *Vertue* have that *Stellas* selfe; yet thus,
>   That *Vertue* but that body graunt to us.

The tone which resolves the "strife" suggests not a choice so much
as a judgment of what "that *Stellas* selfe" really is. But the criterion
Astrophel depends upon keeps the element of choice in the poem: the
determinant reality is his feeling, his desire, because it is concrete.
Opposed to it everything else becomes unreal or absurd.

The change in Astrophel's condition is marked in still another way
by his relation to the society around him. In Sonnet 51 he is fending
off one of the busy wits who would disturb his concentration.

> Pardon mine eares, both I and they do pray,
>   So may your tongue still fluently proceed,
>   To them that do such entertainment need, . . .

The form and procedure are very close to the sonnets on the same
theme in the first section, but the satirical exorcism is performed more
sharply and dramatically and involves an important difference. Astrophel seems to enjoy flapping this bug; the enthusiasm and vigor of
the preceding sonnets are continued here. Furthermore, he turns back,
not to the contemplation of his misery, but to a "sweet comedie." A
similar development is apparent in Sonnet 54, where Astrophel is involved with the ladies of the court. They are just as mistaken as the
curious wits of the earlier sonnets, but their error is significantly
different. They are sure "He cannot love" because he is not acting
like a conventional lover; the specific symptoms he lacks are absurdly
superficial—"set colours" and "lockes of vowed haire"—but at least
by implication he lacks even the symptoms which excited the curiosity
of the wits in the earlier sonnets. The coquettes seem to dismiss him
because he is too normal, too healthy, too sane to be a proper lover.

In Sonnet 58 the phenomenon of "metamorphosis" with which this
second section of the sequence began is restated in rhetorical terms, as
an illustration of the Aristotelian "proof" furnished by the ethos of
the speaker (see above, p. 38): when Stella read his "piercing phrases,"

> O voice, o face, maugre my speeches might,
>   Which wooed wo, most ravishing delight,
>   Even those sad words, even in sad me did breed.

The compliment to the lady's "virtue," her power of "mooving" the

lover, is a way of describing his dilemma: when he is faced with the
"mystery" of such a muse, who not only inspires the poet but transforms his poetry, the only force he can bring to bear is the force of
persona.   The celebration of the mistress-muse, then, provides the
principle behind Astrophel's strategy, the precedence of personality, the
speaker over the speech. Consequently, the poems that follow, like the
poems that follow 44, give a concentrated demonstration of the lover as
naïf, presented as the "proof" of Stella's metamorphic power (she
has transformed him) and at the same time, as an antic role, his chief
defense against it.   Thus, in Sonnet 59 he returns to the method of
45 ("I am not I, pitie the tale of me"),

> Deare, why make you more of a dog then me?
> If he do love, I burne, I burne in love.

Ostensibly Love has turned the lover into the simple-minded sup-
pliant of the convention, but as I pointed out earlier (see above, p. 28),
this performance is designed to laugh the lady into love.   The real
"virtue" of love is expressed by Astrophel's delight in the "sweet
comedie"; he is engaging in a gay dialectic from which emerges a
definition of love that insists on the validity of the individual personality
and the priority of individual feeling to the generalized norms of
convention.

The next four sonnets, continuing the dialectic, present different
versions of the lady's metamorphic power over language, in each case
countered by the lover as naïf. In Sonnet 60 it is the power of the
Petrarchan coquette, and produces the conventional oxymoron.   The
ingenuous lover, bewildered by her perversity, unable to understand
"this fierce *Love* and lovely hate," asks for assistance;

> Then some good body tell me how I do,
>   Whose presence, absence, absence presence is;
>   Blist in my curse, and cursed in my blisse.

In 61 and 62, like the Muse of 44 and the rhetor of 58, she turns his
own terms against him, but her power is now the "virtue" of the
Petrarchan platonique.   The demonstration is particularly full in Sonnet 62, where it is committed to the working out of the rhetorical
figure, *traductio*, or the "tranlacer," a kind of word play in which the
same word is repeated in different forms. Stella, "in whose eyes *Love*
though unfelt doth shine," said that "love she did, but loved a Love
not blind,"

> And therefore by her Loves authority
>   Wild me these tempests of vaine love to flie,
>   And anchor fast my selfe on *Vertues* shore.

"Love" is passed current between them, but by the lady's Platonic manipulation it is falsified, made counterfeit.

> Alas, if this the only mettall be
> Of *Love*, new-coind to helpe my beggery,
> Deare, love me not, that ye may love me more.

The conflict of Love and moral Virtue is being presented here in dramatic terms, as the debate between Astrophel and Stella, with the term "love" exploited in much the same way that "virtue" is exploited in some of the other sonnets, and for the same reason: to contrast the lady's different powers.

The performance of the baffled and exasperated naïf reaches a comic climax in Sonnet 63 where, with a sudden leap of enthusiasm, he seizes an opportunity to turn the tables.

> O Grammer rules, o now your vertues show;
> So children still reade you with awfull eyes,
> As my young Dove may in your precepts wise
> Her graunt to me, by her owne vertue know.

> For late with heart most high, with eyes most low,
> I crav'd the thing which ever she denies:
> She, lightning *Love*, displaying *Venus* skies,
> Least once should not be heard, twise said, No, No.

> Sing then my Muse, now *Io Paean* sing,
> Heav'ns envy not at my high triumphing,
> But Grammers force with sweet successe confirme:

> For Grammer says (o this deare *Stella*, say,)
> For Grammer sayes (to Grammer who sayes nay)
> That in one speech two Negatives affirme.

Here is a metamorphosis indeed. Stella's "owne vertue" in the preceding sonnets, Astrophel argues, has been no more than a capricious tyranny over words, a power that resides in grammar rules and is therefore available to lovers as well as ladies. The amiable absurdity of this, with perhaps an epithalamial suggestion in "Sing then my Muse, then *Io Paean* sing," is its own justification.

The mounting exuberance of the sonnets overflows here in a lyric outburst, the crest of the rising tide of wit and gaiety, the first of the eleven songs.

> Doubt you to whom my Muse these notes entendeth,
> Which now my breast orecharg'd to Musicke lendeth:
> To you, to you, all song of praise is due,
> Only in you my song begins and endeth.

The structure of the song is extremely formal, and constitutes an " envelope," as the last stanza is a repetition of the first—"Only in you my song begins and endeth." The intervening stanzas make up, in question and answer form, the catalogue of the conventional blason.

> Who hath the eyes which marrie state with pleasure?
> Who hath the lips, where wit in fairenesse raigneth?
> Who hath the feet, whose step of sweetnesse planteth?
> Who hath the breast, whose milke doth passions nourish?
> Who hath the hand which without stroke subdueth?
> Who hath the haire which loosest fastest tieth?
> Who hath the voyce, which soule from sences sunders?

The total effect of this general celebration of Stella's "virtues" is one of summing up Petrarchan themes presented earlier in the sequence, drawn together here in the single form. The high formality of structure and the ritualistic hyperbole, insisting on Stella as deity, modify the effect of the sonnets immediately preceding. Having treated her gaily and not altogether respectfully in an effort to make her identify herself as a woman, Astrophel now sings his *Te Deam*. But the glorification is by no means solemn. It is a jubilation.

The dramatic effect of the song, emerging from the sonnets that precede it, is heightened by the marked shift of tone and technique in the sonnets that follow it. Sonnet 64 continues the celebration of Stella's transcendent powers, but in an intensely personal, rather than conventional, way: "No more, my deare, no more these counsels trie . . . do not will me from my *Love* to flie. / I do not envie *Aristotles* wit, . . .

> Nor hope, nor wish another course to frame,
> But that which once may win thy cruell hart:
> Thou art my Wit, and thou my Vertue art.

In contrast to the lyric extravagance of the song, the effect of the sonnet is of utter simplicity, and in place of encomium, an assertion of direct sincerity (see above, p. 24). The first line—". . . no more these counsels trie"—seems to be a reference to the Platonizing admonitions of Sonnets 61 and 62, to which he is responding now not by parody but by appeal. There seems to have been a rediscovery, perhaps through the ritual of the song, of Stella's supreme importance to him, of her real "virtue," and the result is another transformation, a change of persona or perhaps the elimination of it. In contrast to the elaborate roles adopted in the sonnets before the song, the effect here is of no role at all, the lover speaking in his own voice.

The primary function of Sonnet 65 ("Love by sure proofe I may call thee unkind ") is exactly the same, to present Astrophel in propria persona, and the method here goes beyond the limits of the poetical situation to draw upon the values of actual history. This is the sonnet which, through the allegorical form of a complaint to Cupid, makes the identification of Astrophel with Sidney—" Thou bear'st the arrow, I the arrow head " (see above, p. 18). The two sonnets together suggest that, for the moment anyway, the " sweet comedie " is played out; Astrophel is reminding Stella that he has not just been playing a game. To call attention to his " reality " here is to exert the force of personality in a different way, turning him toward the gravity of conventional complaint, though the restraint and control with which the shift is managed, and the personal emphasis, produce an effect that is far from conventional.

The gravity of these two poems is momentary, for the poems which follow start a new movement in which the implied narrative structure is more precise than it has been heretofore, the sonnets more closely integrated with it, and which carries, with mounting intensity, to the end of the central section of the sequence. The new movement is initiated in Sonnet 66—" And do I see some cause a hope to feede? "— by an apparent change in Stella, as if in response to the change in Astrophel. He has caught her eyes upon him,

> while I lookt other way:
> But when mine eyes backe to their heav'n did move,
> They fled with blush, which guiltie seem'd of love.

He recognizes the possibilities of self-deception—" Hope, art thou true, or doest thou flatter me? "—but resolves his doubts by a wry willingness to be so deceived.

> Well, how so thou interpret the contents,
> I am resolv'd thy errour to maintaine,
> Rather then by more truth to get more paine.
>   (Sonnet 67)

The first indication of any real responsiveness on the part of Stella produces an element of willfulness in Astrophel's attitude, a new kind of aggressiveness that seems to supplant the gay, though constantly frustrated, assurance of the earlier sonnets in this section.

His hope is fulfilled in Sonnet 69: " For Stella hath . . . Of her high heart giv'n me the monarchie." His joy bursts out to the friend " that oft saw through all maskes my wo," with an amusing echo of the epithalamial note from Sonnet 63, " I, I, O I may say that she is mine," and is in no way qualified by the terms of Stella's capitulation.

> And though she give but thus conditionally
> > This realme of blisse, while vertuous course I take,
> > No kings be crown'd but they some covenants make.

After the insistence again and again on desire—along with joy, one of the two key terms in this part of the sequence—the casual way in which he accepts the temperance of the Platonic love offered him suggests that the process of maintaining error is continuing. His acceptance of the "vertuous course" is the shrewdness of the strategist, a very worldly "virtue" adopted for practical ends, rather "formidine paenae," than "virtutis amore."[5] It is not surprising, then, that what efforts he makes to observe the terms of Stella's spiritual "don de mercy" are notably unsuccessful. In 71 he celebrates Stella as the Platonic "Idea," using Petrarch, appropriately enough, as his model ("Chi vuol veder quantunque po Natura").[6]

> Who will in fairest booke of Nature know,
> > How Vertue may best lodg'd in beautie be,
> > Let him but learne of *Love* to reade in thee
> *Stella*, those faire lines, which true goodness show.
>
> There shall he find all vices overthrow,
> > Not by rude force, but sweetest soveraigntie
> > Of reason, from whose light those night-birds flie;
> > That inward sunne in thine eyes shineth so.
>
> And not content to be Perfections heire
> > Thy selfe, doest strive all minds that way to move,
> > Who marke in thee what is in thee most faire.

In 72 he addresses Desire as the "old companion" from whose fellowship he must be parted.

> > I must no more in thy sweet passions lie;
> > *Vertues* gold now must head my *Cupids* dart.
>
> Service and Honor, wonder with delight,
> > Fear to offend, will worthie to appeare,
> > Care shining in mine eyes, faith in my sprite:
>
> These things are left me by my only Deare . . .

But in each case the final line completely inverts the "vertuous course" the poem has been taking.

> > But ah, Desire still cries. Give me some food.   (71)

---

5. *Works*, 3, 13.   6. Petrarch, CCXLVIII, p. 565.

> But thou, Desire, because thou wouldst have all,
> Now banisht art, but yet alas how shall? (72)

The reversal technique so prominent in the first part of the sequence reappears here with the source of the powerful effect unequivocally identified; the ambiguities through which teaching and "moving" were contrasted in such sonnets as 68 (see above, p. 35) have been removed: "For who will be taught, if hee be not mooved with desire to be taught?"[7]

The Platonic covenant of Sonnet 69 is clearly doomed. The destruction occurs in the Second Song, which follows Sonnet 72.

> Have I caught my heav'nly jewell,
> Teaching sleepe most faire to be?
> Now will I teach her that she,
> When she wakes, is too too cruell.
>
> Since sweet sleep her eyes hath charmed,
> The two only darts of Love,
> Now will I with that boy prove
> Some play, while he is disarmed.
>
> Her tongue waking still refuseth,
> Giving frankly niggard No:
> Now will I attempt to know
> What No her tongue sleeping useth.
>
> See the hand which waking gardeth,
> Sleeping, grants a free resort:
> Now will I invade the fort,
> Cowards Love with losse rewardeth.
>
> But o foole, thinke of the danger,
> Of her just and high disdaine:
> Now will I alas refraine,
> Love feares nothing else but anger.
>
> But those lips, so sweetly swelling,
> Do invite a stealing kisse:
> Now will I but venture this,
> Who will read, must first learne spelling.
>
> Oh sweet kisse, but ah she is waking,
> Lowring beautie chastens me:
> Now will I away hence flee:
> Foole, more foole, for no more taking.

---

7. *Works, 3,* 19.

This is a more satisfactory "don de mercy," taken instead of given. The terms of the "strife" between Love and Virtue have been reduced to the simplest and most concrete level, and the conquest itself, no longer merely the expression of attitude, has issued directly and dramatically into action.

In eight poems, from the first real indication of the change in Stella's feelings, the relation between the lovers has undergone a major alternation, involving a redefinition of the poetic genre. The redefinition is suggested, before the song, in Sonnet 70, "Sonets be not bound prentise to annoy . . . ," and after it in Sonnet 74 by what is perhaps the broadest parody of the Petrarchan poet-lover in the whole sequence, the burlesque of ingenuousness I discussed earlier (see above, p. 7).

> I never dranke of *Aganippe* well,
>> Nor ever did in shade of *Tempe* sit:
>> And Muses scorne with vulgar braines to dwell,
>> Poore Layman I, for sacred rites unfit.

> Some do I heare of Poets furie tell,
>> But (God wot) wot not what they meane by it:
>> And this I sweare by blackest brooke of hell,
>> I am no pick-purse of another's wit.

In its context this outrageous performance seems to imply that Astrophel feels he can afford such sweeping mockery of the archetype because he has just demonstrated his independence of it. The celebration, in Sonnet 75, of Edward IV, not for any of his regal achievements but for the fact that

> this worthy knight durst prove
> To loose his Crowne, rather than faile his Love,

seems to have very much the same function. Astrophel is identifying a new "tradition," arguing from authority that the sacrifice of "virtue" and the world, which dismayed him in Sonnets 18 and 19 and sobered him in Sonnet 64, is laudable, glamorous, gallant, and finally, "virtuous."

The specific genre to which these sonnets point, and which is introduced by the Second Song, is the "genre du baiser," a genre, Miss Scott points out, that had just received "un très grand développement en France aux mains de Ronsard, et qu'en Italie, on était en train de rivaliser avec le chef de la Pléiade au moment même où Sidney composait son œuvre"; the poems that Sidney devotes to it are interesting, writes Miss Scott,

"parce qu'ils montrent que Sidney n'avait pas limité ses lectures à Pétrarque et à ses imitateurs les plus platoniciens, mais qu'il avait puisé un peu partout. Le poète anglais ne visait pas à donner cette unité de ton qu'on trouve chez le chantre de Laure, ou plutôt, il ne se rendait probablement pas compte de la contradiction qui existe entre la chasteté absolue et le baiser lascif des amoureux." [8]

Of the variety of tone there can be no question, but surely it is mistaken to think that Sidney was in any doubt whatever of the distinction between "la chasteté absolue" and "le baiser lascif." On the contrary, he exploits the very disparity between them as a means of dramatizing the development of Astrophel's attitude from the more or less standard Petrarchan adoration at the beginning of the sequence, through successive stages of more and more personal and passionate intensity, of growing boldness and assurance, with desire becoming increasingly prominent, to the climax in action of frank and even bawdy sensuality. Far from obscuring the distinction, Sidney seems to use the "baiser" because of its difference. The function of the song, as song rather than sonnet, is perhaps to emphasize this difference, to suggest Astrophel's escape from the Petrarchan impasse.

In the group of sonnets from 76 to 82, Stella is treated in the elaborate hyperbole that identifies the conventional deity, but the mode of the convention is controlled by the sensual intensity that has been propelling the sequence. Thus, Sonnet 76, having described Stella as a sun whose heat "No wind, no shade can coole," ends with a prayer "that my sunne go down with meeker beames to bed."

Sonnets 79 to 82, all "baisers," celebrate the kiss in the ritual form of the blason: "Sweet kisse, thy sweets I faine would sweetly endite" (79); "Sweet swelling lip, well maist thou swell in pride" (80); "O kisse, which doest those ruddie gemmes impart, / Or gemmes, or frutes of new-found Paradise" (81);

> Nymph of the gard'n where all beauties be,
>   Beauties which do in excellencie passe
>   His who till death lookt in a watrie glasse,
>   Or hers whom naked the *Trojan* boy did see.
>
> Sweet gard'n Nymph, which keepes the Cherrie tree
>   Whose fruit doth farre th' *Esperian* tast surpasse,
>   Most sweet-faire, most faire-sweet, do not alas,
>   From comming neare those Cherries banish me.
>
>   (Sonnet 82)

The conventional hyperbole, which makes "heav'nly" and "Paradise"

8. Scott, *Les Sonnets Élisabéthains*, pp. 27-8.

almost meaningless counters in the Petrarchan love-game, in conjunction here with the image of the garden seems to have a more than conventional force. It suggests perhaps that these sonnets together comprise a kind of lover's Eden, a suggestion that is reinforced by Sonnet 78.

> O how the pleasant aires of true love be
>> Infected by those vapours, which arise
>> From out that noysome gulfe, which gaping lies
>> Betweene the jawes of hellish Jealousie.
>
> A monster, others' harme, selfe-miserie,
>> Beauties plague, Vertues scourge, succour of lies;
>> Who his owne joy to his owne hurt applies,
>> And onely cherish doth with injurie.
>
> Who since he hath, by Natures speciall grace,
>> So piercing pawes, as spoyle when they embrace,
>> So nimble feet as stirre still, though on thornes:
>
> So manie eyes ay seeking their own woe,
>> So ample eares as never good newes know:
>> Is it not evill that such a Devill wants hornes?

Jealousy, a "sujet à la mode dans la poésie pétrarquiste," comes in here with remarkable precision. The sonnet has the same catalogue form as the "baisers," but constitutes a counterblason, with infernal imagery, devoted to the serpent in the garden. It is a formal exorcism. The reference, obviously, is to Stella's husband, treating him, in terms of the metaphysic established in the first part of the sequence (Sonnet 24), as Evil itself, the lover's Satan. Astrophel is performing the ritual of exorcism in order to perform the ritual of love that follows in the "baisers." The exorcism will not be completely successful, however, until the plea of the last line of the sonnet is satisfied, that is, when the husband has been made a cuckold. Rich, on these terms, is not being treated with the same intensity of feeling as in the earlier sonnets, 24 and 37; the rhetorical technique used here,

> that noysome gulfe, which gaping lies
> Betweene the jawes of hellish Jealousie.

has hitherto been characteristic of Astrophel as parodist. His attitude toward Rich seems to have changed, then, and he looks upon him now as no more than a butt for the familiar Elizabethan joke. The reason is that he is confident that he can actually "exorcise" the husband, that he is on the point of possessing Stella. All of the formal impediments, the restricting conventions, have been eliminated, the social and moral pressures and Stella's conventional defenses, all satirized, "exorcized" from the scene. And finally Lord Rich, reduced to equally conventional dimensions—the stock figure of the jealous husband—is mocked away, leaving the lovers in the "baisers" at their closest proximity, nearest to union. This is the climax of the central section of the sequence.

The climax is achieved by combining the personal, and sensual,

> once more grant me the place,
> And I do sweare even by the same delight,
> I will but kisse, I never more will bite.

with impersonal, ritualistic formality. These two elements in a sense stand for Astrophel and Stella: desire, erotic excitement, on the one hand, the conventional form which restrains or contains it on the other. The structure of this central section has been a process by which Astrophel's individual urgency is constantly adjusted and readjusted to the convention, which is seen on one hand as Stella the coquette or platonique, and so attacked, and on the other as Stella the divinity, and so celebrated. The difference is apparent in the lyric blason of the first song and the dramatic "baiser" of the second.

It is more precise to say that the two elements, desire and formality, represent two attitudes—or two aspects of Astrophel's attitude—which have been alternating throughout this section. The important thing, however, is that the two attitudes are not alternating here at the climax but are approaching fusion. For the formality is not quite the same as in the first song, or the "envelope" sonnet, 50: it belongs to the new "genre du baiser" in which Astrophel can celebrate Stella not as the unattainable goddess but as the woman, divinely desirable but also attainable, almost attained.

The central section of the sequence concludes with a sonnet and a song which illustrate these two fundamental attitudes and so form a kind of summary. Sonnet 83 shifts the tone; the kiss theme is continued but the atmosphere of the garden gives way to one of racy and ironic bawdry.

> Good brother *Philip*, I have borne you long,
>   I was content you should in favour creepe,
>   While craftily you seem'd your cut to keepe,
>   As though that faire soft hand did you great wrong.
>
> I bare (with Envie) yet I bare your song,
>   When in her necke you did *Love* ditties peepe;
>   Nay, more foole I, oft suffered you to sleepe
>   In Lillies neast where *Loves* selfe lies along.

> What, doth high place ambitious thoughts augment?
> Is sawcinesse reward of curtesie?
> Cannot such grace your silly selfe content,

> But you must needs with those lips billing be?
> And through those lips drinke Nectar from that toong;
> Leave that, sir *Phip*, least off your necke be wroong.

As in Sonnet 59, Astrophel is jealous of a pet, but here the specific provocation is the pet's amorous success rather than the lady's attentions to it. The sparrow is the traditional symbol of lechery, and as such it is, like Cupid, a projection of the lover's desire, made more specific with the sparrow as symbol than with "Love." The strategy of the poem resembles that of 46 ("I curst thee oft, I pitie now thy case"): with the lover's attitude objectified in the symbol, he can express an attitude toward it; the structure, as in 46, is ironic, but the irony lies not in his detachment but in his concern. In a sense he is taking the lady's part, defending her virtue against seduction by the lecherous bird. But the joke, of course, is that by threatening the bird with mock ferocity he is warning himself—"Leave that, sir *Phip*, least off your necke be wroong."

The attitude toward Stella in this sonnet—possessive, sensual, ironic, and highly individual—is at one extreme. The attitude in the Third Song, which follows it, is at the other. Like the First Song, the Third is in blason form, a ritual celebration. It presents, in ascending order, Stella's great powers over the inanimate world ("O stones, O trees, learne hearing, *Stella* singeth"), the animal world ("O birds, O beasts, looke Love, lo *Stella* shineth"), and finally over the world of men,

> you with reason armed,
> O eyes, o eares of men, how are you charmed.

The song has the impersonal, generalizing—even universalizing—effect characteristic of the convention.

This hierarchy of hearing, sight, and reason comprises the threefold charm of beauty to which Neoplatonic love is limited. "Love regards as its end the enjoyment of beauty; beauty pertains only to the mind, sight, and hearing. Love, therefore, is limited to these three, but desire which rises from the other senses is called, not love, but lust or madness."[9] The sonnet and the song, then, represent extremes that are mutually exclusive. What they have in common is the lover's jubilation, and on this jubilant note the second section ends.

9. Ficino, *Commentary*, Oration I, iv, tr. Jayne, p. 130.

III

The final "act" of the sequence begins, like the first and second, with Astrophel as poet identifying the source of his inspiration. It is now neither his heart, the introspective symbol of Sonnet 1, nor the mistress-muse of Sonnet 44, but the highway leading him to Stella.

> High way since you my chiefe *Pernassus* be,
>> And that my Muse to some eares not unsweet,
>> Tempers her words to trampling horses feete,
>> More oft then to a chamber melodie,
>
> Now blessed you, beare onward blessed me
>> To her, where I my heart safe left, shall meet;
>
> (Sonnet 84)

The exciting proximity of the "baisers" has been interrupted, but he is hurrying to restore it. Still the king to whom Stella gave the monarchy of her high heart, in anticipation he takes inventory of his domain.

>> let eyes
> See Beauties totall summe summ'd in her face:
> Let eares heare speech, which wit to wonder ties.
>
> Let breath sucke up those sweetes, let armes embrace
>> The globe of weale, lips *Loves* indentures make:
>> Thou but of all the kingly Tribute take.
>
> (Sonnet 85)

The lady is the kingly lover's realm, and he is on the point of complete possession. But the very "virtues" that make the prospect so intoxicating remind us that, as the recurrent rituals have indicated, she is more than subject. She is his very world and the supreme power in that world, and therefore, however regal his approach, his position is implicitly dependent.

The climax so eagerly expected in these two sonnets is presented in the Fourth Song, which follows Sonnet 85.

> Onely joy, now here you are,
> Fit to heare and ease my care:
> Let my whispering voice obtaine,
> Sweet reward for sharpest paine:
> Take me to thee, and thee to me.
> No, no, no, no, my Deare, let be.

The movement is like that which leads to the kiss in the Second Song;

in both cases, as a means of heightening and emphasizing the effect,
the climactic action occurs in a song rather than a sonnet, and in both
cases the song suggests a tradition different from that of the sonnets,
the "nocturne" here, perhaps, related to the medieval serenade.[1]

> Night hath closd all in her cloke,
> Twinckling starres Love-thoughts provoke:
> Danger hence good care doth keepe,
> Jealousie it selfe doth sleepe:
> Take me to thee, and thee to me.
> No, no, no, no, my Deare, let be.

The exorcism of "danger" and "jealousie" suggests the ritual of the
courtly lover, but the solicitation itself, and the *carpe diem* argument
for the opportunity offered by place and time, are as old as love.

> Better place no wit can find,
> Cupids yoke to loose or binde:
> These sweet flowers our [2] fine bed too,
> Us in their best language woo:
>   . . . . .
> Niggard Time threats, if we misse
> This large offer of our blisse:
> Long stay, ere he graunt the same.

The romantic atmosphere of the Second Song, though certainly present
here, is qualified by details that are sharply realistic and concrete; this
seems to be a "real" garden, the exorcism literal—"Feare not else,
none can us spie,"

> That you heard was but a Mouse,
> Dumbe sleepe holdeth all the house:
> Yet a sleepe, me thinkes they say,
> Yong folkes, take time while you may.

The same joke that appeared in the Second Song—"Who will read,
must first learne spelling"—is used again, but with other details that
have an almost comic practicality, as part of a literal seduction.

> Your faire mother is a bed,
> Candles out, and curtaines spread;
> She thinkes you do letters write;
> Write, but let me first endite.

---

1. Scott, *Les Sonnets Élisabéthains*, p. 47.
2. The Folio reading is "on".

In spite of the song form, the immediate, colloquial, matter-of-factness, the atmosphere of realism and urgent practicality, replacing the elaborate lyricism of the "baisers," are responsible for the predominant effect.

There are nine stanzas, all but the last ending with the refrain,

> Take me to thee, and thee to me.
> No, no, no, no, my Deare, let be,

through which the lover's arguments and his advances ("Leave to *Mars* the force of hands") are rejected. In the last stanza, however, the refrain is varied, and with an effect that perhaps recalls the "vertues" of "grammer-rules" suggests that the rejection may not be final.

> Wo to me, and do you sweare
> Me to hate but I forbeare,
> Cursed be my destines all,
> That brought me so high to fall:
> Soone with my death I will please thee.
> No, no, no, no, my Deare, let be.

In the sonnet which follows, Astrophel seems to be uncertain of the appropriate response. He speaks, rather suddenly, in the accents of the Petrarchan lover, making his complaint,

> Alas, whence came this change of lookes? If I
> Have chang'd desert, let mine owne conscience be
> A still felt plague, to selfe condemning me;
> Let wo gripe on my heart, shame load mine eye,
>
> (Sonnet 86)

and he clearly takes this rebuff more seriously than he did the series of rejections, admonitions, and evasions in the second section. There Stella's coldness, with one or two exceptions, was occasion for Astrophel to assume and to satirize the conventional role. His sententiousness here—"O ease your hand, treate not so hard your slave . . . No doome should make ones heav'n become his hell"—suggests the same kind of part, deliberately played, but there are some significant differences, indicated in the last stanza of the song,

> Cursed be my destines all,
> That brought me so high to fall.

Before this Astrophel had been able to assume that Stella's refusals were part of the conventional role she was playing. But he forced her to abandon that pose; his confidence, as king, was possible because he had been accepted as lover on his own, not the conventional, terms. Therefore, her refusal of him now re-creates the mystery of the conventional mistress. The sonnet seems to express his confusion, and it does so by suggesting the Petrarchan lover. Astrophel here is hesitating between the parody characteristic of the previous section and serious acceptance of the conventional role. The king is threatened with slavery.

The intense excitement which hurried Astrophel to the nocturnal meeting in a real garden has been frustrated, not dissipated, by the rebuff. It overflows in a group of five songs which constitute the climax of the whole sequence. The Fifth Song extends and develops the blend of parody and earnestness in Sonnet 86, which it follows. Astrophel is insisting on his righteous indignation. He begins by surveying his good service as a lover.

> While favour fed my hope, delight with hope was brought,
> Thought waited on delight, and speech did follow thought:
> Then grew my tongue and pen records unto thy glory:
> I thought all words were lost that were not spent of thee:
> I thought each place was darke but where thy lights would be,
> And all eares worse than deafe, that heard not out thy storie.
>
> I said, thou wert most faire, and so indeed thou art:
> I said, thou art most sweet, sweet poison to my heart:
> I said, my soule was thine (O that I then had lyed)
> I said, thine eyes were starres, thy breasts the milk'n way,
> Thy fingers Cupids shafts, thy voyce the Angels lay:
> And all I said so well, as no man it denied.

" But now that hope is lost, unkindnesse kils delight "; Astrophel calls upon his muse to help him to vengeance, turning praise to blame.

> Your client poore my selfe, shall Stella handle so?
> Revenge, revenge, my Muse. Defiance trumpet blow:
> Threat'n what may be done, yet do more than you threat'n.
> Ah, my sute granted is, I feele my breast doth swell:
> Now child, a lesson new you shall begin to spell:
> Sweet babes must babies have, but shrewd gyrles must be beat'n.
>
> Thinke now no more to heare of warme fine odourd snow,
> Nor blushing Lillies, nor pearles ruby-hidden row,
> Nor of that golden sea, whose waves in curls are brok'n:
> But of thy soule, so fraught with such ungratefulnesse,
> As where thou soone mightst helpe, most faith dost most oppresse,
> Ungratefull who is cald, the worst of evils is spok'n.

Involved in this résumé is a full awareness of his hyperbolic treatment of Stella, a double awareness including the fact that as she is a woman his praises of her are exaggerations, but that by virtue of her supreme importance to him he cannot exaggerate in praising her.

The song itself is a different kind of exaggeration. The invocation of the vengeful muse has the same dramatic self-consciousness found in Sonnet 47 (". . . go to, / Unkind, I love you not"), a quality that persists through the series of accusations that carry out the threat. Because she has robbed him of his " joyes " Stella is a thief, and the repetition of the charge gives it a comic vehemence.

> Yet worse then worst, I say thou art a theefe, a theefe?
> Now God forbid. A theefe, and of worst theeves the cheefe.

She is a murderer—" Who may and will not save, murder in truth committeth "; a tyrant,

> For thou doest lord my heart, who am not borne thy slave,
> And which is worse, makes me most guiltlesse torments have;

a rebel to Love, by law of Nature and of Reason, vagrant to Venus, a witch of the worst kind, for " No witchcraft is so evill, as which mans mind destroyeth," and finally,

> I say thou art a Devill though clothd in Angels shining;
> For thy face tempts my soule to leave the heav'n for thee,
> And thy words of refuse do powre even hell on mee.

Although this mock cursing is in part a dramatic performance, it has a serious element that distinguishes it from the parodies in the earlier sections. Where before his performance was primarily a sardonic, teasing way of exposing the absurdity and perversity of Stella's behavior, it now implicates Astrophel himself, for it is not entirely by his choosing; he is losing the independence, the freedom of action which allowed him to play as many roles as he liked. The curses involve a vision of the consequences of being so lost in love as he has been. The actual threat, of course, is to Astrophel, so utterly dependent upon Stella that her rejection of him may indeed be a kind of murder and damnation.

The justification for his attitude is fundamentally moral. It is based on the sense of injustice suggested in Sonnet 86—" In justice paines come not till faults do call." The lover who had insisted so blithely on the dissociation of love and virtue now makes the conventional argument that his love is perfect virtue which the lady has traduced. His curses, as a matter of fact, seem to be drawn from Neoplatonic doctrine. Thus, in the doctrine according to Ficino,

> Therefore anyone who is loved ought in very justice to love in

return, and he who does not love his lover must bear the charge of
homicide, nay rather, the triple charge of thief, homicide, and
desecrator. Money is possessed by the body, the body by the soul,
and therefore the man who takes captive a soul, by which both
body and money are possessed, thus seizes all three at once: soul,
body, and money. Hence it happens that, like a thief, homicide,
and desecrator, he is punishable by triple death, and, as though
naturally wicked and immoral, he may be killed by anyone with
impunity, unless he obeys that law of his own accord, that is, by
loving his lover.[3]

What is happening is that the intensely individualistic lover, who had
affirmed the supreme importance of the personal experience and had
attacked so enthusiastically all the institutionalized values, is here being
forced back upon some sort of general norm, some sort of impersonal
authority or standard. In other words, he is forced to invoke the very
convention he had attempted to eliminate.

The last stanza of the song summarizes the accusations and offers
terms for a reconciliation.

> (alas) you still of me beloved,
> You see what I can say; mend yet your froward mind,
> And such skill in my Muse you reconcil'd, shall find,
> That all these cruell words your praises shall be proved.

The Sixth and Seventh Songs are successive celebrations of Stella's
face and voice. In the Sixth Song the strife between the lovers is
replaced by a ritualistic "bate," whether voice or face is the more
beautiful; both are so perfect that choice is impossible, and the formal
and delicate balancing of the verse maintains the balance between them.
In the last stanza reason is invoked,

> Then reason Princesse hy,
> Whose throne is in the mind,
> Which Musicke can in sky
> And hidden beauties find,
> Say whether thou wilt crowne
> With limitlesse renowne.

but the debate is unresolved. The Seventh Song is almost a *reprise* of
the Third, in the same three-stanza structure, involving not stones and
beasts but men so dull of ear and eye as to be unmoved by beauty; let
them learn by seeing and hearing Stella.

Heare then, but then with wonder heare; see but adoring see,

_____

3. Ficino, *Commentary*, Oration II, viii, p. 145.

No mortall gifts, no earthly fruites, now here descended be :
See, do you see this face? a face? nay image of the skies,
Of which the two life-giving lights are figured in her eyes :
Heare you this soule-invading voice, and count it but a voice?
The very essence of their tunes, when Angels do rejoyce.

Both of these songs reassert the attitude characteristic of all the
rituals, and like the Third Song they are confined to the two senses
in which, along with reason, Love alone resides, according to the
Platonist. That is, the desire which has led to Astrophel's rejection is
specifically omitted.

The Eighth Song is the longest and the most important in the sequence, for the whole structure turns upon it. The most striking thing
about it is that it is in the third person, the only such poem in the
sequence. The lovers are seen from a completely objective point of
view, as if at a distance, and from this objective point of view they
appear in a new intimacy; the distinction Astrophel is constantly forced
to make between "I" and "she" is eliminated in the "they" of the
song.

Though Astrophel's appeal is presented more directly than elsewhere,
the terms are familiar from the rituals performed earlier in the sequence : the blason of face and voice, from the First, Third, Sixth and
Seventh Songs; the carpe diem theme of the Fourth Song, "now use
the season"; and the invocation of the standard of the Fifth Song, of
Love as the law of Nature,

> Love makes earth the water drinke,
> Love to earth makes water sinke.

The appeal ends as it does in the Fourth Song,

> There his hands in their speech, faine
> Would have made tongues language plaine ;
> But her hands his hands repelling
> Gave repulse all grace excelling.

Stella's response, however, is far more important. She makes a long
protestation of her own, which was one of the passages omitted until
the publication of the 1598 Folio.

> Then she spake; her speech was such,
> As not eares but hart did tuch :
> While such wise she love denied,
> As yet love she signified.
>
> Astrophel sayd she, my love
> Cease in these effects to prove :

> Now be still, yet still beleeve me,
> Thy griefe more than death would grieve me.
>
> If that any thought in me,
> Can tast comfort but of thee,
> Let me fed with hellish anguish,
> Joylesse, hopelesse, endlesse languish.
>
> If those eyes you praised, be
> Halfe so deere as you to me,
> Let me home returne, starke blinded
> Of those eyes, and blinder minded.
>
> If to secret of my hart,
> I do any wish impart,
> Where thou art not formost placed,
> Be both wish and I defaced.
>
> If more may be sayd, I say,
> All my blisse in thee I lay;
> If thou love, my love content thee,
> For all love, all faith is meant thee.
>
> Trust me while I thee deny,
> In my selfe the smart I try,
> Tyran honour doth thus use thee,
> Stellas selfe might not refuse thee.
>
> Therefore, Deere, this no more move,
> Least though I leave not thy love,
> Which too deep in me is framed,
> I should blush when thou art named.

The role of Stella has suddenly expanded beyond the star; she is completely the woman. It is important that she should be so here, for the nature of her refusal is extremely significant. Astrophel has indeed the monarchy of her high heart; there is no suggestion of coyness or conventional posturing; her refusal seems to come from the heart, with remarkable directness. Consequently, there is a finality about it that alters the relationship of the lovers fundamentally and permanently. Astrophel now has no recourse.

> Therewithall away she went,
> Leaving him to passion rent
> With what she had done and spoken,
> That therewith my song is broken.

The rejection of the despairing and utterly humble lover is the most

conventional of subjects, and the highly wrought, almost incantatory
verse emphasizes the conventional character of its treatment in this
poem. Miss Scott believes there is some resemblance to the " Chants
de Mai ou ' Reverdies' composés par les Trouvères et les Troubadours
lorsqu'un souffle d'amour venait les troubler au printemps." [4] But the
nature of the setting and the ritual performed in it suggest a more
specifically pastoral tradition. The whole atmosphere of the poem is
one of sensuality, but sensuality restrained and purified. The formal
celebrations of Stella which have intervened between the Fourth and
Eighth Songs seem to have exorcised all the realistic details which made
the first appeal so practical and worldly a one: the particular moment in
time, which will pass (" Niggard Time threats, if we misse ") is here a
season, with an effect of timelessness; there are no sudden noises to
startle the lovers, no authority to be deceived, and no suggestion of
bawdiness. Astrophel's desire is explicit, but completely controlled,
transmuted by the ritual formality of the verse.

> Stella soveraigne of my joy,
> Fair triumpher of annoy,
> Stella starre of heavenly fier,
> Stella loadstar of desier.

His appeal is now a prayer—" no fault there is in praying "—and the
" force of hands " which pushed him away in the Fourth Song has
become itself a kind of grace, " all grace excelling."

The purpose in evoking the pastoral atmosphere seems to be to present the lovers in their most universal aspect. The rich texture of
" irrelevance " which has created so solid a world around the lovers is
purged, sublimed away, and they are alone, heart to heart, in the
pastoral garden. The objectivity and the idealization of the garden
reveal their relationship in terms of the timeless, permanent lack of
achievement characteristic of the pastoral world.

The effect of the poem is nevertheless strangely active, far more so
than the elaborate working of the conventional form and materials
would suggest. It emerges as a kind of counterpoint between the ritualistic formality and the pressure of intensely dramatic feeling, built up
through the whole sequence to this point and expressed here in the
forcefulness and directness of the dialogue.

In the Ninth Song there is a return to the first person. Astrophel
reappears and sees himself in the role of pastoral lover, pouring out his
sorrows to his sympathetic sheep.

> Stella fiercest shepherdesse,

---

4. Scott, *Les Sonnets Élisabéthains*, p. 47.

Fiercest but yet fairest ever;
Stella whom o heavens do blesse,
Tho against me shee persever,
Tho I blisse enherit never.

Stella hath refused me,
Stella who more love hath proved,
In this caitife hart to be,
Then can in good eawes be moved
Toward Lamkins best beloved.

He overstresses the pastoral symbols, and makes the pastoral role, as
he made his other roles, a kind of deliberate attitudinizing, a vehicle
for irony, but with the difference noted in the Fifth Song: it is a means
of expressing his awareness that the role is not one he has chosen to
create but one that is forced upon him.   The irony is tacitly comic as
he rejects Stella's protestation of love.

Is that love? forsooth I trow,
If I saw my good dog grieved,
And a helpe for him did know,
My love should not be beleeved,
But he were by me releeved.

The tonal effect resembles that at the end of the first section of the
sequence (in Sonnet 43) and it involves a similar recognition, a kind of
rediscovery, of his situation as that of the conventional lover. The song
ends on a lugubrious note.

Then adieu, deere flocke adieu:
But alas, if in your straying
Heavenly Stella meete with you,
Tell her in your piteous blaying
Her poor slaves unjust decaying.

In the role of woeful shepherd Astrophel mocks himself as the lover
who so recently, in the real garden, was so confident, so colloquial,
and so possessive.

It might be well to pause here to consider briefly some of the questions raised by the presence of the songs in the sequence, and to summarize the effects of the nine that have been commented on so far.
There are eleven songs altogether, all rhetorically elaborate and profuse in phonetic detail, but no two of them have precisely the same
form. Five are iambic, six trochaic, with lines ranging in length from
tetrameter to the fourteener; the stanzas are in four, five, and six lines,
with eight different rime schemes, though eight songs use the device

of balancing masculine and feminine rimes against each other.[5] In structure they vary from narrative and dramatic, as in the Fourth Song, to the completely static ritual of the Sixth. The Third and Seventh resemble in structure the conventional sonnet, with the first two stanzas, like the quatrains of a sonnet, presenting illustrations or examples, the third, like the sestet, a summary and application.

The variety is such that if they are read in a single group the songs seem almost a series of deliberate experiments, a demonstration of technical virtuosity. Following the model of the 1591 quartos, such editors as Grosart have printed all of the songs together at the end of the sequence. By so doing they deny the variety any meaningful function, and in effect relegate the songs to the position of " Certaine Sonets."

In some cases the songs are dramatic necessities, for the decisive action of the sequence occurs in them. The Second Song provides the kiss prepared for in the " Desire " sonnets (71 and 72), and celebrated in the " baisers " which follow it; the Fourth Song is the climax of the anticipation in Sonnets 84 and 85 (" High way. . . . I see the house. . . . Onely joy, now here you are "), and accounts for the shift in tone and attitude in Sonnet 86 (" Alas, whence came this change of lookes? "). In other cases, though a song may be nondramatic in itself, like the First and Third, it produces a dramatic effect through the contrast of form achieving emphasis at points in the development of the story where such emphasis is needed. Thus, the steadily mounting excitement at the end of the central section of the sequence is preceded by the First Song, an overflow of exuberance from the sonnets, and is concluded by the Third Song, a ritual celebrating the beloved so near to possession.

The five songs just discussed, placed at the high point of the sequence, function like a play-within-a-play, a formal and symbolic representation of the whole drama, by means of which the universal values are defined. And they also constitute a kind of ritual purgation through which the gaiety, the confidence, the insistent desire, and the vital individuality of the Astrophel of the first two sections are removed, and he is transformed into the Petrarchan lover who dominates the remainder of the sequence.

In the sonnets following the Ninth Song the structure of the sequence is being readjusted to the climax presented in the songs. In Sonnet 87 Astrophel speaks in a new and rather solemn tone, with the accents of the Petrarchan lover, recounting that " When I was forst from *Stella* ever deere . . . By *Stellas*[6] lawes of duty to depart."

---

5. According to Albert W. Osborne, *Sir Philip Sidney en France* (Paris, 1932), p. 45, Sidney learned this device from the Pléiade.

6. The Folio reading is " iron ".

> Alas I found that she with me did smart,
>   I saw that teares did in her eyes appeare;
>   I saw that sighes her sweetest lips did part,
>   And her sad words my saddest sence did heare.

He is clearly referring to the scene in the Eighth Song, and expressing an attitude toward it quite different from that expressed, via the pastoral role, in the Ninth Song. He is not questioning here, but accepting the total situation with its contradiction of love and rejection, and accepting it as the grounds for the conventional paradox.

> Thus, while the 'ffect most bitter was to me,
>   And nothing then the cause more sweet could be,
>   I had bene vext, if vext I had not beene.

The change is more impressive because more generalized, almost official, in a sonnet such as 89.

> Now that of absence the most irksome night
>   With darkest shade doth overcome my day;
>   Since *Stellas* eyes wont to give me my day,
>   Leaving my Hemisphere, leave me in night;
>
> Each day seems long, and longs for long-staid night,
>   The night as tedious, wooes th' approach of day.

And so forth. The rest of the sonnet keeps the single rime and rings the changes on the paradox.

> living thus in blackest winter night,
>   I feele the flames of hottest sommer day.

The transformation of Astrophel is total: he is as thoroughly conventional a lover as one can imagine, and Sidney, in this sonnet, as thoroughly conventional a poet. In answer to the criticism that it is the worst sonnet in the sequence, Miss Scott defends Sidney by saying that he has done no more than follow the example of his predecessors and " contemporains étrangers." [7] She is undoubtedly right, but the important thing is that he should choose to follow them so slavishly and at this particular point. Astrophel has been forced into the Petrarchan mold by the frustration of the Eighth Song and the ritualistic meditation is his identification. Furthermore, by the use of so obvious an example the whole convention is evoked to emphasize the loss of the unique and independent personality in the general and impersonal system of attitudes it represents.

7. Scott, *Les Sonnets Élisabéthains*, p. 41.

The nature of Sonnet 89 seems to be explicitly acknowledged in Sonnet 90.

> *Stella*, thinke not that I by verse seeke fame,
>> Who seeke, who hope, who love, who live but thee;
>> Thine eyes my pride, thy lips mine history:
>> If thou praise not, all other praise is shame.

Following immediately after 89 it implies that Astrophel is answering, or anticipating, the suspicion of insincerity so imitative a poem must provoke. He does so by reversing the extravagant and witty parody of Sonnet 74,

> And this I sweare by blackest brooke of hell,
> I am no pick-purse of anothers wit.

He does not deny here that he uses conventional materials; on the contrary, he seems to point to the example of the preceding sonnet,

> Ne if I would, could I just title make,
> That any laud to me thereof should grow,
> Without my plumes from others wings I take,

but he does deny that he is therefore insincere. This is another, and the final, use of a sonnet on poetry to mark a shift in the dominant mode of the sequence.

The change is marked further by revision of Astrophel's relation with the wits and ladies of the court: the coquettes who were sure "He cannot love" (Sonnet 54) now seem to find him fair game.

> in brave array heere marcheth she,
> That to win me, oft shewes a present pay.
>> (Sonnet 88)

The implication, perhaps, is that he is displaying, if not "set colours" or "special lockes of vowed haire," then the conventional melancholy of the lover. Similarly, the wits who had been intruders on the lover now seem to be his only contact with Stella, and the loquacity he avoided is replaced by an equally maddening reticence.

> When I demaund of *Phenix Stellas* state,
> You say, forsooth, you left her well of láte,
> O God, thinke you that satisfies my care?
>> (Sonnet 92)

In the Tenth Song, which follows Sonnet 92, Astrophel delegates to "Thought" the action he himself is denied.

O deare life, when shall it be
That mine eyes thine eyes may see?

. . . . .

Thought therefore I will send thee
To take up the place for me;
Long I will not after tary,
There, unseene, thou maist be bold,
Those faire wonders to behold,
Which in them my hopes do cary.

. . . . .

Thinke of my most Princely power,
Which I blessed shall devower,
With my greedy licorous sences,
Beauty, musicke, sweetnesse, love,
While she doth against me prove
Her strong darts but weake defences.

This imaginative wooing, like the meditation on Absence, is a conventional exercise. Thus, in Petrarch,

Ite, dolci penser, parlando fòre
Di quello ove'l bel guardo non se stende.[8]

The effect of it here, however, is a function of the context provided by the earlier sonnets and songs, particularly such a sonnet as 85 ("I see the house"), where Astrophel, in much the same terms as these, anticipated with almost uncontrollable delight his royal possessions. The song constitutes a re-creation of the lover before his rejection, with all his aggressiveness and sensual intensity, and it is perhaps his awareness of the ironic contrast that forces him to break off the fantasy.

O my thought my thoughts surcease,
Thy delights my woes increase,
My life melts with too much thinking;
Thinke no more, but die in me,
Till thou shalt revived be,
At her lips my Nectar drinking.

The imaginative aggressiveness of the song is in pointed contrast to the actual abjectness of the next group of sonnets, the most conventional series in the sequence, and one in which the only variation of the mode is from one ritual to another, from the nocturnal meditation in Sonnets 94-99 to the blasons Stella weeping (Sonnet 100), Stella sick (Son-

8. Petrarch, CLIII ("Ite, caldi sospiri"), p. 384.

nets 101 and 102), and Stella boating on the Thames (Sonnet 103).
With one or two exceptions, these are Sidney's least distinguished as
well as his most conventional sonnets, but the rhetorical excess that
identifies them—"O fate, o fault, o curse, child of my blisse" (93),
". . . the blacke horrors of the silent night" that "Paint woes blacke
face so lively to my sight" (98), the ". . . honied sighs, which from
that breast do rise, / Whose pants do make unspilling creame to flow"
(100)—also identifies the lover; the characteristic weaknesses of the
poems have a dramatic effect in the context as the symbolic vehicle for
the helpless frustration of the lover.

The principal exception is Sonnet 99, where the theme is just as conventional as in the other sonnets but more successfully controlled.

> When far spent night perswades each mortall eye,
>   To whom nor art nor nature graunteth light,
>   To lay his then marke wanting shafts of sight,
>   Clos'd with their quivers in sleeps armory;
>
> With windowes ope then most my mind doth lie,
>   Viewing the shape of darknesse and delight
>   Takes in that sad hue, which with th' inward night
>   Of his mazde powers keepes perfit harmony:
>
> But when birds charme, and, that sweete aire which is
>   Mornes messenger, with rose enameld skies
>   Cals each wight to salute the floure of blisse;
>
> In tombe of lids then buried are mine eyes,
>   Forst by their Lord, who is asham'd to find
>   Such light in sense, with such a darkned mind.

The conventional analogy between natural and unnatural darkness here
does not seem to be forced upon the poem by a rhetorical technique
but upon the lover by his experience. There is no suggestion of either
the strain or the flatness ("Both sadly blacke, both blackly darkned
be") of the other sonnets on this theme. The elaborate artifice through
which the natural processes and phenomena are presented gives a
powerful sense of the world as created and creative, a world of symbolic
forms, from which the lover excludes himself first by the incorporation
of his "mazde powers" with the formless "shape of darknesse" and
then by the act of will with which he shuts himself out from the sacra-
mental vision of the morning, with its suggestion of matins and eyes
uplifted. His mind is darkened by the conventional sorrows, but even
more by his feeling that those sorrows are a source of shame.

Astrophel's final appeal is made in the Eleventh Song, the last in
the sequence, which follows Sonnet 104.

> Who is it that this darke night,
> Underneath my window playneth?
> It is one who from thy sight
> Being (ah) exiled, disdayneth
> Every other vulgar light.

This song, like the Fourth, is a " serenade," but the tone and the atmosphere have been radically altered; the change in Astrophel has been demonstrated in the preceding sonnets in perhaps too much detail, but the change in Stella has not been prepared for. There is a sudden harshness in her surprise at finding Astrophel.

> Why alas, and are you he?
> Be not yet those fancies changed?

Where in the Fourth Song the urgency was Astrophel's, here it is Stella's,

> Peace, I thinke that some give eare:
> Come no more, least I get anger.

The coquetry is gone, and the ambiguous refrain—" No, no, no, no, my Deare, let be "—is replaced by a brusque and utterly final dismissal.

> Well, begone, begone I say,
> Lest that Argus eyes perceive you.

The dialogue of this song represents the final version of the conflict between Love and Virtue, but the dramatic center has shifted; the relative positions of lover and lady have been transposed: now it is she who provides the dramatic force, and he the ritualistic form and manner which resist it. As the situation has ceased to be a " practical " one— that is, one in which his suit has some hope of success—the " practical " arguments of the central section have given way to an affirmation of the Petrarchan absolutes. Astrophel's responses, reiterating the terms of the conventional sonnets, constitute a catechism of the virtues of Love.

> Deere, when you find change in me,
> Though from me you be estranged,
> Let my chaunge to ruine be.
>
> . . . . .
>
> Time doth as the subject prove;
> With time still the affection groweth
> In the faithfull Turtle dove.
>
> . . . . .
>
> Deere, do reason no such spite;

> Never doth thy beauty florish
> More then in my reasons sight.
>
> . . . . .
>
> Blisse, I will my blisse forbeare,
> Fearing, sweete, you to endanger,
> But my soule shall harbour there.

The song presents the two facts of the Petrarchan impasse: the lady's implacable resistance and the lover's helpless devotion. From this situation there is no escape, and the concluding sonnets are devoted to Astrophel's acceptance of it as permanent.

> *Stella* since thou so right a Princesse art
> Of all the powers that life bestowes on me,
> That ere by them ought undertaken be,
> They first resort unto that soveraigne part;

Astrophel asks leave to return to the world of affairs he had rejected at the beginning of the sequence—

> on my thoughts give thy Lieftenancy
> To this great cause, which needes both use and art

—to return not released from passion, but as the Petrarchan lover, passion's slave.

> On servants shame oft Maisters blame doth sit;
> O let not fooles in me thy workes reprove,
> And scorning say, see what it is to love.
>
> (Sonnet 107)

The sequence ends in Sonnet 108 with Astrophel rehearsing his woes in the accents of the tradition of which he has become a part.

> So strangely (alas) thy works in me prevaile,
> That in my woes for thee thou art my joy,
> And in my joyes for thee my only annoy.

IV

It is a common view that *Astrophel and Stella* ends inconclusively and is therefore unfinished. The conclusion that Sidney intended, according to the argument, is supplied by the two poems published among the " Certaine Sonets " in 1598, " Thou blind mans marke, thou fooles selfe chosen snare " and " Leave me o Love, which reachest but to dust." But it is difficult to see how such a conclusion can be accepted without distorting the unified structure of the sequence.

That structure, from the point of view I have been taking, is one of analysis and synthesis, with the Petrarchan convention as its subject matter. The Petrarchan convention throughout the sequence has delimited the world of Astrophel as lover, as contemporary affairs of state delimit the world of citizen and courtier. It functions as the universal to which, as lover and as poet, he must relate himself, and that relationship is in part one of self-assertion, in part one of self-discovery. At first he imposes himself on the convention in an effort to overcome and eliminate it; it is public and impersonal and consequently the antagonist of the individual lover, who asserts the primacy of his unique personality over its generalizations, its assumptions, and its manners. His technique is that of the orator and advocate, attacking the conventional " vice " in its various forms, praising virtue, and identifying himself as his " proof." By asserting himself through this technique he eliminates the superficial and therefore falsifying aspects of the convention, discovers and finally reaches Stella. By the end of the sequence, through his relation to Stella, Astrophel has been made aware of the nature of Love as the Petrarchan universal: he has discovered himself as part of the convention, which, by virtue of his participation in it, has acquired permanent validity.

Sonnet 108, then, is not conclusive in the sense of a complete resolution, but that very fact constitutes its dramatic function. It concludes the portrait of the conventional lover and the definition of the genre, ending the sequence with the acceptance of a frustration that can have no end. The effect of permanence, symbolized in the pastoral setting of the climax, is the essential one, essential to the dialectical as well as the dramatic organization. Sidney's achievement in *Astrophel and Stella* ("our English Petrarke," as Sir John Harington called him) is not only in the excellence of the individual sonnets but in the arrangement of the sequence to exploit the different modes of the convention in such a way that the generalized forms acquire specific significance in a single poetic structure.

BEN JONSON'S MASQUES

by W. Todd Furniss

For

Ruth Pine Furniss

The Arms of James I
From James I, *Workes*, 1616

Preface

THE MASQUES of Ben Jonson have long been studied and admired for the ingenuity of their stage effects, for the charm of their songs, and for the splendor of the occasions on which they were presented. Introduced to the masques by Oscar J. Campbell and C. Beecher Hogan, I approached them through the existing studies, finding much that was stimulating in the material that had been made available. Later, under the direction of Charles T. Prouty, I began to discover that what had been concluded about the masques thus far came short of explaining Jonson's great interest in the form, expressed directly and seriously in the prefaces to some of the masques and indirectly in the careful attention he gave to their publication. However, when a new approach, suggested by the recent work of E. W. Talbert, D. J. Gordon, and A. H. Gilbert, was pursued, the puzzling inconsistencies began to disappear and a pattern underlying all Jonson's masques and justifying his interest and attention emerged. With the guidance of Louis L. Martz, I was able to present to the Graduate Faculty of Yale University a dissertation designed to demonstrate this pattern. The following chapters cover the material in the original thesis, omitting only a detailed study of the imagery of monarchy and a number of the extended illustrations.

I wish to express my gratitude to the Graduate School of Yale University for the award of the Lewis-Porter Fellowship in 1948 and to the Graduate School of the Ohio State University for its contribution toward the costs of publication. To the staffs of the Yale University Library and the Henry E. Huntington Library for their patient help, I owe a great debt. Finally, those who know his work will recognize instantly my good fortune in having had the imaginative, learned, and generous counsel of Professor Martz.

W. T. F.

Columbus, Ohio

Index of Jonson's Masques and Entertainments

Introduction

> Princes ar Gods. Oh do not then
> rake in their graues to proue them men.
> —*An Epitaphe upon King James* [1]

JONSON'S *Oberon* (1611) opens on a pastoral scene with satyrs and their leader Silenus. Waiting to see Oberon and his knights come from his palace, they have been passing the time by dancing and tormenting the Sylvans who guard the gates. Finally Oberon appears and one of the Sylvans calls for silence:

> This is a night of greatnesse, and of state;
> Not to be mixt with light, and skipping sport:
> A night of homage to the *British* court,
> And ceremony, due to ARTHVRS chaire,
> From our bright master, OBERON the faire. (320-4) [2]

Oberon and his knights and attendants have come to pay their annual vows to "this only great, / True maiestie, restored in this seate," that is, King James, seated on a throne in the center of the hall. Yet in the fable James is both Arthur, the greatest of the English kings, and a modern version of Arthur whose presence is a restoration of England's Golden Age. Taking his cue from the Sylvan, Silenus speaks up, calling on the satyrs to recognize the fact that James is "aboue your reach" by nature, not merely by position.

> He is a god, o're kings; yet stoupes he then
> Neerest a man, when he doth gouerne men. (344-5)

The king is the link between men and gods in the universal hierarchy and yet, for all his majesty, he is a gentle philosopher who attempts "To teach them by the sweetnesse of his sway, / And not by force." His reign is the dream of foreigners less lucky than his own subjects. More than that,

> 'Tis he, that stayes the time from turning old,
> And keepes the age vp in a head of gold. (350-1)

---

1. *Dr. Farmer Chetham MS.*, ed. A. B. Grosart, Chetham Society (1873), p. 195.

2. C. H. Herford, Percy and Evelyn Simpson, *Ben Jonson*, 11 vols. Oxford, The Clarendon Press, 1925-52. The masques are collected in Vol. *7*; the commentary on the masques is in Vol. *10*. All subsequent references to Jonson's text and to H & S are to this edition.

Here the implications are very suggestive: his power can arrest time so that the Golden Age does not fade away as it did in ancient myth; his head is gold-encircled with a crown at the same time that it is golden—"of most value"—for its wisdom; he is the "golden" head of the state. These ideas are reinforced in the next lines:

> That in his owne true circle, still doth runne;
> And holds his course, as certayne as the sunne.   (352-3)

The true circle is the crown as well as the ancient symbol of perfection and unity. Allied with the sun because of his stability and because the sun is also a ruler and golden, he is given more of its attributes:

> He makes it euer day, and euer spring,
> Where he doth shine, and quickens euery thing
> Like a new nature: so, that true to call
> Him, by his title, is to say, Hee's all.   (354-7)

The images used here of the king, whether Arthur or James or both, form a paean which mounts to a crescendo with the words "Hee's all." Notice that the Sylvan has said that the ceremony is "due to ARTHVRS chaire," that is, the office of a British king. By the end of the speech, the office of the king has become a symbol of the proper working of the universe, the king is a "new nature," and the celebration widens its application to include everything in nature.

Is this flattery? Is it poetry? Over the years a tradition has grown up of looking at Jonson's masques as "bubbles and butterflies and rainbows" (H & S, 2, 334), minor efforts of a great poet and dramatist in which all such passages as that quoted above are deplorable examples of abject flattery. In recent years, however, such writers as Allan Gilbert, D. J. Gordon, Ernest W. Talbert, and Dolora Cunningham have adopted a new point of view toward the masques which is most concisely summed up in the conclusion of Talbert's "The Interpretation of Jonson's Courtly Spectacles":

> I suggest, consequently, that if Jonson's courtly entertainments are to be interpreted in accordance with his own words, if his purpose and his long preoccupation with the *genre* are to be fully understood, the critic should examine carefully the voice and sense of each masque. And the voice of Jonson's masques, I submit, is that of the panegyric *laudando praecipere*; the sense, that of precepts *de regimine principum* enlarged by the ethical-poetical *credo* of a staunch Renaissance humanist.[3]

---

3. *PMLA, 41* (1946), 473. Allan H. Gilbert, *The Symbolic Persons in the Masques of Ben Jonson*, Durham, N.C., Duke University Press, 1948. D. J.

In addition to examining the voice and sense of each masque that I discuss, this study will concern itself with a third element, the masques' ritual form. But following first Talbert's lead we may ask if such passages as those from *Oberon* reflect a particular tradition in their language or voice. The effect of the passages depends upon the imagery and upon the presence of a king—not necessarily of King James. Together they suggest a world centering in the office of monarchy, which is itself patterned on a universal philosophy. Obviously Jonson is talking here to some degree in terms of an ideal monarchy rather than of the actual British court. If we start from this point and assume that the picture given here is that of an ideal monarchy and not the real one, we may ask where Jonson found the picture. A survey of the imagery traditionally associated with kings shows that it existed twenty centuries before Jonson was born, and a glance at some of the literature of Jonson's day shows that it persisted and was conventional.

From the works of classical writers available to scholars of the early seventeenth century it is possible to compile a dictionary of the images of monarchy. In books of instruction for princes, in panegyrics, in legal documents, we find the same images used again and again. They are related by a philosophy, that expressed most fully in the works of the Platonists, and when they are codified they fall into categories which correspond to the links in the Great Chain of Being. Kingly images are not to be dissociated from the pattern of the universe; they are of the pattern, and the force of any single image depends on its relationship to the pattern.

Within a state based on universal harmony, the functions of the king are expressed in various ways. Thus, in the top category in the hierarchy of being, we find images dealing with the king's relations with the gods or God.[4] While the king is occasionally called a god, most often he is a kind of lesser god directly representing the supreme God, or his power is shown as a gift from the gods while he himself is the vice-regent and prophet of God, God's statue or image, the son of Zeus, and the like. Martial ascribes full divinity to Domitian, calling him Master and God, Lord of the Earth and God of the Universe, says that

Gordon, " The Imagery of Ben Jonson's *The Masque of Blacknesse* and *The Masque of Beautie*," *Journal of the Warburg and Courtauld Institutes, 6* (1943), 122-41; "*Hymenaei*: Ben Jonson's Masque of Union," ibid., *8* (1945), 107-45; " Ben Jonson's 'Haddington Masque': The Story and the Fable," *MLR, 42* (1947), 180-7. Dolora Cunningham, " The Jonsonian Masque as a Literary Form," *ELH, 22* (1955), 108-24.

4. The catalogue of kingly images which follows is treated at length and documented in my unpublished dissertation, " Ben Jonson's Masques and Entertainments " (Yale University, 1951), ch. 1.

his power is divine and sacred, and speaks of his sacred life and name
(Domitian had, it is true, ordered that he should be referred to in
official documents as *Dominus et Deus noster*). Whether or not the
king is considered to be a god, he is usually associated with heavenly
bodies and godlike functions. For example, he is the sun or a star, he
provides various kinds of light, and he can hurl thunderbolts. His
presence protects the hind from the hounds, and even the great turbot
is glad to be caught for Domitian's table. He is a giver of increase, lord
of the seasons, and god of the sea.

The king is not always described in supernatural terms, however.
On a civic level he becomes not only sovereign but also prince of princes
and even senator. From the family group the king assumes the title of
father, one of the most common of the images of monarchy. He is also
a husband to his people, a household manager, field manager, and
master. In the image in which the state becomes analogous with the
human body, the king is the head. Lower in the scale of being we find
that the animal kingdom provided writers with the images of the king
as a bull, a ram, king bee (i. e. queen bee), boar, cock, lion, and eagle.
In the world of inanimate nature we find the king as gold, ornaments,
a fountain of light, and a mirror reflecting either the image of God or
abstract qualities of virtue for the benefit of his subjects.

By far the largest group of images is that which likens the king to
men carrying out the duties of their occupations. In most of these
images is implied a relationship to another individual or body of indi-
viduals which may represent the state or the king's subjects. The
principal image is that of the king as a shepherd, but he is pictured too
as a pilot or helmsman of the ship of state, as a physician, a charioteer,
a trainer of athletes, a general, the steward of an estate, a guardian
and protector. He is a hero or champion, a prophet, and an actor on
the stage. And writer after writer calls him the restorer of the Golden
Age.

That these images were familiar and conventional from classical
times to the early seventeenth century can be demonstrated by reference
to such sources as the *Laudes Regiae* of the ninth century and later,
in which the king acquired titles which more appropriately belonged to
Christ, to the Pope, or to a Roman conqueror.[5] John of Salisbury's
Policraticus (1159) as well as *The Buke of the Governaunce of
Princes*[6] and George Buchanan's *De Jure Regni apud Scotos* (1579,

5. Ernst H. Kantorowicz, *Laudes Regiae: A Study in Liturgical Acclamations
and Medieval Ruler Worship*, University of California Publications in History,
33 (Berkeley and Los Angeles, 1946), 29-30, 47, 56-8, 74, 96.

6. In *Gilbert of the Haye's Prose Manuscript* (A.D. 1456), ed. J. H. Stephen-

although written 1567-68) contain images of the sort we have been concerned with here. To the traditional imagery from classical times were added through the years images associated with the English Golden Age, the time of King Arthur, and with the Robin Hood myth, the pastoral version of the English Golden Age. Along with these literary accretions to the tradition came the kind of visual mythology represented in such iconographies as that of Cesare Ripa in which not only are kings and tyrants portrayed in pictures but abstract qualities are given visual forms and attributes. Thus a body of visual symbols of honor, virtue, love, harmony, unity, and the like was created.

Besides the literary and iconographical traditions on which Jonson drew, the Christian tradition with its mythology also lay at hand. Only in a few isolated instances, however, does Jonson draw upon this material for his imagery, and his use of the tradition appears mostly in the imitation of some of the characteristics of the Psalms in his hymns to the king. When Jonson deals with the functions of the king as head of the church, protector of the faith, and defender against popery on the one hand and Puritanism on the other, he does so in terms other than biblical.

In illustrating the use of the conventional imagery of monarchy in Jonson's day, we may turn to broadside ballads, speeches delivered to James on his progresses, sermons to which James listened, and a wide variety of poetry and drama. As a single example from another source, James's first speech to the English Parliament in 1603 will serve to show not only the persistence of the imagery but the way in which it could be used for a particular occasion.[7] The speech was important in that it was necessary for James to make a strong impression on the magistrates of his new realm. In it he lays the foundation of the attitudes he expects his subjects to hold toward him and, although his interpretation of monarchy was far stricter than that of Elizabeth, by use of the traditional images he was able to make it seem on the surface that he would be the kind of king who had received approval for two thousand years. At the center of the speech is the idea that in his person James symbolizes the blessings of God, that is, foreign and civil peace and their concomitants. He himself, he says, is the living example of the blessings of union, since in him is mirrored the union of York and Lancaster and of England and Scotland. He introduces and develops at length the images of father, husband, shepherd, and head of the body. In the body of which he is the head the judges and magistrates

son, Scottish Text Society, Vol. *62* (Edinburgh and London, 1914), *2*, 100-1, 145-56, 163.

7. *The Political Works of James I*, ed. Charles H. McIlwain, Harvard Political Classics, No. 1 (Cambridge, Mass., 1918), pp. 269-80.

are the eyes and ears. If his person symbolizes all good things, then the persons of his heirs symbolize the continuity of these things. Cleverly he introduces the image of himself as a servant, but quickly says that he is the servant of the commonwealth of which he is also the head and governor. He even brings in obliquely the Golden Age, implying that he has restored it to England.

James's use of the images of monarchy was calculated to impress on his hearers a single conception of the office of the king, but traditionally the same images had been used to express every kind of monarchy from tyranny to a modified republicanism. By the time Jonson was ready to work consciously with the images, each one was so loaded with meanings that his job was more that of definition than anything else, and in each masque Jonson defines in traditional images part of a theory of kingship: a king's duties, a subject's obedience, the place of love in a monarchy, the necessity of celebrating the office of a king. This kind of thing we have already glimpsed in the passages from *Oberon*. But there is danger in overemphasizing the imagery that has been discussed here, although it is the chief characteristic of the " voice " of the masques. The masque is more than its voice, more than a definition of kingship. It involves a stage and both royal and noble dancers, professional actors, music and scenery, a specific occasion, and a number of other elements we cannot afford to ignore. The masques may "constitute almost a King's Mirror," as Gilbert says,[8] but they are also poems, and poems written under circumstances which tended to control their forms.

In *Neptune's Triumph* (1624) Jonson attests to the power of Dame Expectation in determining what a masque was to present. In a dialogue between the Cook and the masque-writing Poet, the Cook says:

> I am by my place, to know how to please the palates of the ghests; so, you, are to know the palate of the times: study the seuerall tasts, what euery Nation, the *Spaniard*, the *Dutch*, the *French*, the *Walloun*, the *Neapolitan*, the *Brit[t]an*, the *Sicilian*, can expect from you.
>
> ### POET.
>
> That were a heauy and hard taske, to satisfie *Expectation*, who is so seuere an exactresse of duties; euer a tyrannous mistresse: and most times a pressing enemie.
>
> ### COOKE.
>
> She is a powerfull great Lady, Sir, at all times, and must be satisfied: So must her sister, Madam *Curiositie*, who hath as daintie a palate as she, and these will expect.   (48-60)

---

8. *Symbolic Persons*, p. 26.

It would not be surprising to find extensive use of the imagery of monarchy in the texts of masques presented before Jonson was hired to write for the court, as well as some indication of what it was that the monarchs expected. To accumulate conclusive evidence on either of these points is, however, impossible, for the material is too varied and the texts too few for certainty. Although we review all the English texts referred to in Enid Welsford's and Mary Steele's lists,[9] we can come away with only one impression, that the masque had existed in England in a bewildering multitude of forms and that no one form had been established by 1605. Among the purposes or ends of the earlier entertainments we can see the presentation of gifts for good will, dancing for the amusement of both the participant and the spectator, supplication to the monarch, advice to the king or to others in command, the teaching of virtue and wisdom generally, the justification of possibly doubtful claims to the throne, placation or criticism of a monarch, dressing up for its own sake, the introduction of jousts, providing splendor for the increased majesty of the sovereign, a compliment to him, and sheer amusement divorced from other purposes.[1]

Among the means employed in accomplishing these ends are found first various treatments of allegory: an unexplained procession of familiar allegorical figures, a playlet explained by a Truchman (interpreter), or one participated in by two or more speakers, a combination of speakers and symbolical scenery and costume, allegory expressed in mythological, religious, or other figures with their accepted attributes, or emblematic scenery alone. Besides allegory, we find other means of accomplishing the various ends, such as dancing by professionals, nobles, or the king, masked or unmasked, in formal figures or in "ballroom" freedom from formality. We find also the use of speeches in prose or poetry, blank verse or song, expressing moral values or romantic tales. There may be no scenery or it may be the most lavish imaginable. Costumes may be merely splendid or outlandish or emblematic and they may be worn by people of any rank.

Can this welter of means and ends be ordered to show any lines of development leading up to the Jacobean masque? Every attempt that has been made has proved that these traditional entertainments alone cannot explain the elaborate masques produced at the court of James. It is far better to accept the fact that the masque throughout its life was a fluid form, taking a different shape under each writer who dealt

---

9. Enid Welsford, *The Court Masque*, Cambridge, 1927. Mary S. Steele, *Plays & Masques at Court during the Reigns of Elizabeth, James and Charles*, New Haven, 1926.

1. A documented review of the ends and means of earlier court entertainments will be found in my dissertation, pp. 63-80.

with it; only in this way can we understand what happened to it in the hands of Jonson.

If the history of the masque cannot tell us specifically what the queen, as Dame Expectation, wanted when she asked for a masque, what then determined Jonson's choice of sense, voice, and form from this mass of traditional elements? In the choice of sense, the determining factor was that Jonson could speak directly to King James. As Gilbert puts it, " The masque enjoyed an almost incredible advantage over tragedy in that it was intended only for presentation before the monarch and his peers. If ever poet could expect to touch the center of influence, here was his opportunity " (*Symbolic Persons*, p. 25). For a learned poet the problem of finding a subject fit for the king's ears was solved in his reading. It had been the best poet's duty always to advise the ruler on matters of virtue and good government; witness the works of the greatest writers, who applied their talents to the instruction of the king. Tradition then supplied the sense as well as the voice of the masque. But in what form were they to be embodied? A *Mirror for Magistrates* was not appropriate for the masque, nor were the forms of panegyric, satire, or epigram unless they could be altered to provide a framework which would permit the teaching to be delightful enough for Dame Expectation and forceful enough to be accepted by the audience for whom it was designed.

I suspect that Jonson's choice of form for his masques is partly the result of a challenge delivered by Samuel Daniel in the masque which he published in 1604 as *The Vision of the Twelve Goddesses*. In his preface Daniel claims that even though the masque " was not inferiour to the best that euer was presented in Christendome," certain " captious Censurers " had criticized his work on the grounds that Daniel " could giue no reason for what was done." [2] Of the censurers he says, " If their deepe iudgements euer serue them to produce any thing, they must stand on the same Stage of Censure with other men, and peraduenture performe no such great wonders as they would make vs beleeue." Whether Jonson was one of the censurers or not, the following passage seems to apply to him: " And whoeoeuer striues to shew most wit about these Pun[c]tillos of Dreames and shewes, are sure sicke of a disease they cannot hide, and would faine haue the world to thinke them very deeply learned in all misteries whatsoeuer." We may oppose to this Jonson's claim in the preface to *Hymenaei*, published two years later, that the important part of the masque is its " soul," which should have reference to " remou'd *mysteries* " based on " solide *learnings* " : " And, howsoeuer some may squemishly crie out, that all endeuour of

2. Samuel Daniel, *Works*, ed. A. B. Grosart (5 vols. London, 1885-96), *3*, 195.

learning, and *sharpnesse* in these transitorie *deuices* especially, where
it steps beyond their little, or (let me not wrong 'hem) no braine at all,
is superfluous; I am contented, these fastidious *stomachs* should leaue
my full tables, and enioy at home, their cleane emptie trenchers, fittest
for such ayrie tasts " (19-25).

To one familiar with Jonson's masques the first and last impression
of the *Vision* is that Daniel missed more opportunities than he developed. The fable in outline is not impossible to work with, but the
interrelationship of theme and imagery and action with which Jonson's
readers are familiar is lacking here. Basically what Daniel's masque
sets out to do is to raise a contemporary fact, peace between England
and her old enemies, to a symbol of monarchy acting according to
divine principle. But his allegorical figures are the merest emblems
and at that not very accurate; he presents no conflict to heighten the
value of peace; and if his poetry is mechanical, the prose spoken by
some of the characters is far worse. But we see in this entertainment
the germs of the Jonsonian masque and can point out in its elements
some advantages which Jonson developed to the full.

First of all, the fable is based on one of the images of monarchy,
that of the king as Prince of Peace. We find similar images in Jonson
as the basis of the fable. For example, in *Hymenaei* King James is
" the *king,* and *priest of peace!*" (92). The advantages of making the
imagery of monarchy the center of the masque are manifold: it is sure
to meet with the royal approval, its scope is very broad, and its tradition
guarantees that it will be appropriate.

The introduction of goddesses and allegorical figures in the *Vision*
is justified by Daniel's fable, and is, of course, a device that Jonson
uses. But the mingling in the masque of apparently unrelated figures
seems to have been one of the things Daniel was derided for; his preface
is devoted chiefly to explaining his use of them and he claims that even
if they are not completely accurate " the mythologers " themselves are
not agreed on the special virtues and attributes of the figures he uses.
The first impression we receive from some of Jonson's masques is as
puzzling as that produced by Daniel's. Except in the few cases when all
the figures on stage are obviously related by a special myth, it is necessary to delve into all the classical and pseudoclassical attributes of a
given figure before we can see the full point of the masque. For usually
Jonson is perfectly aware that the mythologers do not agree, yet he
does not force himself to select only a single attribute; on the contrary,
often he makes use of all the attributes he finds listed in his sources in
order to extend the meaning of his characters into several otherwise
unrelated spheres.

Aside from their value as symbols, the gods and goddesses in Jon-

son's masques perform another important function : they speak directly
to the king.   A god may do this where a man frequently may not,
especially when he attempts to show the king his duties.

The mythological or pseudomythological fable has other advantages
besides the ones we have noted.   For example, it makes an intellectual
as well as a visual appeal possible.   Jonson counted on the court to
be learned enough to grasp immediately the various significances of
mythological figures.   But if one were to expect this, one had to be
accurate in presenting them.   The chief source of Jonson's quarrel with
Jones was that the architect had appareled the masquers " as noe
thought can teach / Sense what they are!" (H & S, *8*, 404).

Another important element in Daniel's masque—probably the most
important in the light of Jonson's work—is the ceremony which the
Goddesses are undertaking, a pseudoclassical rite in which a sibyl calls
on supernatural beings to give their virtues to the reigning king.
Whether Jonson took his lead from Daniel in this or not, the ritual
ceremony forms a part of every masque he wrote.   The ceremonies
vary in kind from Roman marriage rites (*Hymenaei*) to the annual
celebrations of the coming of spring (*Chloridia*) to the paying of
homage to the king by his lowliest subjects (*Christmas*), with all
shades in between.   The full value of ritual in the masque was apparent
to Jonson as it was not to Daniel, if we can take Daniel's results as an
indication of his awareness of the possibilities.   For example, the ritual
provided a ready-made framework for a performance in which were
already integrated verbal, musical, and visual symbols, dancing, singing,
the serious and the comic, dignity without pomposity.   Traditionally a
religious ritual permits reference not only to supernatural beings and
ideas but to events in one's own day as well.   In the masque, a ritual
form can express both the ideals of a perfect monarchy and the pleasures
of a particular reign within the same framework.   It is also extremely
flexible and allows even the introduction of the weird and ugly figures
which the Queen later insisted on and which Jonson called antimasquers ; they are brought in as the profaners of the rites, as the powers
to be exorcised, and as the devils who by implication in every religious
ritual are always lurking just over the horizon as a threat.   Another
of the advantages of ritual is that it allows everyone to be promoted :
the king is converted into a god, the courtiers into princes.   And it
satisfies the requirement that the masquers should not speak, because
in the ritual there are priests and other celebrants who speak for them.
The question of flattery is neatly solved, for it is necessary for celebrants
to praise and thank their gods even if at the same time they remind
them of their duties.

Many other benefits of which Daniel seems unaware lurk in the ritual form, but until we come to the analysis of Jonson's masques we need mention here only that religious or civil ritual brings with it a language unlike that ordinarily used. This is the language which Jonson uses in the main masques (as distinguished from the antimasques), the language of the classical religious festivals, of the Triumphs of the emperors, even of the hymns of the Church of England; to this he welds the imagery of monarchy, which might also be called the imagery of ritual worship because the epithets applied to gods and kings are to a great extent the same. Jonson takes advantage of this tradition in the masques; the form of ritual permits him to use the voice and sense appropriate to the delight and instruction of a king and his court.

The plan of building the masque on a ritual celebration and around a fable based on one or more of the images of monarchy is so flexible that it can be the foundation of a work without appearing on the surface. Daniel complains that the surface of his masque distracted attention from its meaning. The enormous variety shown on the surface of Jonson's masques has frequently deluded his readers. We must try to see the pattern common to them all, though I should not like to suggest that in each masque we see such a well-defined ritual as that in *Hymenaei* or that the imagery of monarchy is always as prominent as that of the king as the sun in *Blackness*. These elements are like the warp in a piece of cloth: while they determine to a great extent the nature of the cloth, they do not necessarily determine its appearance, which may result from the use of any kind of fiber in the weft. We shall see that the weft which makes the masques appear so varied is provided not only from the traditions of the masque in England but from Jonson's reading in classical and contemporary literature and from his observation of life in James's realm.

The most complete information available about the production of each of Jonson's masques and entertainments is to be found in the commentary of Herford and Simpson. A brief summary here will give a general picture of Jonson's activities in writing for the court. Between 1605 and 1631 he produced twenty-five masques. To one of these, *Pleasure Reconciled to Virtue*, he added for the second performance a new antimasque which was printed as *For the Honour of Wales*. Another, *Neptune's Triumph*, was not performed and in the following year was revamped by the substitution of a new antimasque and some changes in the masque as *The Fortunate Isles*. The complete text of the masques, therefore, is comprised of twenty-seven separately titled works.

Although most of the masques were written for King James, the two final ones, *Love's Triumph* and *Chloridia*, were produced for Charles I, and *Lovers Made Men* was designed for the honor of the Baron de la Tour, the French ambassador. Except when I am talking of these three productions I shall speak of James as the person for whom the masques were written, only to avoid the cumbersome qualifications necessary to include Charles and the Baron. With the exception of *The Gypsies Metamorphosed*, which was performed three times in the country, and possibly *Pan's Anniversary* (H & S, *10*, 604), all the masques were given in one or another of the banqueting-houses in London.

There are ten "Entertainments." One of these is Jonson's *Panegyre* to King James, welcoming him to England in 1604. Another, *Black-friars*, was written in 1620 for the christening of the Earl of Devonshire's son in the presence of the Prince of Wales. The others are shows to be performed, unlike the masques, at the expense of the king's hosts as a way of welcoming him to the city (as in the case of the London entertainments of 1604) or more usually to a nobleman's country house. Jonson thought of the word "entertainment" in the sense of welcome or of providing for a guest (*OED*, "Entertainment" † 11). One of the productions included under "masques" in the 1640 Folio, *The Gypsies Metamorphosed*, has some relation to the entertainments for it was produced twice at the expense of noblemen; but because it was performed a third time at Windsor and because it is not particularly concerned with welcoming the king, it properly appears with the other masques.

Every writer who has dealt with the mass of these works has treated them chronologically for reasons connected with his thesis. This is not a satisfactory arrangement here because it makes the relating of masques unnecessarily difficult. However, it is not easy to establish categories on other foundations, for while a masque may be predominantly pastoral and thus might appear with other pastoral masques, yet it may have elements which make it closely akin to a nonpastoral masque of a contemporary Golden Age. The groups, therefore, are not to be considered mutually exclusive. The masques are here divided into four categories: the Golden Age, the Pastoral, the Triumph, and the Combats of Concepts. In each category I deal only with representative masques, since a detailed analysis of all thirty-five masques and entertainments becomes repetitious and therefore unnecessarily tedious. I have omitted several important masques from the discussion because they have been thoroughly dissected by others, although in some cases I have commented on the work that has been done. And I have tried to combine with my analysis a study of those elements which deserve attention in every masque—verse, music, scenery, dancing, Jonson's use of the king as the central symbol. Although these are handled separately, they apply equally to all the masques.

1

Masques in the Tradition of the Golden Age

> Here are kingdomes mixt
> And nations ioyn'd, a strength of empire fixt
> Conterminate with heauen; The golden veine
> Of SATVRNES age is here broke out againe.
> —*Prince Henries Barriers*

THE tradition of the Golden Age, associated with the imagery of monarchy, was very much alive in Jonson's day. In classical writing we find the myth of the Golden Age being used in several ways. For example, Seneca uses it as a means of expressing the principles of good government; Plato illustrates with it the inevitable sequence of change from monarchy to other forms of government; in Horace it serves to point up the rewards of righteousness or to indicate the excellences of the reign of Augustus; Juvenal uses it for contemporary satire; and Tibullus, while satirizing his own world, evokes a measure of nostalgia for the good old days which the myth of Golden Age suggests.[1] In the centuries between the classical writers and Jonson two particularly English ideas became a part of the myth in literature. First, the idea arose that the times of King Arthur were the English Golden Age, and with it such links with the past as the name Troynovant for London were established. In addition, the Robin Hood myth assumed some of the characteristics of the Golden Age in the suggestion of a life of ease in the forest. The Golden Age was for Jonson a powerful symbol: it appears directly or indirectly as a central idea in fifteen of the masques and many of the entertainments, usually in combination with other traditions. Let us take as a first example *Time Vindicated* (1623), which centers on this symbol. At first glance the masque appears to be completely divided between a biting satire against George Wither and a mythological representation of the glories of the Golden Age. The careful reader will discover, however, that in both sections, the antimasque and the masque, there is a unity brought about by the imagery of time in each. This imagery is based

---

1. Seneca, *Epistles*, 90. 5. Plato, *Republic*, 8. 546-7. Horace, *Epodes*, 16. Juvenal, *Satires*, 6. 1-20. Tibullus, 1. 3. 37-50.

on the conception of the king as Saturn, the god of the Golden Age, and branches out into the traditional attributes of Saturn, of Kronos his Greek ancestor, of Chronos (Time) with which Kronos was etymologically confused early in his Italian history, and finally into conventional phrases and usages of the word "time": the times, clock time, and the like. King James, who sits throughout the performance on a throne in the center of the hall among the spectators, does not take part in the action of the masque, although he dominates the proceedings by his presence and is in some instances the equivalent of Saturn or Time; a professional actor plays the part of the real Saturn who appears in the clouds above the stage.

The unity which the imagery of time produces in the masque is more than verbal, for there is a deeper unity which is predicated on the idea that there is a "time for everything." The entertainment is divided not so much into masque and antimasque as into three parts of equal importance if not equal length. The first introduces us to the Curious (Eyes, Eares, Nose), who are driven away by a group of Jugglers and Tumblers called up by Fame. Fame comments on them:

> Commonly,
> The curious are ill-natur'd, and like flies,
> Seeke *Times* corrupted parts to blow upon.   (265-7)

In the second part of the masque Fame introduces to the king the Glories of the Time, hidden by Hecate in obscure regions and now freed by Saturn,

> As being fitter to adorne the age,
> By you restor'd on earth, most like his owne.   (285-6)

That is, of course, the Golden Age, which James has brought back to earth. The part of the masque which follows lasts the longest. During it the king is praised as the Lord of Time and the begetter of this court, in which such glories find their rightful home. The masquers dance in a display of their agility, beauty, and skill and then, urged by Cupid and Sport, they dance with the ladies of the court. The scene is one of gaiety and happiness. The suggestion is that under such a king everyone and everything is good and beautiful and that this ceremony, beauty, and magnificence are the outward signs of a sound, peaceful, and self-sufficient monarchy. The dancers justly celebrate the king and his comfortable world.

Thus, this part of the masque presents the positive value of harmony and joyousness and beauty in the court of James. But the final section introduces a sudden conflict. It is interesting that Jonson prepares us for this only in the first section when he has Fame say that Hecate has been jealously hiding the Glories of the Time up to the moment when Saturn freed them. In the second section no reference is made to any higher value than is being presented: Saturn, Venus, Fame, the Chorus, and the masquers themselves seem thoroughly pleased by the celebration and willing to accept it as an ultimate good. Then, as the dance with the ladies ends, the chorus introduces a disturbing element:

> The Courtly strife is done, it should appeare,
> Betweene the Youths, and Beauties of the yeare,
> Wee hope that now these lights will know their spheare,
> And strive hereafter to shine ever here:
>
> > Like brightest Planets, still to move
> > In th'eye of *Time*, and orbes of *Love*.   (450-5)

Superficially this is an expressed hope that the glories will no longer live away from the court but will inhabit it permanently, in the eye of the king (the Lord of Time) and orbs (eyes, orbits) of Love. The jarring note comes first in the suggestion that this beauty and youth is transitory: "of the yeare," not of all time. It also appears in the suggestion that the court had been without glories up to this moment. And finally, if we interpret "these lights" as referring to the actual courtiers who are taking part in the masque, there is a strong implication that up to now they have *not* been shining "like brightest planets."

The Chorus' song works two ways, then: it looks back (in terms of the masque) to the value of the glory which justifies and dignifies a court, but it looks ahead to the next action, the appearance of Diana, the Hecate who had hung as an unacknowledged threat over all the proceedings. She and her assistant, the chaste Hippolitus, deny that she had kept the glories away with "purpose to defraud/ The *Time*, of any glories that were his."

HIPPOLITVS.

To doe *Time* honour rather, and applaud
His worth, hath beene her study.

DIANA.

And it is.
I call'd these Youths forth, in their bloud, and prime
(Out of the honour, that I bore their parts)
To make them fitter so to serve the *Time*
By labour, riding, and those ancient arts,
That first enabled men unto the warres,
And furnish'd Heaven with so many Starres:

HIPPOLITVS.

As *Perseus, Castor, Pollux*, and the rest,
Who were of Hunters first, of Men the best.   (489-98)

According to Diana, then, the place of the young courtiers is not in
revels but rather in more serious activity, principally in hunting. They
may achieve the status of the heroes "if the *Time* give leave" (i. e.
if the king allows, if this present age permits it, and if they are given
enough time for martial studies and not kept from pursuits of greater
value by the pleasant, happy, but essentially unproductive activities of
dancing and dalliance). Saturn (Time) agrees to Diana's request and
the Glories leave the hall to return to her school of the chase while
the Chorus qualifies the meaning of "hunter."

> Turne Hunters then,
>   agen.
> Hunting it is the noblest exercise,
>   Makes men laborious, active, wise,
> Brings health, and doth the spirits delight,
>   It help's the hearing, and the sight:
> It teacheth arts that never slip
>   The memory, good horsmanship,
> Search, sharpnesse, courage, and defence,
>   And chaseth all ill habits thence.   (514-23)

Yet these results are of no value unless they are applied in particular
ways.

> Turne Hunters then,
>   agen,
> But not of Men.
> Follow his ample,
> And just example,
> That hates all chace of malice, and of bloud:
>   And studies only wayes of good,
>   To keep soft Peace in breath.
> Man should not hunt Mankind to death,
>   But strike the enemies of Man;
>   Kill vices if you can:
> They are your wildest beasts.
> And when they thickest fall, you make the Gods true feasts.
>   (524-36)

The hunting is not an end in itself, nor is the wisdom, sharpness, or
courage which hunting develops. The specific duty of the hunter is to

kill vices. In this he is imitating Christ's "ample and just example" as well as James's (for these lines are a clear reference to James's love of hunting and of peace); the Christian application grows in this stanza up to the last line when it is neatly twisted to round out the essentially classical fable on which the masque is based with the idea that killing vices is to offer the best sacrifices to the gods.

This interpretation of the masque depends to a great extent on our recognition of Jonson's use of the king in the masque. In every masque at which James was a spectator there are at least three kinds of reference to him. In the first place he has a role in the story. In this case, as we have noted, although he is not on the stage he is a member of the cast in being the Lord of Time or in sharing the identity of Saturn or Time. Secondly, he is an example of kingship whose very presence insists on certain attitudes from the masquers. Finally he is James, King of England. Corresponding to these roles of the king are the roles of the courtiers who dance: in the fable they have a special identity (here the Glories of the Time); but they are also the idealized courtiers of the example of kingship and are expected to act as tradition says courtiers should; and finally they are Prince Charles, the Duke of Buckingham, the earls, and others, who are, outside the masque, the actual residents of the court. It is this triple set of identities which we must keep in mind when we read such a passage as the song of the Chorus at the turn of the theme. It is useful, too, in reading the antimasque.

Thus far we have seen the masque "laying hold on more remou'd *mysteries*"; we must now consider how it is "taught to sound present occasions." Most pressing on the reader's attention is the identification of Chronomastix in the antimasque with George Wither. Herford and Simpson are representative of those who have discussed the masque when they say, "The chief object of the antimasque is to castigate George Wither for attempting satire" (H & S, *10*, 651). Certainly on January 19, 1623, the court understood the satire, so that "Ben Iohnson they say is like to heare of yt on both sides of the head for personating George withers a poet or poetaster as he termes him, as hunting after fame by beeing a crono-mastix or whipper of the time, wch is become so tender an argument that yt must not be touched either in iest or earnest." [2] Simpson's extensive notes summarize the de· tails of the antimasque which apply to Wither and we need repeat only a few of them here to show the kind of satire Jonson uses. There are a number of references to the frontispiece of *Wither's Motto* (1621) which showed Wither in an emblematic setting and crowned with

2. John Chamberlain in a letter to Sir Dudley Carleton, H & S, *10*, 648.

laurel: Jonson calls him " The gentleman-like Satyre," and has Wither speak of his " glorious front, and word at large, / [which] Triumphs in print at my admirers charge." And since Wither had dedicated *Abuses Stript, and Whipt* (1613) to himself, Jonson labels him " selfe-loving Braggart." For the most part the details of the satire are chosen from such minor but characteristic lapses in taste exhibited by Wither in his printed works.

But is this treatment of Chronomastix only a piece of personal invective designed to discredit Wither at court? It seems to me that the test lies in the question whether we are able to read the satire as a proper part of the masque as a whole or whether it loses touch with the theme. One indication of its unity with the parts of the masque we have examined will be seen in its use of the imagery of time as a counterpart to the Saturn-Kronos-Time imagery on which the fable is based. Chronomastix does not appear until the Curious have set the stage. Jonson points out the evil nature of the Curious by showing them possessed by a predilection for " *Times* corrupted parts." They speak of the attributes of Saturn and Time which, even if traditional, are somewhat lurid: the fact that Saturn eats his children, that he carries a scythe (which they turn into a fencer's sword), that he is a pagan god, and that he presides over the Saturnalia, which they see as a Shrove Tuesday rout in which " men might doe, and talke all that they list. . . . Slaves of their lords. . . . The servants of their masters . . . . And subjects of their Soveraigne " (43-6). It is this aspect of the Curious which offends Fame the most, the irresponsible tongue-wagging of the ignorant, their predisposition always to see the worst and talk of it. At this point Chronomastix enters, " Lo, I, the man, that hate the time," who with his whip lashes the age. Lapsing into the royal use of " we " he says, " If you would see *Time* quake and shake, but name us, / It is for that, we'are both belov'd, and famous." Being informed that the lady present is Fame, his haughty manner drops and cringingly he offers her his devotion, but she rebuffs him as an imposter: " *Fame* doth sound no trumpet / To such vaine, empty fooles." Chronomastix turns then to the Curious and complains at this treatment: is he not popular with the fishwife and the button boy? does he deserve to be scorned? while Eares comments, " Rare! how he talkes in verse, just as he writes! " Now Chronomastix calls forth those who love him, including a degraded justice, a penurious printer and his compositor, and a schoolmaster who translates Chronomastix's poetry into Latin and forces it on his pupils, and, joined by the Curious, they perform a dance of adoration to Chronomastix and carry him off in triumph.[3]

3. This scene appears in lines 65-189.

When the Curious return to the stage, they insist that Fame keep her promise of showing them the spectacle which Saturn had sent her to introduce. She asks them what they would like, and they answer, " I had now a fancie / We might have talk'd o'the King. . . . Or State. . . . Or all the World. . . . Censur'd the Counsell, ere they censure us. . . . We doe it in *Pauls*. . . . Yes, and in all the tavernes! " (206-12) Again we see their desire to censure and to speak only of the evil they imagine they see. Fame's answer as she has the Curious driven off is the point of the antimasque:

> A comely licence. They that censure those
> They ought to reverence, meet they that old curse,
> To beg their bread, and feele eternall Winter.
> Ther⟨e⟩'s difference 'twixt liberty, and licence. (213-16)

If we see Chronomastix as one of those who, for the sake of fame and personal glory, "censure those they ought to reverence," rather than as a man who kills vices for the sake of God, as the hunters are told to do later, his position in the masque is justified. The Curious and Chronomastix are witty, to be sure, but ridiculous and essentially ignorant and evil.

We may ask why Jonson did not express this aspect of his theme in some other way; there are many examples of viciousness just as ridiculous which could have been contrasted with the masque-figures. The emphasis in the antimasque here falls on the question of speaking against the king or talking about affairs of state. Jonson, I feel, counted on contemporary circumstances to give this part of the masque a political as well as a moral and personal significance. In 1620 James issued a proclamation making it punishable to speak of affairs of state.[4] In 1621 the Commons began to discuss matters which James felt were out of its province. Spain had attacked Frederick, Prince of Bohemia, James's Protestant son-in-law, and the Commons was ready to provide money to send him immediate aid. However, at that time Spain was England's closest ally, her ambassador Gondomar was James's chief adviser, and her princess was to be married to Prince Charles. Under these conditions the Commons sent James a petition asking him to abjure Spain and go to the help of Frederick. Even before he had received it James had replied that such considerations were beyond the authority of the Commons and that he would prosecute any member of

---

4. The information in this paragraph is drawn from Godfrey Davies, *The Early Stuarts:1603-1660*, corr. ed., Oxford History of England (Oxford, The Clarendon Press, 1949), pp. 22-7, and Samuel R. Gardiner, *History of England . . . 1603-1642* (10 vols. London, 1883-84), *4*, 117, 246-71.

Parliament who discussed these affairs. Throughout the next year, and until Parliament was dissolved without having obtained a clarification of its rights, the question of free speech was uppermost in the political tangles of England. *Time Vindicated* presents the king's side of the argument on the grounds that when the ignorant and inquisitive (the Curious) talk of things they do not understand they inevitably work against harmony and order.

The antimasque serves, then, less as a vehicle for Jonson's feelings about Wither than as a link in the chain of values which the masque as a whole presents. As a satire of Wither specifically it has no organic relation to the whole. As a satire of those who ignorantly speak against the Crown it illustrates the side of the coin of which the masquers represent the reverse. It holds a position in this masque akin to the satire of Sporus and Atticus in the " Epistle to Dr. Arbuthnot " : it is necessary dramatically.

In the antimasque the references to time center naturally on Chronomastix, the Whipper of the Time, just as in the masque the references center on Saturn. In both parts of the masque we find allusions to time in the sense of " the age " (" The knaveries of the *Time*," 52), time as a person (" The *Time* hath sent me with my Trumpe," 37), or a triple reference such as clock time and the present moment and time as a person in " I'le fit you, though the *Time* faintly permit it " (260). It is a minor point but at almost every appearance of the word " time " it is italicized for emphasis.

The unity we have observed in this masque—in its imagery, its theme, and its dramatic elements—is borne out in its use of verse forms and in its changes of tone. For example, the speeches of the Curious are a broken iambic pentameter, emphasizing the flylike character of the speakers which Fame has pointed out. Rather than give them short prose speeches Jonson provides a regular rhythmic line which they split up among themselves in their capricious, incoherent, and fragmentary way :

> EIES.   We come to spie.
> EARES.   And hearken.
> NOSE.   And smell out.
> FAME.   More than you understand, my hot Inquisitors,
>   ⟨Is it not so?⟩
> NOSE.   We cannot tell.
> EIES.   It may be.   (10-16)

And although they use local reference and colloquialisms their speech is not entirely of the streets, for Jonson is showing their universal characteristics of ignorance and pettiness.

Chronomastix, who next appears after the Curious, speaks in heroic couplets, imitating Wither's own use of the same " soft ambling verse " which Chronomastix so admires in this passage, his answer to Fame's condemnation of his motives:

> O, you the *Curious*,
> Breath you to see a passage so injurious,
> Done with despight, and carried with such tumor
> 'Gainst me, that am so much the friend of rumor?
> (I would say *Fame*?) whose *Muse* hath rid in rapture
> On a soft ambling verse to every capture,
> From the strong guard, to the weake childe that reades me,
> And wonder both of him that loves, or dread's me!
> Who with the lash of my immortall pen
> Have scourg'd all sorts of vices, and of men!
> Am I rewarded, thus? have I, I say,
> From *Envies* selfe torne praise, and bayes away,
> With which my glorious front, and word at large,
> Triumphs in print at my admirers charge.   (103-16)

The rime itself is an imitation of Wither's satires, and the weakness of the feminine endings in the first eight lines above is designed to characterize the verse as soft and ambling and unfit for satire. In the next lines the hesitancy of " have I, I say " makes even more ridiculous the commonplace quality of the preceding lines which deal feebly with Wither's immortal pen. Thus his big phrases which are supposed to make his hearers quake and stand in awe merely show him as a prosy buffoon.

With the entrance of the masquers we meet a different variety of verse. The speeches of Saturn, Venus, and Diana are in a more dignified style. Fully aware of the presence of the king, the deities neither stand in awe of him nor stoop to familiarity: this is the case of god talking to god.

VENUS.

> Beside, that it is done for *Love*,
> It is a worke, great *Time*, will prove
> Thy honour, as mens hopes above.

SATURNE.

> If *Love* be pleased, so am I:
> For *Time* could never yet deny
> What *Love* did aske, if Love knew why.   (292-9)

Apparently Venus and Saturn have been caught here at the end of a long conversation and have reached a godlike agreement. Compare the conversational dignity of the lines above with the reaction of the Chorus and Votaries to the presence of the fabulous masquers:

CHORUS.

What griefe, or envie had it beene,
That these, and such had not beene seene,
   But still obscur'd in shade!
Who are the glories of the *Time*,
Of youth, and feature too, the prime,
   And for the light were made!

VOTARIES.

1 Their very number, how it takes!
2 What harmony their presence makes!
  3 How they inflame the place!   (317-27)

Here is awe and wonder; the Votaries especially seem to be on their knees before the spectacle of the masquers, who in turn borrow value from the homage being paid.

The appearance of Cupid and Sport, who coax the masquers to dance with the ladies, introduces another tone which suggests that of Chronomastix and therefore a continuing need for control. While they maintain on the surface their respect for the king, they are thoroughly impudent. Note especially the abruptness of the opening line addressed to the king:

CU[I]PID.

You, Sir, that are the Lord of *Time*,
Receive it not as any crime
'Gainst Majesty, that *Love* and *Sport*
To night have entred in your Court.

SPORT.

Sir, doubt him more of some surprise
Vpon your selfe. He hath his eyes.
You are the noblest object here,
And 'tis for you alone I feare:
For here are Ladyes, that would give
A brave reward to make *Love* live
Well, all his life, for such a draught.
   And therefore, looke to every shaft,
   The Wag's a Deacon in his craft.   (374-88)

Is it proper for a subject to put his king in a class with ladies who are so eager to fall in love that for one shot of his arrow they would support Cupid in the highest style?

While it is necessary that we be able to see the differences in verse in the masque, it is more important that we recognize Jonson's working on two or three levels of meaning at once. For example, when Fame banishes the Curious, she turns to James and says:

> For you, great King, to whom the *Time* doth owe
> All his respects, and reverence . . . (275-6)

The remark has relevance to each of the king's three roles in the masque. First, in the world of the fable, the god Saturn (or Time) owes this great king, for whose honor he has brought back the Golden Age, respect and reverence. In the king's second role, that of the ideal monarch ruling an ideal state, the subjects naturally (i. e. by heavenly law) owe him respect and reverence (this assumes that " The Time " is the equivalent of " the times " as we use it to refer to people in a contemporary age). And third, the courtiers who are dancing before him and every one of his subjects throughout the realm depend on James himself for whatever well-being they have. In return they owe him respect and reverence.

One final point of unity in this masque is its ritual or ceremonial element. In the fable itself we have homage being paid to the Lord of Time by the glories of the court, assisted by the votaries. The singing of praises, the dancing, and the direct help of the gods mark this as a kind of ritual. By contrast the antimasque presents the heretic's ritual: the antimasquers " adore " Chronomastix in the first dance before they carry him off in triumph, while in the second they are driven away ignominiously rather than led to something higher, Diana's school. There are other elements of unity which we could show: the changes of scene, for example, and the question of the masquers' symbolic costume. However, since the principle on which these work is the same in other masques and since in some of the other masques the costumes and scenery are described in great detail (in *Time Vindicated* we depend on sources outside the text), it is better to wait. It is perhaps sufficient at this point simply to remember that, although we may agree with Swinburne that Jonson's lyrics are lovely, their beauty derives from the fact that they carry the burden of the masque as a whole.[5]

Let us now turn to consider *The Golden Age Restored*, which uses

5. A discussion of the importance of the lyric to early Stuart drama is to be found in William Bowden's *The English Dramatic Lyric, 1603-42*, Yale Studies in English, Vol. *118*, New Haven, 1951. Bowden shows that the lyrics are not merely decorative but perform several dramatic functions. In the masques their importance is even greater.

again the Saturn-Time idea but subordinates it to imagery based on the mineral content of various epochs: the Golden and the Iron Ages. The basic story of the two masques is the same: after a long period of evil, good returns to the earth in contemporary times graced by the heroes of the original Golden Age.. In *The Golden Age Restored*, however, there are some significant changes. The most striking of these at first glance is that when the masque opens the age has not been restored: the Iron Age still holds sway and the spectators are inhabitants of it, "offending mortalls." Pallas speaks first:

> Looke, looke! reioyce, and wonder!
>   That you offending mortalls are,
>   (For all your crimes) so much the care
> Of him, that beares the thunder!
>
> Iove can endure no longer,
>   Your great ones should your lesse inuade,
>   Or, that your weake, though bad, be made
> A prey vnto the stronger.
>
> And therefore, meanes to settle
>   Astraea in her seat againe;
>   And let downe in his golden chaine
> The age of better mettle.   (1-12)

In the Iron Age, then, the strong exploit the weak, and because Jove cannot stand this he is going to restore the Golden Age—out of his duty as a god, as Pallas says, rather than as a result of man's good deeds.[6] This is far from flattering to the king and the spectators. But before they have time to brood upon it, Iron Age herself enters with "a tumult and clashing of armes" and Pallas retires. In Iron Age's speech we begin to see the development of the central imagery of the masque which was suggested in Pallas' lines, "let downe in his golden chaine / The age of better mettle." The pun on the last word suggests that at least part of the masque will contrast various kinds and uses of metals and mettles. Iron Age calls out her evils to make war on Jove: Grandame Vice, Avarice, Fraud, Slander, Ambition, Pride, Scorn, Force, Rapine, Smooth Treachery, Folly, and Ignorance, along with "Corruption with the golden hands." Here Jonson brings in a favorite paradox which he uses more fully in Epigram LXIV.

---

6. The next two stanzas of this song contain the most difficult lines in all of Jonson's masques; the single variant recorded by Herford and Simpson does not help us to sort out the pronouns and tenses. This difficulty does not constitute a full-scale Jonsonian crux, however, because the general import of the lines is clear.

> Not glad, like those that haue new hopes, or sutes,
> With thy new place, bring I these early fruits
> Of loue, and what the golden age did hold
> A treasure, art: contemn'd in th'age of gold.[7]

The double standard represented by gold, first as a symbol of value and second as a symbol of avarice, is of course extremely common as a literary figure. In this masque Jonson develops it into the business of buying and selling, while he enlarges the idea of gold as one of the metals. Iron Age calls on her evils to fight Jove:

> Whom, if our forces can defeat,
>   And but this once bring vnder,
> Wee are the masters of the skyes,
> Where all the wealth, height, power, lyes,
>   The scepter, and the thunder.   (49-53)

Note that Iron Age's first interest in heaven, if we are to believe her speech, is in its wealth. But the whole speech carries this out. In the next lines she asks the spectators,

> Which of you would not in a warre
> Attempt the price of any scarre,
>   To keepe your owne states euen?   (54-6)

Notice the way she puts honor in terms of price and money, and thus tends to degrade it. Addressing her evils again, she says:

> But, heere, which of you is that hee,
> Would not himselfe the weapon bee,
>   To ruine IOVE and heauen?
> About it then, and let him feele,
> The iron-age is turn'd to steele,
>   Since he begins to threat her:
> And though the bodies here are lesse
> Then were the Giants; hee'l confesse
>   Our malice is farre greater.   (57-65)

Each of the evils is a steel weapon to turn against Jove. The battle is symbolized by a dance, and Jove wins through the agency of Pallas' shield, traditionally a symbol of virtue.[8] Pallas turns the evils to another kind of mineral, stone, and then calls on Astraea and Golden Age to descend,

---

7. " To Robert Earle of Salisbvrie," H & S, *8*, 47, lines 1-4.
8. H & S, *10*, 558, quoting Lydgate and Peele.

> And as your softer times diuide the aire,
> So shake all clouds off, with your golden haire.   (80-1)

The times, the pleasant moments, divide the air as the minutes divide
the hour. The two goddesses come down clad in gold and with golden
hair. When they are assured that Jove plans to restore justice and
mercy they are dubious of the reception mercy will get:

> ASTRAEA. AGE.
> 2. But doe they know,
>   How much they owe,
>   Belowe?
> 1. And will of grace receiue it, not as due?   (92-6)

Even here we have the suggestion of gold as money in the words "due"
and "owe." Pallas assures them that "if not, they harme themselues,
not you," and the choir sings "Let narrow Natures (how they will)
mistake, / The great should still be good for their owne sake."

Objecting that they cannot reign without retainers, Astraea and
Golden Age are told that they will be provided with the poets Chaucer,
Gower, Lydgate, and Spenser, "To waite vpon the age that shall your
names new nourish, / Since vertue prest shall grow, and buried arts
shall flourish" (119-20). And here in the buried arts we have a treasure waiting to be dug up in the Golden Age.

As the action of the masque progresses the gold-mineral-money
images multiply. The time has come to reveal the masquers, semigods
who retired to obscure shades when the old Golden Age died and now
are being provided to defend justice and sustain the age. Pallas' shield
is again brought into play and the masquers are revealed. Never again
will there be "Tumour of an yron vaine"—imagery joining the idea
of disease with the double suggestion of vein. "But, as of old, all now
be gold." After the first dance, which now takes place, the song deals
with the physical characteristics of the old Golden Age, drawn from
Ovid, Hesiod, and Vergil (H&S, *10*, 559). It is implied that the new
Golden Age which is in the process of developing under James's rule
will take on these characteristics. To assist the change, the four greatest
English poets are called upon to persuade the masquers to dance with
the ladies. They tell of love in golden times when

> The male and female vs'd to ioyne,
> And into all delight did coyne
>   That pure simplicitie.   (182-4)

as pure ore is coined into money.

The last two songs are designed to entice the courtiers into their
"sphere" where they will sit in a circle, the symbol of unity, around

Astraea. The songs were printed in different arrangements in the first
and second Folios, the arrangement in the second being dramatically
the better and that adopted by Herford and Simpson. Following this
order, first Pallas sings of the future, saying that in return for the help
of the masquers in sustaining the age, Astraea

> vowes, against or heat or cold,
> To spin you garments of her gold,
>   That want may touch you neuer,
> And making garlands euery hower,
> To write your names in some new flower,
>   That you may liue for euer.   (212-17)

The golden garments will be the signs of their worth and they will be
protected from the "touch" of "want" by these, i. e. by gold and by
Astraea's power. Finally, in the spirit of Ovid, the masquers will be
metamorphosed into flowers and thus live forever. The closing words
are Astraea's:

> Of all there seemes a second birth,
> It is become a heau'n on earth,
>   And *Ioue* is present here,
> I feele the Godhead: nor will doubt
> But he can fill the place throughout,
>   Whose power is euery where.   (228-33)

Although the primary reference is to the presence of the god Jove, there
is of course the suggestion that James is the deity whose godhead
Astraea feels, for he has made the court bloom into gold:

> This, this, and onely such as this,
> The bright *Astraea's* region is,
>   Where she would pray to liue,
> And in the midd'st of so much gold,
> Vnbought with grace or feare vnsold,
>   The law to mortals giue.   (234-9)

The central difference between this masque and *Time Vindicated*, that
in this one the age is not restored at the opening of the masque, is in
part resolved here as the divinity of King James is finally suggested.
Throughout the performance every reference to the audience has been
a slighting one, and we must recognize this openly expressed antagonism of Pallas and her crew as a dramatic device designed to do two
things: first, to emphasize Pallas' condemnation of "your great ones"
who oppress the weak, and second, to make the redemption of the court
more strikingly the result of the inborn divinity of the king rather than

of anything they have been able to do during the masque to atone for their sins.

The ritual in this masque finds its peak in the dancing. The masquers are told:

> Moue, moue then to these sounds.
> And, doe, not onely, walke your solemne rounds,
> But giue those light and ayrie bounds,
> That fit the *Genij* of these gladder grounds.   (149-52)

This is a dance of Genii, the Roman "spirits," in a happy ceremony. The word "grounds" has several meanings. It refers of course to the court; but it suggests also the plot of ground on which the ceremony is to be held in the fable, and it has a third meaning drawn from music, "these happier strains." This dance is gladder by contrast with the dance of Iron Age and her evils, a performance conceived in hell.

In the two masques we have reviewed we have seen Jonson stressing respectively the Saturn-Time and the gold-money-metal imagery of the Golden Age. In each case he uses the king as a character in the masque, drawing him in as a divine symbol of the heavenly hierarchy and giving him the role of a new Saturn, the restorer of the Golden Age. In *Prince Henries Barriers*, written as a part of the ceremonies attending Prince Henry's creation as the Prince of Wales (1610), Jonson was forced to use the legends of King Arthur because Henry had some time earlier delivered a formal challenge to the knights of the realm in the name of Meliadus, a lover of the Lady of the Lake. Jonson translates the ancient Golden Age into its English equivalent, the Age of Chivalry, and makes King James its restorer.

Although the barriers was a form of entertainment in which prowess in battle was the central element, Jonson manages to subordinate this element to its opposite, a classical love of peace. To do this he has Merlin interpret for the prince the pictures painted on a shield which was the gift of the ancient King Arthur to the new Prince of Wales. The pictures show England's famous warrior princes in action, and one would expect that they are presented as models for Prince Henry to emulate. But in each case Merlin points out that the models, while admirable, did not escape faults of pride and carelessness. Merlin then calls attention to James, saying

> But all these spurres to vertue, seedes of praise
> Must yeeld to this that comes. Here's one will raise
> Your glorie more, and so aboue the rest,
> As if the acts of all mankind were prest
> In his example.   (335-9)

James is the epitome of all virtues. And as Merlin has chosen incidents

from the lives of his historical figures, so he chooses carefully the
virtues and actions of James which are germane to the theme. The
next lines are built on James's arms, which, it will be remembered,
include in the quarterings the three leopards of England, the single lion
of Scotland, the fleurs-de-lys of France, and the harp of Ireland; above
or below are the rose and the thistle of England and Scotland (frontispiece). To Merlin, as to anyone familiar with this common heraldry,
the shield represents the unity of Great Britain:

> Here are kingdomes mixt
> And nations ioyn'd, a strength of empire fixt
> Conterminate with heauen; The golden veine
> Of SATVRNES age is here broke out againe.
> HENRY but ioyn'd the *Roses*, that ensign'd
> Particular families, but this hath ioyn'd
> The *Rose* and *Thistle*, and in them combin'd
> A vnion, that shall neuer be declin'd,
> *Ireland* that more in title, then in fact
> Before was conquer'd, is his *Lawrels* act.　(339-48)

The positive value of unity is stressed by making James's arms, and
therefore James, the embodiment of the various unities which Merlin
sees in the English world: the unity of the houses of York and Lancaster; of the countries of England and Scotland; of Ireland, England,
and Scotland in the British Isles; and of the British Isles and heaven.
In this last union can be seen the Golden Age of Saturn, which also
joined heaven and earth in the same bonds. James has restored not
only Elizabeth's wall of shipping, which had been allowed to decay, but
the Golden Age and "by actions hard and high" has become the
"goale for all posteritie to sweat, / In running at" (354-5).

Merlin's summary of James's qualifications is more notable for what
it omits than for what it includes:

> This is the height at which your thoughts must fly.
> He knowes both how to gouerne, how to saue,
> What subiects, what their *contraries* should haue,
> What can be done by power, and what by loue,
> What should to *Mercie*, what to *Iustice* moue:
> All *Arts* he can, and from the hand of *Fate*
> Hath he enforc'd the making his owne date.
> Within his proper vertue hath he plac'd
> His guards 'gainst *Fortune*, and there fix'd fast
> The wheele of *chance*, about which Kings are hurl'd,
> And whose outragious raptures fill the world.　(356-66)

Since this speech is part of the introduction to a combat, we should expect some exhortation to battle; at least Merlin ought to say that James knows how to fight at barriers, and that therefore Henry should imitate him. However, in Merlin's whole speech, even when dealing with the traditionally exceptional warriors, he has emphasized the necessity of avoiding wars. The only just use of arms is defensive, and it is necessary to keep in trim. But a wise man ought to be able to keep out of wars, and it is far more important to know how to govern than how to fight. The symbolic nature of the barriers has been subordinated to the symbol of the wise and peaceful king who sits *unarmed* in the center of the hall. After the combat Merlin interrupts and makes his point again in the closing speech:

> Nay, stay your valure, 'tis a wisdome high
> In Princes to vse fortune reuerently.
> He that in deeds of *Armes* obeyes his blood
> Doth often tempt his destinie beyond good.
> Looke on this throne, and in his temper view
> The light of all that must haue grace in you:
> His equall *Iustice*, vpright *Fortitude*
> And settled *Prudence*, with that *Peace* indued
> Of face, as minde, alwayes himselfe and euen.
> So HERCULES, and good men beare vp *heauen*. (405-14)

The Prince's feats of arms will not make him a symbol of heaven; only the practice of justice, fortitude, prudence, and peace can achieve the union of man and heaven of which James is the symbol.

This is not the first time that we have seen the value of the masquers' actions obscured by reference to something greater. At the end of *Time Vindicated*, although the longest part of the performance is their dancing, the Glories of the Time are sent back to the school of virtue as their proper place. In *Prince Henries Barriers* the combats lasted from ten in the evening until the next morning and yet the text plainly points out that the revival of chivalry is a poor thing compared with the acquisition of a wisdom which sees battle as the worst way to settle difficult questions.

It is the wedding of the English to the classical traditions which allows this change to take place smoothly. If the barriers were solely in terms of the Arthurian tradition and the English historical traditions of their warrior kings, which ennoble or enshrine the warrior, the result would have to be an exhortation to battle. But Jonson has successfully combined the Arthurian material with the traditions of the Golden Age, which in classical eyes was primarily a peaceful time; and he has added his and King James's essentially classical love of peace and moderation. The shift in emphasis is marked at the beginning of Merlin's speech when he says that the shield will not show the deeds of the traditional Arthurian knights, but rather of men. He tells Meliadus in effect, " If you came here to play at fighting giants, please grow up. You must deal with men." He goes on, speaking of Henry:

> His arts must be to gouerne, and giue lawes
> To peace no lesse then armes. His fate here drawes
> An empire with it, and describes each state
> Preceding there, that he should imitate.   (175-8)

And if there is to be no romantic nonsense about the Arthurian material, the same is true of the handsome shield which normally was a symbol of battle. The pictures must be studied in their relationships to each other and to the art of government.

In treating so fully the three masques in this chapter I have tried to show how Jonson pulls together widely differing experience. Classical tradition, local tradition, contemporary events, predetermined conditions of the actors and the stage, and many other elements are given a unity through his use of the presence of King James, the ancient imagery of monarchy, and the form of the ritual. In later chapters some of these individual aspects of the masque will be given more extensive treatment at the expense of exhaustive analysis of each masque. First to come under scrutiny is the pastoral tradition.

2

The Pastoral Traditions

PAN is our All, by him we breath, wee live,
Wee move, we are.
                          —*Pan's Anniversary*

IN the three masques of the Golden Age we have seen developed
the imagery of time, of gold, and of war and peace, but in none
of them is there any great emphasis on the physical aspects of
the Golden Age as we find them described in the ancient accounts of
Hesiod, Ovid, and others. The greatest concentration of this material
is in *The Golden Age Restored*, and it is slight. Pallas, speaking of the
future age, says:

> Then earth vnplough'd shall yeeld her crop,
> Pure honey from the oake shall drop,
>   The fountaine shall runne milke:
> The thistle shall the lilly beare,
> And euery bramble roses weare,
>   And euery worme make silke.

> QVIRE.

> The verie shrub shall *Balsame* sweat,
> And *Nectar* melt the rocke with heat,
>   Till earth haue drunke her fill:
> That she no harmefull weed may know,
> Nor barren *Ferne*, nor *Mandrake* low,
>   Nor *Minerall* to kill.   (163-75)

The scene is, of course, predominantly pastoral. The Golden Age preceded the Age of Gold; buying and selling, commerce, cities, travel,
luxury, and riches are all products of later ages. The original Golden
Age was rural. But though it was rural the pastoral life was not necessarily rude, and in even the ancient writers we find a division among
the inhabitants which persists in pastoral literature to this day. The
principal characters in Theôcritus' pastoral idyls are sometimes real
rustics, sometimes shepherds and cowherds who are by nature so noble
that their speech and their ideals are those of the highest cultural levels.

In Jonson's pastoral masques this division is reflected in the differences between the antimasquers and the masquers.

But for Jonson to have adhered solely to classical traditions for both masque and antimasque would have been to ignore the rich country entertainment traditions in England and the dramatic possibilities they offered. Here Jonson looked directly at country practice as well as at the literary traditions of English pastoral. Among the latter would be the stories of Robin Hood and Oberon; among the former he would find a number of customs which he might turn to good use. Chief of these are the three forms of group entertainment connected with the passing of the old year and the rebirth of the new: mumming, the sword dance, and the morris dance.[1] The element common to the three entertainments is a basis in ancient fertility rites. Mumming, as practiced in England, generally signaled the death of the old year and the beginning of the new at Christmas time and was usually presided over by Father Christmas. The sword dance, which has definite connections with the rites for Mars performed by the Roman Salii, represents a ritual in which sacrifice and resurrection is the dominant theme. It was generally danced by armed boys, one of whom was symbolically decapitated and then healed. The morris dance was the only form of these entertainments which had no dramatic speeches. It was danced in summer as an incitement to the growth of crops, and the dancers sometimes bore symbolic swords. In all cases, it will be remembered, these performances were, in Jonson's day, folk shows and no longer a part of the ritual of higher classes.

In Jonson's pastoral masques we find the classical division between noble and rustic. In some cases, courtiers are disguised as rustics coming to pay their respects to a fertility god, and in others, the chief actors are truly lowborn figures whose attitude is a combination of rudeness and respect for their betters. Within the first group, which includes *Oberon* (1611), *Pan's Anniversary* (1620), *Vision of Delight* (1617), and *Chloridia* (1631), the pattern is much the same. In a beautiful country setting, a group of noble people (the masquers) have convened to celebrate the power which has made possible their happy existence. In each of the masques the rites are interrupted or postponed while rude people display an imperfect (or incomplete) attitude toward them, either by challenging the higher powers directly or by expressing inappropriate feelings. In all four masques the spokesmen for the interrupting groups are tolerated and their actions forgiven.

1. For the following remarks I am indebted to R. J. E. Tiddy, *The Mummer's Play*, Oxford, The Clarendon Press, 1923, and Jessie L. Weston, *From Ritual to Romance*, Cambridge, The University Press, 1920.

It will be remembered that in *Time Vindicated* and *The Golden Age Restored* the profaners of the rites were banished. The milder fate in the pastoral masques emphasizes another element which we notice immediately: the spirit of these masques is far lighter than that of the masques discussed in the first chapter. This spirit is achieved in many ways. Most obviously, the country setting in sunlight or moonlight and the appearance of the classical figures of satyrs, shepherds, and nymphs help to set the tone. Besides these, each masque is divided into two parts which react on one another in such a way as to keep the masque light, and, although in each masque it is stated early that the purpose of the celebration is serious, the seriousness is qualified almost immediately by comedy.

Let us look at *Pan's Anniversary* as a representative example. The action is simple: in Arcadia three nymphs and an old Shepherd prepare a place for the annual rites paid by the Arcadian shepherds to Pan. The preparation completed, the shepherds (the masquers) appear and are about to start the ceremonies when a Fencer interrupts, introducing a group of "Boyes from Boeotia" who assert that in dancing and singing they can outdo the shepherds. When they have demonstrated their prowess, the Shepherd sends them away and calls on the Arcadians, who dance their homage to Pan (James) while hymns of praise are sung. After they have danced with the ladies of the court they are again interrupted by the Fencer who brings in his group, now metamorphosed into sheep for their rudeness and stupidity, to perform another antic dance. The Chorus and the Shepherd then close the ceremonies with a hymn. There is here no double standard of values: at the beginning the shepherds are setting out to perform an uncomplicated act of devotion. At the end they accomplish this and it is approved. The conflict in the masque is only hinted at and it never gets beyond the stage of fun.

Before we examine the main masque, with its careful balancing of the duties of king and subject, let us look at the part of the performance which precedes it and sets the tone for it. Potentially the Fencer and his Boeotians are serious threats to the proceedings, but in actuality they are tolerated because they provide amusement through their dancing and through the apparent nonsense of the Fencer's imagination. Yet nonsense is not quite a correct description. In the speeches of the Fencer—and in the opening speech of the Shepherd in this masque, in the talk of the satyrs in *Oberon*, of Delight and Phant'sie in the *Vision of Delight*, and of the Postilion in *Chloridia*—we find a very special device, a way of using a snowstorm of words to set the tone of the whole masque. As *Pan's Anniversary* opens, the nymphs are strewing flowers and they sing of the shepherds' holiday which is about

to begin. The old Shepherd then tells them to gather a second load
of flowers:

> Then hence: and fill
> Your fragrant prickles [2] for a second shower,
> Bring Corn-flag, Tulips, and *Adonis* flower,
> Faire Oxe-eye, Goldy-locks, and Columbine,
> Pinkes, Goulands, King-cups, and sweet Sops-in-wine,
> Blew Harebells, Pagles, Pansies, Calaminth,
> Flower-gentle, and the faire-hair'd Hyacinth,
> Bring rich Carnations, Floure-de-luces, Lillies,
> The chequ'd, and purple-ringed Daffodillies,
> Bright Crowne-imperiall, Kings-speare, Holy-hocks,
> Sweet *Venus* Navill, and soft Lady-smocks,
> Bring too some branches forth of *Daphnes* haire,
> And gladdest myrtle for these postes to weare
> With Spikenard weav'd, and Marjoram betweene,
> And star'd with Yellow-golds, and Meadows Queene,
> That when the Altar, as it ought, is drest,
> More odour come not from the Phoenix nest;
> The breath thereof *Panchaia* [3] may envie,
> The colours *China*, and the light the skye.   (27-45)

The richness of this passage is created not by an appeal to the eye, for
it is almost without color, nor by an appeal to the nose, though Jonson
uses "sweet" and "odour." The effect is produced by the overwhelming mass of suggestive names which carries us along, letting us
catch sparkles and hints of regions beyond our own lives (after all, this
is Arcadia), partly classical (Adonis, Hyacinth, Venus, Daphne), allied
with the majesty of the court and the trappings of chivalry (corn-flag,
king-cups, lilies, fleur-de-lys, crown-imperial, kings-spear and meadows-
queene), and yet associated with the traditions of yielding lovers couched
in softly seductive bowers (goldy-locks, fair-haired Hyacinth, sweet
Venus navel, soft lady-smocks, Daphne's hair). In one sentence of
eighteen lines the Shepherd manages to set a scene of lush magnificence
out of a mere list of flowers—and yet a list carefully chosen to suggest
richness, beauty, and the dalliance of lovers. If we look closely at the
passage we realize he has told us nothing at all about the scene: these
are the flowers which the nymphs are to collect and strew at a later
time and he does not explain why each flower is appropriate. Yet we
would not question the value of these lines in preparing us for a pastoral
rite.

2. *Prickles*, baskets.
3. *Panchaia*, a fabulous land of spices. Claudian, *De Raptu Proserpinae*, 2,
81-2. (H & S, *10*, 399.)

At the conclusion of the Shepherd's speech the scene opens to reveal the Arcadians sitting around the Fountain of Light, and the musicians below them dressed as the Priests of Pan. Before they can begin their ceremonies, the Fencer bursts in. His speech is, appropriately, in prose, for he is a rude character, and while talking with him the Shepherd also lapses into prose. But note the Fencer's style:

> Roome for an old Trophie of Time; a Sonne of the sword, a Servant of *Mars*, the Minion of the Muses, and a Master of Fence. One that hath showne his quarters, and plaid his prizes at all the games of *Greece* in his time; as Fencing, Wrestling, Leaping, Dauncing, what not? And hath now usher'd hither by the light of my long-sword certaine bold Boyes of *Boeotia*, who are come to challenge the *Arcadians* at their owne sports, call them forth on their owne holy-day, and Daunce them downe on their owne Greene-swarth. (52-60)

Here for comic purposes is much the same rhetorical device as that used in the Shepherd's speech: the multiplication of names (trophy, son, servant, minion, master), and the nonstop rush of words, reinforced by repetition of the grammatical construction and the use of alliteration. In a moment we recognize the Fencer as the kind of person who can overcome opposition merely by a flood of verbiage. His subsequent speeches bear this out as he describes the boys he has brought with him: tinker, tooth-drawer, juggler, corn-cutter, bellows-mender, tinder-box man, clock-keeper, maker of mousetraps, tailor, and clerk. Much of the humor of the Fencer's speeches arises from his juxtaposing these characters from the streets of London with their supposedly Theban background. When the Shepherd says that the solemnity will include dancing, the Fencer answers:

> Enough: They shall be met with instantly in their owne sphere, the sphere of their owne activitie, a daunce. But by whom, expect: No *Cynaetheian*, nor *Satyres*; but (as I said) Boyes of *Boeotia*; thinges of *Thebes*, (the Towne is ours, Shepheard) mad merry Greekes, Lads of life, that have no gall in us, but all ayre and sweetnesse. A Tooth-drawer is our Foreman, that if there be but a bitter tooth in the company, it may bee called out at a twitch; he doth command any mans teeth out of his head upon the point of his Poynard; or tickles them forth with his ryding rod: Hee drawes teeth a horse-backe in full speed, yet hee will daunce a foot, he hath given his word: He is yeoman of the mouth to the whole Brotherhood, and is charged to see their gummes bee cleane, and their breath sweet, at a minutes warning. Then comes my learned

Theban, the Tinker I told you of, with his kettle Drum (before
and after) a Master of Musique, and a man of mettall; He beates
the march to the tune of Tickle-foot, *Pam, pam, pam*, brave *Epam*
with a *nondas*. That's the straine.   (82-100)

The flow of detail in this passage, finally reducing itself to the non-
sensical drumbeats of the last lines, tells us practically nothing necessary
to our understanding of the fable. The total effect of the speech depends
on more than the massing of detail, however, and it would be well to
consider the role of the Fencer in relation to the masque as a whole.

The thing that strikes us first on his appearance is the inappropriate-
ness of a fencer in the pastoral setting, but Jonson has only slightly
varied two pastoral traditions which we have noticed: those of the
Roman Salii and the English sword dance. Fundamentally Jonson is
keeping decorum. But once the swordsman is accepted as part of the
pastoral scene, Jonson makes every detail of the Fencer's speeches a
careful pointing up of the pastoral versus the antipastoral. For example,
on the pastoral side, the boys come from Boeotia, a country made
famous by Hesiod's *Works and Days* as a stronghold of pastoral industry; but on the antipastoral side they are boys from the city of Thebes,
made famous for its warriors by the general Epaminondas. But the
division lies deeper than this and can be discovered in details which at
first glance seem to be nonsense. For example there is a contrast
between the boys of Boeotia, who are presented as tradesmen and
artisans such as might be found anywhere in London, and the court in
which they appear (Pan's court, or James's court): the Tooth-drawer
is called "yeoman of the mouth to the whole Brotherhood"; in this
Jonson has kept a court title but ludicrously changed the functions of
the titleholder, for James's Yeoman of the Mouth was an official of the
pantry, not of the dentist's office (H & S, *10*, 610).

In one aspect, then, the Fencer and his crew are purely pastoral
figures and thus appropriate to the action, for from the English traditions of the rustic dances they acquire their rudeness, and from the
Roman tradition their right to take part in the religious celebration.
On the other hand, as London tradesmen and apprentices, antipastoral,
anticlassical and city-bred, they are effective profaners of the rites of
Pan and are justly removed when the rites are to be performed. It is
probably worth while to notice too that the Fencer, in being a swordsman, is opposed to the policies of James (not Pan) who was known to
dislike the sight of drawn swords (H & S, *2*, 325). The upshot of these
considerations is only the intensification of our conviction that the
Fencer and his boys are funny and that their banishment is consequently
not harsh. By the time they leave the stage the way is thoroughly

prepared for the masquers. The scene has been set by the Shepherd as one of richness, and the tone has been set by the Fencer as one of lightness. Thus, when the Shepherd calls forth the Arcadians, we are prepared for the joyousness of the hymns. Here is the first:

> 1. Of PAN we sing, the best of Singers, *Pan,*
> That taught us swaines, how first to tune our layes,
> And on the pipe more aires then *Phoebus* can.
> CHO. Heare, O you groves, and hills, resound his praise.
> 2. Of *Pan* we sing, the best of Leaders, *Pan,*
> That leads the Naiad's, and the Dryad's forth;
> And to their daunces more then *Hermes* can.
> CHO. Heare, O you groves, and hills, resound his worth.
> 3. Of *Pan* we sing, the best of Hunters, *Pan,*
> That drives the Hart to seeke unused wayes,
> And in the chace more then *Sylvanus* can.
> CHO. Heare, O you groves, and hills, resound his praise.
> 4. Of *Pan* we sing, the best of Shepherds, *Pan,*
> That keepes our flocks, and us, and both leads forth
> To better pastures then great *Pales* can.
> CHO. Heare, O you groves, and hills, resound his worth.
>   And while his powers, and praises thus we sing,
>   The Valleys let rebound, and all the rivers ring.   (172-89)

The repetition of the pattern in the four stanzas suggests incantation or ritual while it focuses attention on the places where the pattern is varied, the important points for which Pan is being praised: he is a singer, leader, hunter, and shepherd. It is hardly necessary to note that these lines apply not only to the mythological Pan but to James himself, whose favorite pursuits were hunting and poetry and who as king was leader and shepherd. There is no suggestion in this hymn of any threatening evil: it is all lightness and celebration of the good. An important point about the hymn and its companion pieces which follow is that Jonson has maintained strictest decorum in the imagery: every image of every hymn is drawn from the pastoral life or the pastoral landscape. This is not true in the case of the Fencer's speeches, as we have seen; in them the humor is derived fundamentally from the intrusion of contemporary London in a classical visor which keeps slipping awkwardly over its nose. Here the illusion is perfect because it is pure.

The masques have often been called fragile. The reason is, I think, that the requirements of the court often forced on them the kind of pseudomythological fable we have seen Jonson using, and in order to maintain the illusion it was absolutely necessary to keep decorum. The slightest slip undermines the structure, as we shall find later in Jonson's own *Chloridia*. Thus it is important to see how Jonson's hymns maintain decorum not only in their pastoral imagery but in keeping a single point of view.

In other senses, too, Jonson keeps decorum. His Hymns to Pan in their formal structure reflect the literary conventions of hymns or songs of praise: we may compare the refrain and concluding lines of the hymn above with the refrains of Spenser's " Prothalamion " and " Epithalamion." The hymns show also a strong kinship to the Psalms and liturgy of the Church of England. It is not inappropriate that these new hymns be sung to King James, for the equivalence of Pan and Christ was traditional enough for Milton to use it in " On the Morning of Christ's Nativity " (88-90), and the extension of this equivalence to the King is foreshadowed in E. K.'s gloss on " Syrinx " (*Shepheardes Calender*, Aprill, 92) : " But here by Pan and Syrinx is not to bee thoughte, that the shephearde simplye meante those Poetical Gods: but rather supposing (as seemeth) her graces progenie to be diuine and immortall . . . could deuise no parents in his iudgement so worthy for her, as Pan the shepheards God, and his best beloued Syrinx. So that by Pan is here meant the most famous and victorious King, her highnesse Father, late of worthy memorye, K. Henry the eyght. And by that name, oftymes (as hereafter appeareth) be noted kings and mighty Potentates: And in some place Christ himselfe, who is the verye Pan and god of Shepheardes."

In the second hymn the double responsibility of the king and his subjects is stated in terms of the Arcadians' duty to Pan:

> PAN is our All, by him we breath, wee live,
> Wee move, we are; 'Tis he our lambes doth reare,
> Our flocks doth blesse, and from the store doth give
> The warme and finer fleeces that we weare.
> > He keepes away all heates, and colds,
> > Drives all diseases from our folds:
> > Makes every where the spring to dwell,
> > The Ewes to feed, their udders swell;
> > But if he frowne, the sheepe (alas)
> > The Shepheards wither, and the grasse.
> Strive, strive, to please him then by still increasing thus
> The rites are due to him, who doth all right for us.
>
> (192-203)

Although it might be possible to translate these pastoral images into contemporary references (" our lambes doth reare " into " gives preferment to our children at court " for example), the poem not only does not insist upon it but rather rejects any too close interpretation beyond the recognition that James, like Pan, had in an absolute sense extreme powers over the lives of the masquers and in more than a superficial way was "our All." The hymn is interesting for other considerations, however, and in it we can see a strong link between the masque and the antimasque. We notice first that Jonson brings to the Arcadians' praise of James the authority not only of pagan but again of Christian religious tradition; the first lines echo Acts 17:28, "For in him we live, and move, and have our being."[4] The development of the idea is in terms which antedate any authority I can give and are reminiscent of what Jessie Weston has to say about the traditional ideas of the influence of the king (whether the Fisher King or his equivalent) on every area of life and particularly on fertility (ch. 5). The influence of Pan, and therefore James, on the increase of the flocks and on the healing of diseases (a reference perhaps to the King's Evil?), on the bringing of the spring and the withering of the grass, suggests not only the Christlike power of the king but his specific role as the object of worship in the fertility rites. And here we see a link between the masque and the antimasque, for, as we have pointed out, the sword dance is another form of a fertility rite, and through the Roman equivalent in the rites to Mars Jonson was likely to have known this.

The third hymn, which serves to bring the masquers to the "silver-footed fayes" of the court for the next dance, is an echo-song, very light in tone. This is followed by a reappearance of the Fencer, whose boys, now changed into sheep, dance and are again sent away. The appropriateness of the Boys of Boeotia as antimasquers becomes even greater here: Jonson adds to their other qualities the tradition in which "Boeotian sheep" was synonymous with stupidity (H & S, *10*, 610). After they have danced, the Chorus ends the rites with the final hymn:

> Great *Pan*, the Father of our peace, and pleasure,
>> Who giv'st us all this leasure,
> Heare what thy hallowd troope of Herdsmen pray
>> For this their Holy-day,
> And how their vowes to Thee, they in *Lycaeum* pay.
>
> So may our Ewes receive the mounting Rammes,
> And wee bring thee the earliest of our Lambes:
> So may the first of all our fells[5] be thine,

4. This is now used also in the form for Family Prayers in the *Book of Common Prayer*, but it does not appear in the 1604 Prayer Book, as it came from the Hampton Court Conference.

5. *Fells*, fleeces. *Beestning*, the first milk after bearing young. *Tode*, fox. *Brock*, badger. (H & S, *10*, 611.)

And both the beestning of our Goates, and Kine:
    As thou our folds dost still secure,
    And keep'st our fountaines sweet and pure,
    Driv'st hence the Wolfe, the Tode, the Brock,
    Or other vermine from the flock.
That wee preserv'd by Thee, and thou observ'd by us,
May both live safe in shade of thy lov'd *Maenalus*.

(255-69)

The role of the king as the god of fertility could not be more heavily
stressed. As the first hymn was a song of praise and the second a
testament of Pan's power, this is the contract between the shepherds
and their god and between King James and his courtiers. The purpose
of the contract is mutual safety in their pastoral home. Its form combines elements of the legal contract with the regular solemnity of an
ecclesiastical chant or a courtroom reading of a piece of legal liturgy:
" So may . . . ; So may . . . ; As . . . ; That we . . . and thou
. . . may." And yet, prepared as we are by the second coming of the
Fencer, the solemnity of this hymn is not overpowering and the masque
is still predominantly light in tone.

The same lightheartedness appears in *The Vision of Delight*. Although the opening scene is " A Street in perspective of faire building,"
the masque belongs properly among the pastoral masques, for this city
scene is designed to emphasize a contrast between the delights of the
city and the superior delights of the country. As the first speaker,
Delight, says,

    Let us play, and dance, and sing
      let us now turne every sort
    O' the pleasures of the Spring,
      to the graces of a Court.   (9-12)

The emphasis will be on the ability of the Spring to transform the court
to something better than it is. Delight, for the amusement of the spectators, immediately produces an antimasque, " A she Monster delivered
of six *Burratines*, that dance with six *Pantalones*." [6] Having prepared the spectators for fun and pleasure, Delight then calls on Night
to preside over the evening's festivities and Phant'sie to provide them,
for at night all Phant'sie's

      figures are allow'd,
    and various shapes of things;

---

6. "*Burratines*. Apparently puppets which the She-monster produced and
handed over to the Pantaloons . . . *Pantalones* . . . These would be old men in
contrast to the young Burratines." (H & S, *10*, 571.)

> Create of ayrie formes, a streame:
>   it must have bloud, and naught of fleame,
> And though it be a waking dreame;
>
> *The Quire.*
> ⎤ Yet let it like an odour rise
> ⎟   to all the Sences here,
> ⎨ And fall like sleep upon their eies,
> ⎟   or musick in their eare.   (46-54)

The masque which follows consists of two scenes or dreams which
Phant'sie creates. The first is a fantastic one, actually another dance
of "Phantasmes" like the first one of Burratines and Pantalones. Introducing this dance, Phant'sie, like the Shepherd and the Fencer in
Pan's Anniversary, floods us with speech. She coins delight out of a
rush of the imagination in which she lets her mind dance from one
object to another over almost invisible bridges of connecting impression
rather than by a marked path of consecutive thought. When Night
calls on Phant'sie for a delightful dream, she answers:

> Phant'sie, I tell you, has dreams that have wings,
> And dreams that have honey, and dreams that have stings;
> Dreames of the maker, and Dreames of the teller,
> Dreames of the kitchin, and Dreames of the Cellar:
> Some that are tall, and some that are Dwarffes,
> Some that are halter'd, and some that weare scarffes;
> Some that are proper, and signifie o' thing,
> And some another, and some that are nothing:
> For say the French Verdingale, and the French hood
> Were here to dispute; must it be understood,
> A feather, for a wispe, were a fit moderator?
> Your Ostritch, beleeve it, 's no faithfull translator
> Of perfect Utopian; And then 'twere an od-piece
> To see the conclusion peepe forth at a cod-piece.   (61-74)

To trace the progress of Phant'sie's thought as she speaks is amusing.
For example, "wings" suggests the rime "stings" which in turn suggests "honey." Or "maker" as a translation of "poet" (one of
Jonson's favorite words in *Discoveries*[7]) suggests "teller," suggesting
the rime "cellar" and consequently "kitchin." There is no logical connection of thought, though we can see threads leading from one image
to another. After fifty-six lines of this kind of rambling, during which
Phant'sie has put us in a mood to accept the Phantasmes of the second

---

7. "*A Poet* is that, which by the Greeks is call'd . . . a Maker, or a fainer."
Discoveries, lines 2347-8. (H & S, *8*, 635.)

antimasque, she says: "but mum; a thread may be drawne out too long." Later, commenting on the dance, she says:

> Why, this, you will say, was phantasticall now,
> As the Cocke, and the Bull, the Whale, and the Cow;
>   But vanish away, I have change to present you,
> And such as (I hope) will more truly content you:
>   Behold the gold-haird *Houre* descending here,
> That keepes the gate of Heaven, and turnes the yeare,
>   Alreadie with her sight, how she doth cheare,
> And makes another face of things appear.   (118-25)

The change in the scene is immediately reflected (in the fifth line above) in a change of meter: the swift anapestic verse gives way to the more dignified iambic pentameter, and the imagination comes more under control. To mark the change visually, the Bower of Zephyrus appears and a new character, Peace, sings the introductory song to. the pleasures that she brings. The Choir responds:

> We see, we heare, we feele, we taste,
> we smell the change in every flowre,
> we onely wish that all could last,
> and be as new still as the houre.   (136-9)

The question of the cause of these metamorphoses is given to Wonder to ask; she compares the delights of the scene with images drawn from classical pastoral tradition:

>   It showes
> As if *Favonius*, father of the Spring,
> Who, in the verdant Meads, doth reigne sole king,
> Had rowsd him here, and shooke his feathers, wet
> With purple-swelling Nectar? and had let
> The sweet and fruitfull dew fall on the ground
> To force out all the flowers that might be found?   (142-8)

To this paean of surprise, which has its parallel in the image-laden speeches of the Fencer and Phant'sie, Phant'sie comments:

> How better then they are, are all things made
> By WONDER! But a while refresh thine eye,
> Ile put thee to thy oftner, what, and why?   (167-9)

And as good as her word, she produces the Glories of the Spring (the masquers) sitting in a bower. Wonder greets the spectacle with an overwhelming series of questions implying that these masquers are too wonderful to be comprehended. In the final lines of her speech, combining images of music and nature, she asks, "Whose power is this? What God?" And in answer, Phant'sie says immediately:

> Behold a King
> Whose presence maketh this perpetuall *Spring*,
> The glories of which Spring grow in that Bower,
> And are the marks and beauties of his power.   (201-4)

Whether we look on this statement as referring to the king of the fable or to James I in his court, the masquers depend on him for their "perpetuall Spring." The Choir develops the idea in pastoral terms:

> The founts, the flowers, the birds, the bees,
> The heards, the flocks, the grasse, the trees,
> Do all confesse him.   (208-10)

and then calls on the masquers to dance:

> Advance, his favour calls you to advance,
> And do your (this nights) homage in a dance. (214-15)

And the masque becomes the ritual celebration with which we are now familiar, directed to a king-god who is the wellspring of the pleasant life which the masquers lead.

The elements of the pastoral which we have observed in *Pan's Anniversary* and the *Vision of Delight* are present also in *Oberon*, a successful masque, and in *Chloridia*, a failure. The failure of *Chloridia* does not result from the fact that by the time Jonson was hired to write this last masque for the court the importance of the antimasque required him to provide for eight "entries"; he handles these well and they fit the pastoral decorum. It lies rather in the introduction at the end of the masque of the figure of Fame, supported by Poetry, History, Architecture, and Sculpture. Jonson describes the scene in his "Expostulation":

> Th'ascent of Lady Fame which none could spy,
> Not they that sided her, Dame Poetry,
> Dame History, Dame Architecture too,
> And Goody Sculpture, brought w^{t}h much adoe,
> To hold her vp.   (35-9)

It is probably a safe assumption that Fame was introduced at the request of Inigo Jones, who was familiar with Parigi's "The Palace of Fame," produced in Italy in 1608, in which Fame was drawn into the Air.[8]

8. Herford and Simpson (*10*, 682) call attention to Welsford, *The Court Masque*, p. 218, in which this source was first reported.

But whether this was the case or not, the reason that *Chloridia* fails is that there is no real link between the careful simplicity of the pastoral scene of the main masque and the grandeur of the ascent of Fame. We have seen Jonson introduce apparently discordant elements into the pastoral masque, but, like the Fencer in *Pan's Anniversary*, they turn out to have a fundamental relationship to the pastoral, and where the discord appears it is developed for its effect on the theme. The heroic-allegorical tradition from which Fame derives is not reconciled in any way with the classical pastoralism of the main part of *Chloridia*, and even without the difficulties encountered by Jones in staging the ascent the masque is not unified.

We have seen in the pastoral masques the importance of keeping the decorum in the serious parts in order to avoid the kind of blunder which *Chloridia* shows. In the antimasques, on the other hand, part of the method of setting a lighthearted tone is the breaking of the pastoral decorum; pastoral images (especially the classical details and characters) are set against details of contemporary London life for a comic effect. This aspect of the pastoral masques is what Jonson develops in the four masques and five entertainments which exhibit a predominance of the rude over the polite character we are familiar with in the masque proper. Most noticeable about the rude characters is that whether or not they are actually country figures they are treated as pastoral—that is, they are characterized by an attitude derived from conventional pastoral tradition. Thus in the first part of the *Althorp Entertainment* there is a very impudent and knowing satyr whose speeches to Queen Anne, in whose honor the entertainment was performed, border on lese majesty. But following the convention he soon demonstrates that, although he cannot be a courtier in his speech, his respect for the gods of his world—the royal persons—is deep and honest. The respect is expressed chiefly in Jonson's careful attention to tone. Therefore the characteristic of this group of masques which will concern us most is the use of prose and verse to distinguish between the kinds of characters being presented and to set the tone for each masque.

In the variety of poetic forms, *The Gypsies Metamorphosed* (1621) is the most ambitious masque Jonson ever undertook, and its unity is almost entirely poetic. No elaborate machinery gives underlying unity; there is not even a single locale, for the masque was performed three times in different places. Indeed, there is hardly any fable at all; the masque pretends to happen spontaneously as a natural thing to occur at Burley-on-the-Hill on any day.

And yet the masque is not merely a collection of songs. Its unity lies in its changes of tone, which are called for by the two elements we have pointed out in every masque: the ritual nature of the masque and the traditions of reference to the monarchy. These changes constitute a consistent pattern which shows us the subject's duties to the king and a segment of the universal hierarchy (peasant, noble, royalty, God) in its functional order. The changes of tone which make it possible to interpret the masque are controlled to a great extent by the changes in verse form. A recognition of the qualities assumed to be inherent in certain kinds of verse is necessary if we are to see the unity of this masque.

Jonson, had he wished to justify his use of verse, need not have gone farther than a copy of George Puttenham's *The Arte of English Poesie* (1589).[9] Puttenham is telling his reader how to write proper verse for polite ears and consequently he speaks slightingly of popular verse. A survey of Book II of his work will show us that in many respects his judgments are paralleled in Jonson's practice. For example, Puttenham holds that verses of ten syllables are " very stately and Heroicall," of six " very sweete and delicate," of eight " no lesse pleasant than that of sixe," of two, usually bad, but can on occasion be " very passionate and of good grace," depending on their placement in the stanza. Verses of odd numbers of syllables are usually bad unless the writer is careful to see that they have feminine endings (ch. 4). Rime used both in the middle and at the end of a verse should not be countenanced, " vnless it be in toyes and trifling Poesies, for it sheweth a certaine lightnesse either of the matter or of the makers head " (ch. 10). Of the various ways of arranging the rimes of verses, the shorter the distance between rimes the more easily the stanza moves; large distances between riming verses (more than four lines between) are not good for the " rude and popular eare " but delight the ear which is " learned and delicate " (ch. 11). Finally, of the various sorts of feet, among those of two syllables the iamb is the best, " sweete and harmonicall," and the trochee comes second (ch. 18). Of the eight varieties of trisyllabic feet only the dactyl is acceptible and then only in sparing use, for if many are used together you " make your musike too light and of no solemn grauitie " (ch. 15).

It is not my intention to illustrate in detail Puttenham's dicta by reference to Jonson's masques, but the similarity of the preaching of the one and the practice of the other cannot escape our notice. Nor is it my intention to claim that Jonson followed Puttenham. By his own quotations Puttenham shows that he built his theories on what he insistently calls " our vulgar," the practice of the poets of his day writ-

9. *Elizabethan Critical Essays*, ed. G. Gregory Smith (2 vols. Oxford, 1904), *2*, 1-193. The references given here are to chapters in Bk. II of Puttenham's work.

ing in English; his sources represent the tradition in which Jonson worked.

The story of *The Gypsies Metamorphosed* is simple: fortunetelling gypsies come as if by accident upon the King's party and tell the fortunes of sixteen of them.[1] Then, during a dance, a group of country people come in; their fortunes are told comically, they are thoroughly robbed, and the gypsies leave while the rustics discover their losses. In a very ungypsy-like gesture the gypsies reappear, return the stolen goods, and are transformed into the courtiers that they really are. The metamorphosis does not have an elaborate explanation: in a final speech, with very engaging candor, it is confessed that the explanation is " a thing not touchd at by o^r *Poet*; / Good *Ben* slept there, or else forgot to showe it " (1477-8); rather, the metamorphosis was brought about by the barber and the tailor who changed the gypsies' makeup and their clothes. After the metamorphosis, tribute is paid to the king, and the masque closes.

As a way of distinguishing the varieties of verse, let us look at the ranks of men as they appear in the masque. We start with the introduction of the gypsies, go on the fortunes of the king and his party in descending order of rank, meet then the rustics where the lowest figures in the scale are presented, and end with the metamorphosis of the gypsies into courtiers and a set of hymns which puts the whole group of characters into its proper relationship with God and the universe.

The masque opens with the entrance of the gypsies, introduced by the Jackman:

> Roome for the fiue Princes of *Aegipt*, mounted all vpon one horse, like the fower sonnes of *Aymon*, to make the miracle the more by a head, if it may bee. Gaze vppon them as on the ofspringe of *Ptolomee*, begotten vppon severall *Cleopatra's* in theire seuerall Counties; especiallie on this braue sparke strucke out of *Flinteshire* vppon Iustice Iugges daughter, then Sheriffe of the Countie . . . (58-64)

The contrast on which Jonson plays here, between the mysterious and rather wonderful origin of the gypsies and their local character as thieves and bad company, is maintained throughout the masque. This is reflected particularly in their speech, which except for one characteristic is in the diction of the court. The single exception is their occasional use of the jargon of gypsies and thieves, as in the Jackman's opening speech:

---

1. W. W. Greg, *Jonson's Masque of Gipsies*, London, 1952, sorts out the speeches as they were given at the three performances.

Therefore (till wth his painefull Progenitors he be able to beate it on the hard hoofe to the *ben bowse* or the *stauling Ken*, to nip a *Ian* and *cly the iarke*) 'tis thought fitt he marche in the Infantes equipage.[2]

Although prose is not their exclusive way of talking, for the gypsies vary their speech according to the people they talk to, it is appropriate for their introduction: they will be the middle characters between the heights represented by the king and the depths represented by the country folk.

After the prose introduction the gypsies' first important function is telling the fortune of King James. To build up to it they spend a short while preparing the scene in an apparently inappropriate mood with a song about their sleight of hand and their fortunetelling in a "low" verse form exploying consciously rough terms:

> ffrom the famous *Peake of Darby*
> And the *Devills arse* there hard by,
> Where we yearelie keepe o^r musters,
> Thus th' *Aegiptians* throng in clusters.   (121-4))

Without any question Puttenham would call this verse a kind of "ryme dogrell," with its strained rime (Darby—hard by. And further on in the poem, wallnutts—small-nuttes; linen—winne in, tell yee—bellye) and its insistently regular trochaic tetrameter. It is not of the lowest order, however, because although it uses such references as "Devills arse" (a feature of the local landscape) the diction is that of educated people.

Following the song, one of the gypsies, the Patrico, sings in still another verse form:

> Stay, my sweete singer,
> The touch of thy finger
> A little, and linger
> For me, that am bringer
> Of bound to the border,
> The *Rule*, and *Recorder*,
> And mouth of yor *order*,
> And Preist of the game
> And Prelate of the same.   (146-54)

Jonson is here developing the definition of "Patrico," in beggar's

---

2. Lines 80-3. Herford and Simpson (*10*, 616) translate the jargon as follows: *ben bowse*, good drink; *stauling Ken*, tippling house, or house that will receive stolen wares; *nip a Ian*, cut a purse; *cly the iarke*, to be whipped.

parlance a hedge-priest, one who without authority functions as a priest for beggars and gypsies (H&S, *10*, 617-18). The Patrico takes it upon himself to introduce the "Gentry-coue," gypsy-jargon for the gentleman who is James's host. In the verse and the number of rimes we are reminded of Skelton whom Jonson considered a comic poet.[3] In a stanza like the one above, it is the insistence on metrical regularity that seems to contribute the greatest comic element, a regularity which can obscure difficulties of rime or word order and which sometimes obscures meaning.

In the prose of the opening and in the "lower" forms of these two songs, Jonson is setting the stage for the first fortune of the king. We have noticed that he does not allow the gypsies to become real rustics; he accomplishes this by keeping their diction that of educated people. In the next song he adds to this a mock-heroic use of the heroic couplet. The third gypsy sings:

> *Captaine,* if euer at the bowsing *ken*
> You haue in draughtes of *Darby* drilld yo[r] men,
> And we haue seru'd there armed all in ale
> W[th] the browne bowle, and chargd in braggatt stale;
> If musterd thus, and disciplind in drincke,
> In o[r] longe watches wee did neuer wincke,
> But, so commaunded by you, kept o[r] station
> As we preserud o[r] selues a Loyall Nation,
> And neuer yett did braunche of statute breake
> Made in yo[r] famous *Pallace* of the *Peake* . . .   (234-43)

Here is trivial material expressed in a form usually reserved for weightier matters: the comedy depends on the normal use of the heroic couplet. We recognize the gypsy as making a false use of the form, while at the same time he gains a bit in stature because he knows the form at all.

A dance performed just before the king's fortune is told is accompanied by the very familiar song, "The faery beame vppon you" (262-71), which is a kind of charm. With it Jonson leads away from the roughness of his earlier songs by shifting the imagery suddenly from English rustic to a kind of literary pastoral. The regularity of the "comic" meters gives way to a variation more usually associated with lyric poetry than with balladry. The diction is neither formal nor low ("The Boy with the bowe," "the luckier lott").

If we have followed the changes of tone up to this point in the

3. See the antimasque of *The Fortunate Isles,* in which Skelton appears singing his comic "The Tunnyng of Elynour Rumming."

masque as they have been reflected in the changes in the verse, we are
prepared to see in the king's fortune both the roughness of common
people and the delicacy of the better bred. The two attitudes come out
clearly, and each is distinguished by its own verse form, for Jonson has
manipulated his plot so that the Captain of the gypsies starts telling
the king's fortune without knowing it is the king he is speaking to;
when he discovers who his "client" is he retires to compose himself
and returns with the remainder of the fortune. The first half of the
fortune is characterized by anapests:

> Wth you, lucky bird, I begin; lett mee see,
> I aime at the best, and I trowe you are hee.
> Here's some lucke, alreadie, if I vnderstand
> The groundes of my Art. Here's a Gentlemans hand.
>
>   (275-8)
>
> You are no greate wencher, I see by yor table,
> Although yor *Mons Veneris* sayes you are able.   (287-8)

Although he recognizes the king as the best of the group he still demonstrates a country rather than a courtly background in his attitude
toward him. When he has discovered the king's identity the change in
his attitude is signaled not only by greater politeness but by a change
of meter. In place of the anapests we find iambs, but since he is, after
all, still a gypsy, the iambs are in tetrameters which are (according to
Puttenham) "sweete and delicate," and in stanzas of six verses, "very
pleasant to th'eare."

> Could any doubt, that sawe this hand,
> Or who you are, or what commaund
>   You haue vpon the fate of things,
> Or would not say you were let downe.
> From heauen, on earthe to be the Crowne
>   And top of all yor neighbour kinges?   (316-21)

The king is then painted as the master of his own fortune and of the
fortunes of his subjects.

The next section of the masque presents an interesting kind of
diminuendo from the height reached in the king's fortune. Where in
the divided fortune of King James the Captain shows first rudeness and
then respect, in the subsequent fortunes both elements are combined and
as the rank of the people whose fortunes are being told becomes less, so
the boldness of the gypsies grows and their respect diminishes. The
change which takes place is reflected again in the verse.

In illustration of these points let us look at two of the sixteen fortunes. About halfway down the list is the fortune of the Countess of
Exeter:

> Madame, wee knewe of yor cominge so late,
> Wee could not well fitt you a nobler fate
> > Then what you haue readie made.
> > > An old mans wife
> > > Is the light of his life,
> > A young one⟨s⟩ is but his shade.
> > > You will not importune
> > > The chaunge of yor fortune,
> > For, if you dare trust to my forecastinge,
> 'Tis presentlie good, and it wilbe lastinge.   (481-90)

In its over-all tone this is respectful to the Countess, but it is rude in that it touches on matters which perhaps it would have been better to ignore, particularly the fact that her husband was thirty-eight years older than she (H&S, *10*, 622). The reason that it is not offensive is that it is part of a comedy and in Puttenham's light the verse would reflect the comic character of the "matter," for it is irregular. Yet it is not "ryme dogrell," for in many ways it fits Puttenham's recipe for court verse: in the length of the stanza, the rime scheme, and the variation in the length of line.

In the Earl of Buccleuch's fortune the Patrico is less careful, and while he compliments him at the end, he bases the fortune on the Earl's apparent reputation as a woman chaser:

> A Hunter you have bin heretofore,
> And had game good store;
> > But ever you went
> > Upon a new scent,
> > And shifted your loves
> As often as they did their Smocks, or their Gloves.
> But since that your brave intendments are
> > Now bent for the Warre,
> > The world shall see
> > You can constant bee,
> > One Mistris to prove,
> > And court her for your love.
> *Pallas*, shall be both your *Sword*, and your *Gage*;
> *Truth*, bear your *Shield*, and *Fortune* your page.
> > > > (664-77)

Because of its many verses of odd numbers of syllables and its use of irregular feet, in Puttenham's terms this is a less polished stanza than that for the Countess of Exeter, just as its comments on the Earl are harsher than those on the Countess.

As soon as the fortunes are told, the " Clownes" or country people
enter and the next part of the masque begins. Immediately we come
into a world of rustic characters. It is reflected in the song of the
Patrico and the Jackman as they determine to gull the country folk:

Patr.	Why, this is a sport,	
	See it Northe, see it Southe,	
	For the tast of the Court,	
Iack.	For the Courts owne mouthe.	
	Come *windsor* the Towne,	
	Wth the *Maior*, and oppose,	
	Wee'l put 'em all downe,	
Patr.	Do-do-downe like my hose.	(707-14)

The verse uses metrical devices we are familiar with in broadside balladry and in the mummers' plays, with repetition ("For the Courts
owne mouthe") and the conventional tag ("See it Northe, see it
Southe"). The clowns speak mostly in prose of a sort that is not
dialect yet gives the impression of the speech of unlearned people; this is
Jonson's usual way in his comedies of having low characters try to
speak a higher language than they can manage. Thus Towneshead
says, " Admirable tricks, and he do's 'hem all *se defendendo,* as if he
would not be taken in the trap of authoritie by a fraile fleshlie Constable " (1244-6). The inkhorn term, the legal phrase, the ecclesiastical
expression are mixed in the rustics' speech with the common phrases of
their everyday life as members of a country village. Aside from this
kind of prose, two verse forms appear in the long section of the masque
dealing with the rustics. The Patrico, addressing the clowns, uses the
verse we have seen earlier, reminiscent of Skelton:

> Sweet doxies and dells,
> My *Roses* and *Nells*,
> Scarce out of the shelles,
> Yo^r hands, nothing elles.
> Wee ringe you no knelles
> Wth o^r *Ptolemees* bells,
> Though wee come from the fells;
> But bring you good spells,
> And tell you some chances, . . .   (803-11)

As a comic effect added to what we have seen before in this meter,
Jonson plays the " ells " rime as a *tour de force,* a device he uses frequently in this section of the masque. In the face of it, it is hard to
concentrate on what the Patrico is saying, and we rightly conclude that
what he is saying is really less important than the way he says it.

These are verbal gymnastics intended to confuse the country people. And eventually they are confused and allow themselves to be robbed.

In the course of the scene with the clowns a long ballad is sung explaining the meaning of "The Devills Arse" and how it happened to get its name:

> *Cock-Lorell* would needes haue the *Diuell* his guest,
>   And bad him into the Peake to dinner,
> Where neuer the ffeind had such a feast
>   Prouided him yet at the charge of a sinner.
>
> His stomacke was queasie (he came thither coach't)
>   The iogging had made some Crudities rise:
> To helpe it, he calld for a *Puritan* poach't,
>   That vsed to turne vp the eggs of his eyes.   (1062-9)

Although Jonson has the gypsies use the ballad as a satirical device against such groups as the Puritans mentioned in the second stanza, the ballad form and the references to Cock-Lorell, a traditional thief, help to keep the poem on the level of a broadside for the people. Thus he manages to entertain the court with a satire while ostensibly entertaining the country folk with a lurid story in a form they are familiar with.

As the movement from the fortune of the king has been a diminuendo, the movement from the metamorphosis of the gypsies, which now takes place, is a crescendo. As soon as the change is complete the Patrico proposes that a song be sung to the king's senses. The meter of these verses matches the meter of the explanatory song at the opening of the masque. After the king's senses have been praised, without a pause the verse changes and with it the tone of the singers. The change is worth quoting in full, beginning with the last lines of the song to the senses:

> From a needle or a thorne
>   I' the bed at euen or morne,
> Or from any Goutes least grutching,
>   Bless the soueraigne, and his *Touching.* /
>
> Bless him too from all offences
>   In his sportes, as in his sences,
> From a boy to crosse his way,
>   From a fall, or a foule day. /
>
> Bless him, ô blesse him, heau'n, and lend him long
>   To be the sacred burthen of all song,
> The Actes and yeares of all o^r *Kings* to outgoe,
>   And, while hee'is mortal, wee not thinck him so. /
>   (1378-89)

In these three sections Jonson makes a neat transition from the light
to the weighty both in thought and in verse. The middle passage would
have been more acceptable to Puttenham for its trochaic foot and eight-
syllable verse and for its simple rime and short stanza than the stanza
before; but the final lines are in the "stately and Heroicall" iambic
pentameter in rimed couplets reserved by Puttenham for the highest
things. These lines lead through a short introduction to the final hymns
of the masque. The verse from here to the close is all iambic and varies
between the heroic couplets of the opening hymn:

> Glorie of o^rs, and Grace of all the earthe,
>   How well yor figure dothe become yor bir⟨the,⟩
> As in you forme and fortune equall stood
>   And onelie *vertue* gott aboue yor blood.   (1405-8)

and the irregular iambic lines which always seem associated with high
thoughts, as we have noticed in *Time Vindicated* and will see again in
Pleasure Reconciled to Vertue; these appear to be a kind of ode:

> O that we vnderstood
>   Our good!
> There's happiness indeed in blood,
>   And store,
>   But how much more,
>   When *vertues* flood
> In the same streame dothe hitt!
> As that growes highe wth yeares, so happiness wth it. /

Captaine. /

> Loue, Loue his fortune then, and *vertues* knowne,
> Who is the top of men,
>   But make⟨s⟩ the happiness o^r owne:
> Since, where the Prince for goodnes is renownd,
>   The subiect w^th *felicitie* is Crownd. /   (1457-70)

Sung by the gypsies and the country people, this final song is not only
a paean of praise for James but an expression of the central thought
on which the whole masque has been based: that is, the place of the
king in the universal hierarchy as the pattern of virtue, as the real
controller of fortunes for those on earth. The gypsies may tell fortunes
but the king is above all such necromancy: he takes his cue from heaven,
from which he was "let downe . . . on earthe to be the Crowne," and
his is the hand which moves the wheel of fortune for the courtiers, the
gypsies, and the country people.

    This idea is not suddenly proclaimed at the end of the masque. It has been developed from the beginning as the gypsies have first shown their own level of existence and then, through their treatment of the king, the court, and the country people, mirrored the universal hierarchy. We have discovered their attitudes toward their superiors and inferiors not so much through dramatic action as through the verse they use in speaking to them. Were we not able to recognize the variations as they appear we should probably miss the point of the masque, for the fable and the setting give us little information. The unity of the masque is a poetic unity.

3

The Triumphs: Spectacle vs. *Sense*

O Showes! Showes! Mighty Showes!
The Eloquence of Masques! What need of prose
Or Verse, or Sense t'express Immortall you?
You are yᵉ Spectacles of State! Tis true
Court Hieroglyphicks! & all Artes affoord
In yᵉ mere perspectiue of an Inch board.
    —"Expostulation with Inigo Jones"

IT is by now well known that the quarrel between Jonson and Inigo Jones was based on the latter's refusal to accept the poet's direction in designing the visual elements of the masques. It is hard to remember, however, that Jonson had many words of praise for Jones's scenery during much of their association and that in his first entertainments for the king the scenery was very important. The group of masques which are based on the Roman Triumph will illustrate Jonson's methods of using scenery, music, and dancing, because the Triumph, more than any other form Jonson uses, depends for much of its effect on spectacle.

The origin of the Triumph lies in the Roman practice of honoring successful generals in a procession which moved from the Campus Martius to the Capitol.[1] Amid cries of " Io triumphe!'" a chariot decked with laurel and drawn by four horses carried the conquering general dressed in the purple and gold of Jupiter and bearing in his hands a branch of laurel and a scepter surmounted by an eagle; over his head was held Jupiter's crown. Although the procession tended to be rowdy, for the soldiers were allowed to sing scurrilous songs, it ended on a more solemn note when the general offered the laurel to Jupiter in thanks. On these traditions Jonson drew for one group of his masques and entertainments.

Common to all the masques in this group is the idea of victory: in *Mercury Vindicated* (1616), Nature triumphs over artifice; heroic love defeats false love in *Love's Triumph through Callipolis* (1631); Albion's homecoming after conquering the difficulties of the ocean is

---

1. Cf. Theodor Mommsen, *Römisches Staatsrecht* (3 vols. Leipzig, 1871-88), *1*, 124-36.

celebrated by his father in *Neptune's Triumph* (1624). In all of this group except *Mercury Vindicated* the celebration of the victory takes the form of the traditional procession: in the *Masque of Queens* (1609) the twelve queens circle the stage in chariots to the wheels of which are tied the witches they have defeated. In *Neptune's Triumph* and *The Fortunate Isles* (1625), which have a common main masque, the procession is not in chariots but on a moving island. *Mercury Vindicated* expresses the Triumph in a dance with symbolic figures paying tribute to the agent of victory, James, as the sun.

The Triumph by its nature allows a double standard of perfection: in Rome both the general and Jupiter received praise, with Jupiter ultimately getting most of it. For Jonson's purposes this was useful when he had to write a masque celebrating one of the actors. In *Love's Triumph* King Charles was the chief masquer, playing the part of Heroic Love going in triumph through the City of Beauty to lay the laurel at the feet of the Queen of Beauty (Henrietta Maria). In *Neptune's Triumph* and *The Fortunate Isles* Albion is praised for the success of his trip (Charles's trip to Spain) but in turn pays homage to his father, Neptune (James), whose wisdom directed him.[2]

The nature of the main masque, the celebration of a great action after which the victor finds a reason to make obeisance to an even greater power than himself, suggests that the antimasque will display a false hero worshiping false gods. In the antimasques of the *Masque of Queens, The Fortunate Isles*, and *Mercury Vindicated* Jonson presents witches, Rosicrucians, and alchemists. He shows these as devotees of unnatural sciences, worshipping at the altars of greed and ignorance. Even the antimasque of *Neptune's Triumph*, which on first reading may appear to be merely a friendly conversation about their jobs between a cook and a poet, turns into the presentation of characters much like those in the *Staple of News* who

> Know all things the wrong way, talke of the affaires,
> The clouds, the cortines, and the mysteries
> That are afoot, and, from what hands they haue 'hem . . .
> They are our *Quest of enquiry*, after newes.   (247-55)[3]

A characteristic of the Roman scene closely associated with the Triumph was the commemorative arch. In 1604, when Jonson was first commissioned to entertain the king, arches of triumph were well known as a device for welcoming a monarch to a city. The plan of providing

---

2. The Triumph is of course not the only form which allows the praise of the masquers as well as the king. Cf. *Oberon.*

3. That is, they discuss the masque and its staging (*cortines*, curtains) as if they knew something about them.

arches for James's first trip through London had been decided on before
Jonson was hired to provide the idea for two of them and a poetic excuse
for a third which had already been built. When the king's procession
arrived at Fen-Church the arch was covered with a curtain on which
clouds were painted, signifying that before the king's coming all was
obscured. At the approach of the king, the curtain was drawn and the
arch revealed. Under a large representation of London with all its
buildings appeared twelve figures in order of their importance, each
dressed symbolically and designated on the arch by a " word " or Latin
phrase summarizing his duties. The persons were: Monarchia Britannica, beneath whom was Theosophia (Divine Wisdom), below whom
came Genius Urbis supported by Bouloutes (the city council) and
Polemius (the city's military force). Under these appeared Tamesis,
the river Thames, and his six daughters, representing gladness, venera-
tion, promptitude, vigilance, loving affection, and unanimity. As an
example of the symbolic nature of these figures the description of
Monarchia Britannica is worth quoting in full. Jonson says of her:

The highest person aduanc'd therein, was

MONARCHIA BRITANNICA,

and fitly: applying to the aboue mentioned title of the citie, THE
KINGS CHAMBER, and therefore here placed as in the proper seate
of the empire: for, so the glorie and light of our kingdome M.
CAMDEN, speaking of *London*, saith, shee is, *totius Britanniae Epitome, Britannicique Imperij sedes, Regumque Angliae Camera,
tantum inter omneis eminet, quantum (vt ait ille) inter viburna
Cupressus.* Shee was a woman, richly attyr'd, in cloth of gold
and tissue; a rich mantle; ouer her state two crownes hanging,
with pensile shields thorow them; the one lim'd with the particular
coate of *England*, the other of *Scotland*: on either side also a
crowne, with the like Scutchions, and peculiar coates of *France*,
and *Ireland*. In her hand shee holds a scepter; on her head a
fillet of gold, inter-wouen with palme and lawrell; her hayre bound
into seuerall points, descending from her crownes; and in her lap
a little globe, inscrib'd vpon

ORBIS BRITANNICVS.

And beneath, the word

DIVISVS AB ORBE.

To shew, that this empire is a world diuided from the world, and
alluding to that of *CLAV.

—Et nostro diducta Britannia mundo.*

And V<small>IRG</small>.

—*Et penitus toto diuisos orbe Britannos.*

The wreathe denotes victorie and happinesse. The scepter and
crownes soueraignetie. The shields the precedency of the countries, and their distinctions.

* *De Mallij Theodor. cons. Panegyri. Eclog. I.*

(24-53)

Monarchia Britannica speaks through her appearance and her symbols
only, and yet with this description her position is clear. All the figures
except Tamesis and Genius Urbis are mute, and Tamesis merely
expresses his confusion when the king and queen approach. Genius
Urbis finally welcomes the royal pair in a speech which draws for its
imagery on the visual symbol of welcome and unity which the arch
affords. For example, addressing Tamesis he says:

Vp thou tame R<small>IVER</small>, wake;
And from they liquid limbes this slumber shake:
Thou drown'st thy selfe in inofficious sleepe;
And these thy sluggish waters seeme to creepe,
Rather than flow. Vp, rise, and swell with pride
Aboue thy bankes. " Now is not euery tyde . . ."

(302-7)

In this speech Tamesis becomes symbolic of the great mass of Lon-
doners who for this occasion must rouse themselves from their usual
sluggish ways to praise the king. Jonson explains his use of the visual
element in this entertainment in the following words:

Thus farre the complementall part of the first; wherein was not
onely labored the expression of state and magnificence (as proper
to a triumphall Arch) but the very site, fabricke, strength, policie,
dignitie, and affections of the Citie were all laid downe to life:
The nature and propertie of these Deuices being, to present alwaies
some one entire bodie, or figure, consisting of distinct members,
and each of those expressing it selfe, in the owne actiue spheare,
yet all, with that generall harmonie so connexed, and disposed,
as no one little part can be missing to the illustration of the whole:
where also is to be noted, that the *Symboles* vsed, are not, neither
ought to be, simply *Hieroglyphickes, Emblemes,* or *Impreses,* but
a mixed character, partaking somewhat of all, and peculiarly apted
to these more magnificent Inuentions: wherein, the garments and
ensignes deliuer the nature of the person, and the word the present
office. Neither was it becoming, or could it stand with the dignitie
of these shewes (after the most miserable and desperate shift of

the Puppits) to require a Truch-man, or (with the ignorant Painter) one to write, *This is a Dog*; or, *This is a Hare*: but so to be presented, as vpon the view, they might, without cloud, or obscuritie, declare themselues to the sharpe and learned: And for the multitude, no doubt but their grounded iudgements did gaze, said it was fine, and were satisfied.   (243-67)

The meaning of the arch is to be read in the arch itself and does not require an interpreter for the "sharpe and learned." This attitude seems to play directly into Jones's hands: Jonson is asking the reader to read the meaning of the entertainment "in yᵉ mere perspectiue of an Inch board." But even in this entertainment in which the arch is so important the scenery expresses a complex idea supplied not by the architect but by the poet; the architect's job is to fit his work to the idea, not to invent some other plan. And most of all, if the arch can speak to the "sharpe and learned" without an interpreter, it must be accurately designed.

In such entertainments as this the visual elements are proportionately more important than they are in the triumphal masques. If we look at a characteristic masque from this group we see that the scenery, whi'e it plays a positive role in expressing the theme, is subordinate to the poetry, in which the theme is most completely developed. The action of *Neptune's Triumph* takes place between two pillars marked "NEP. RED." and "SEC. IOV." which Jonson expands as "Neptvno Redvci" and "Secundo Iovi," referring to James, as the masque makes clear. The opening of the masque depends on the pretense that the performance has not yet started: the first figure on the stage is the Poet passing out the "argument" of the masque, a printed summary of what will take place. He is approached by the king's Cook, whose province is also the banqueting-house and who points out the similarity between their professions in that they both must produce something to fit a wide variety of taste and expectation. After questioning the Poet about the masque, the Cook decides to present the antimasque himself in the form of an "olla podrida" (emphasizing "podrida," rotten), which is dumped out on stage, pouring forth the comic dancers of the first antimasque, those who "know all things the wrong way." After the antimasque the scene opens to reveal the masquers on a moving island on which they have made the hazardous trip from Celtiberia. As they debark, Saron, Proteus, and Portunus sing a song of thanksgiving for their safe return, saying that it is symbolic of "all the glories" of Neptune's "great designes." After the first dance the scene changes to a "prospectiue of a maritime Palace, or the house of Oceanus," and after the next, changes again to a "prospect of the Sea," on which some time later "the Fleete is discouered." While this scene

fills the background the Cook appears again and presents an antimasque
of sailors. The final dance of the masquers closes the proceedings.

The link which holds the masque together is the idea that what occurs
on stage is symbolic of James's (Neptune's) power. It is appropriate in
a Triumph that all its elements shall concentrate on the display of the
power of the gods, through which the hero is seen to be ennobled. The
first scene, the island, is described by the Poet in his conversation with
the Cook.

> A *Delos:*
> Such, as when faire *Latona* fell in trauaile,
> Great *Neptune* made emergent.

> COOKE.
> . . . Ha' you nothing,
> But a bare Island?

> POET.
> Yes, we haue a tree too,
> Which we doe call the Tree of *Harmonie,*
> And is the same with what we read, the *Sunne*
> Brought forth in the *Indian Musicana* first,
> And thus it growes. The goodly bole, being got
> To certaine cubits height, from euery side
> The boughes decline, which taking roote afresh,
> Spring up new boles, & those spring new, & newer,
> Till the whole tree become a *Porticus,*
> Or arched Arbour, able to receiue
> A numerous troupe, such as our *Albion,*
> And the Companions of his iourney are.
> And this they sit in.   (180-207)

The bower or arbor, a common pastoral scene, becomes a symbol of
harmony. The thought is developed further when at the appearance
of the island the heavens open, revealing the musicians dressed as muses,
along with Apollo, Mercury, and the goddess Harmony. Apollo and
the Chorus explain that the return of Albion on the island is symbolic
of Neptune's wisdom and the harmonious relationship among all the
members of his court. The next scene, the house of Oceanus, symbolizes
the importance of the son of Neptune. The Poet points this out:

> Behold the Palace of *Oceanus!*
> Hayle, Reuerend structure! Boast no more to vs
> Thy being able, all the Gods to feast;
> We haue seene enough: our *Albion* was thy guest.
>   (458-61)

The Palace is impressive only because Albion has been there, and the visual effect of the scene is made to contribute to Albion's glory. The next scene, the open sea, is designed to produce awe for Neptune in the spectators, and when the ships sail out on it the spectators see

> a part of *Neptunes* strength.
> See, yond', his fleete, ready to goe, or come,
> Or fetch the riches of the *Ocean* home,
> So to secure him both in peace, and warres,
> Till not one ship alone, but all be starres.   (509-13)

In these scenes we see the theme of the masque, a tribute to the power of James (Neptune) and Charles (Albion), reinforced by the impact of the spectacle, the magnificence, ingenuity, and beauty of which are interpreted as manifestations of James's reign.

In Jonson's Triumphs, spectacle is used specifically to express the excellence of the two principal figures: the person in whose honor the Triumph is held and the god to whom the hero offers his thanks. And in every case, whatever the fable of the particular entertainment, the full effect depends on the presence of the king. At the center of each of these performances is not the spectacle itself but the idea that the king is a hero or a god in whose person are to be seen reflected the virtues which have their seat in heaven. Jonson takes many details from the traditions of the Triumph, but its recognition of the hierarchy which puts the hero over the common people and a god over the hero is its most important contribution to the masque. It is this idea, developed in the poetry, that the spectacle is made to serve.

That the music and dancing are, like the scenery, subordinate to the poetry in the masque is suggested by Jonson's treatment of spectacle, but there is more convincing proof. If the music and dancing were to Jonson centrally important elements they should appear to be so in the texts. But in most of the masques music is not mentioned at all. Where there is some reference to it, Jonson usually speaks of actions taking place to loud music (generally the opening of a scene), or soft music (a gentle introduction), or confused and martial music (as in the war-like antimasque of the *Golden Age Restored*). Occasionally he mentions that the music of the main masque in its concord symbolizes the harmony which the graceful dangers also represent; in *Love Restored*, when Cupid introduces the masquers, he says:

> As *musique* them in forme shall put,
> So they will keep their measures true,
> And make still their proportions new,
> Till all become one *harmonie*.   (260-3)

In the masques of *Blackness* and *Beauty* Jonson tells us whether the songs are sung by tenors or basses. In a few masques he gives Lawes, Ferrabosco, or Lanier credit for writing the music,[4] and in one he praises John Allin for his singing (*Queens*, 740 f.). The latest lists include settings for songs in ten of Jonson's masques, but the complete score of a masque has not survived.[5] This is not much information. Where Jonson has mentioned the music, it has been as a subordinate element designed to catch the attention, provide auditory discord to support the discord of the antimasque, or represent a harmony growing out of the theme. The only other reference to music in the masques is a curious one in that its real importance seems to be outside the history of Jonson's masques. *Lovers Made Men* (1617) is the only one of Jonson's masques not designed for presentation before royalty and for this reason we shall have to examine it more closely. But it is also known to musicologists as the first English opera, on the evidence of the lines in which Jonson says, "And the whole Maske was sung (after the Italian manner) *Stylo Recitativo*, by Master *Nicholas Lanier*; who ordered and made both the Scene, and the Musicke" (26-8). Of the other masques, only one, *The Vision of Delight* (1617), has the same notation: "DELIGHT / spake in song (*stylo recitativo.*) " (8). The only other possible candidate for this style would be *Love's Triumph*, because there is no prose and all that we have of the masque is designed to be sung: the antimasque is missing. The effect of these masques in performance must have been different from the effect of masques which included prose, but from the texts about all that can be said with certainty is that Jonson did not feel called upon by the Italian style to make the other elements of the masque Italianate.

Jonson subordinates dancing to the poetry of the masques almost as thoroughly as he does music; but while he frequently ignores the music entirely, he almost never ignores the dancing but rather incorporates it into his theme. We have seen in the pastoral masques that variations of the traditional sword dance are used in the comic parts of the entertainments; in the *Masque of Christmas* this is the only dance that takes place. In most of the masques there is also dancing by the noble masquers, usually as a part of the ritual observance paid to the king, a kind of tribute to him having its origin in antiquity: the dancing in

---

4. In the masques of *Blackness, Beauty, Hymenaei, Haddington*, and *Lovers Made Men*.

5. H & S, *11*, 605-9, supplemented by John P. Cutts, "Original Music to Browne's Inner Temple Masque, and other Jacobean Masque Music," *N & Q*, N. S. I (1954), 194-5, and Macdonald Emslie, "Three Early Settings of Jonson," *N & Q*, *198* (1953), 466-8.

Pan's Anniversary is of this sort. Sometimes the masquers perform both a ridiculous and a stately dance, as in the *Irish Masque*, to signify a change which the influence of James has wrought in them. In still other masques, among them *Pleasure Reconciled to Virtue* and *Hymenaei*, the dancing is one medium in which the working out of the theme takes place. As Gordon has shown in his article on *Hymenaei*, the dancing of the eight Humours and Affections with the eight powers of Juno in the figures of a chain and a circle represents the consent of heaven to the " grand union " which has taken place in all the spheres of life. The chain is a representation of the great chain between heaven and earth and the circle is the familiar symbol of perfect unity. In *Pleasure Reconciled to Virtue* the dancers' figures represent the labyrinths of love and beauty and the successful negotiation of them by the virtuous. But we must not let the importance of the dancing in these two masques outweigh the importance of Jonson's poetry. The dances, like the costumes and scenery, have a symbolic function which they must perform as part of the development of the theme. And as we have seen, the theme is always in some way a celebration of the king's power so that the dances contribute to this celebration. Neither dance nor music is central to the masque, but rather with the scenery they are languages in which parts of the masque are expressed. The most important of the languages is, however, poetry.

One other element of Jonson's masques which deserves some attention along with his use of spectacle, music, and dancing is his learning. D. J. Gordon's studies of the masques of *Blackness* and *Beauty* and of the *Haddington Masque* and *Hymenaei*, E. W. Talbert's article on the *Masque of Augurs*, and my own on the *Masque of Queens* all demonstrate that Jonson's learning was real and sound, although we must not assume that when he quotes or cites a classical authority he is necessarily familiar with it; more often than not he has found his reference in one of the Renaissance compendia of knowledge which were plentiful in his day. In all these masques too he shows a familiarity with contemporary literature on many kinds of abstruse subjects and his erudition must be credited with scope not only in time but in breadth of subject. The display of learning was not, however, an end in itself; it served rather as a means of presenting a worthy theme to a worthy audience, a means of finding the appropriate voice and sense for an address to the king.

The best detailed exposition of Jonson's ability to control the spectacular elements of the masque through the exercise of his learning is still D. J. Gordon's article on *Hymenaei*, a masque which, while not a Triumph, depends on a Roman ritual for its form and is developed in many ways like the masques which are Triumphs. In it, as Gordon

shows, the elements of scenery, costume, music, and dance are subordinated to the fable and thus to the theme. I should like, however, to
go one step beyond Gordon. His conclusion is that *Hymenaei* is a
failure:

> Jonson chose to translate the current image of the marriage
> of the kingdoms into terms of a Roman marriage, and make its
> interrupted but triumphant celebration, crowned by the epiphany
> of the goddess [Juno] and her participation in the rites through the
> action of her powers [the masquers], into a symbolic representation
> of the union the king so greatly wanted. This choice implies an
> attempt to make spectators, and readers, see the Union in a new
> way. It implies the apprehension of a relationship between the
> Union and these classical forms, historically conceived: a relation-
> ship which, once it is seized by the audience, will make them see
> the Union in a fresh light. And it is here that *Hymenaei* fails, in
> the relationship it states between the classical forms and the politi-
> cal event, between past and present. The effect of failure is pro-
> duced by the very cleverness with which Jonson has worked out
> the relationship. He did it, as we have seen, through the figure
> of Juno, whose name could be read, anagrammatically, as *Unio*.
> This was very clever. Too clever indeed, for his Juno is a crypto-
> gram and never a potent symbol. The relationship between Juno
> and her rites and the king's Union is an intricate riddle—no more
> than this. The historical conception of the Roman forms does not
> enter into the situation, does not modify or recreate the Union,
> setting it in a new light. These historical forms remain apart; the
> historical approach produces only an interest in history, in the
> accurate reconstruction of the past: a pure archaeological interest.
> History has not become symbol.   (p. 132)

In labeling *Hymenaei* a failure Gordon chooses Juno as the central
symbol. She hovers over most of the proceedings, and her "powers"
dance out the hieroglyphic of union with the Humours and Affections.
Again the spectacle—costumes, scenery, music, dancing, the splendor
of the masquers—tempts us to find among the actors on stage the
embodiment of the virtues which the masque celebrates. The Roman
ritual on which *Hymenaei* is based suggests that the highest figure is the
goddess Juno. But here, as in many of his other masques, Jonson shifts
the central symbolism from one of the characters to the king. This
shift is prepared for near the beginning of the masque when Hymen, as
soon as he appears, feels that there is something special about the
temple of Juno on this night:

What more then vsuall light
(Throughout the place extended)
Makes Ivno's *fane* so bright!
Is there some greater *deitie* descended?

Or raigne, on earth, those *powers*
So rich, as with their beames
Grace Vnion more then our's;
And bound her *influence* in their happier streames?

'Tis so: this same is he,
The *king*, and *priest of peace!*
And that his *Empresse*, she,
That sits so crowned with her owne increase!

O you, whose better blisses
Haue proou'd the strict embrace
Of Vnion, with chast kisses,
And seene it flow so in your happie *race*;

That know, how well it binds
The fighting *seedes of things*,
Winnes *natures, sexes, minds*,
And eu'rie discord in true musique brings:

Sit now propitious *Aides*,
To *Rites*, so duely priz'd;
And view two noble *Maides*,
Of different sexe, to Vnion sacrific'd.

In honour of that blest *Estate*,
Which all good *minds* should celebrate.   (83-108)

Hymen states clearly that as symbols of union the king and queen are
superior to both Juno and himself. After the masque has presented its
Roman marriage and its dance of the powers of Juno with the Humours
and Affections, Reason, who has ordered the dancing, says to the
dancers:

Vp *youths*, hold vp your lights in ayre,
And shake abroad their flaming hayre.
Now moue vnited, and, in gate,
As you (in paires) doe front the *state*,
With gratefull *honors*, thanke his *grace*
That hath so glorified the place:
And as, in *circle*, you depart
Link'd *hand in hand*; So, *heart in heart*,

> May all those *bodies* still remayne
> Whom he (with so much sacred payne)
> No lesse hath bound within his realmes
> Then they are with the OCEANS streames.
> Long may his VNION find increase
> As he, to ours, hath deign'd his peace.[6]

It is not to Juno that the masquers are to look to see perfect union represented, for she represents only part of it. In James and Anne, however, appears not only the union of marriage but also the political union of England and Scotland, the perfect union of humors and affections under the powers of love and reason, and the union of heaven and earth and of God and man.

6. Lines 417-30. *in gate*, apparently a dancing term, like *in circle* below, but the closest meaning given in *OED* is " to be on the way to, to be bound for " (*sb²*, 2).

4

Combats of Concepts

Read him as you would doe the booke
Of all perfection, and but looke
    What his proportions be;
No measure that is thence contriv'd,
Or any motion thence deriv'd,
    But is pure harmonie.
            —*News from the New World*

THE shift of the central symbol from a character on the stage to King James is common in Jonson's masques, although it appears most clearly in the final group which I have labeled "Combats of Concepts." That the masques in this group have appealed least to modern readers is proven by the readiness with which critics call them failures. One characteristic they have in common is that the bones of allegory and personification gleam whitely through the thin flesh of fable. Characteristically, too, these masques have as their basic form the debate ending in a reconciliation through the intervention of a third party. But none of Jonson's masques is simply a static debate between allegorical persons. The closest to such a standard is probably the debate between Eros and Anteros in the *Challenge at Tilt* (1614), in which the question for discussion is that of the relative values of the man's love and the woman's love in marriage. The rest of the masques and entertainments in this group, while they discuss a normally philosophical question of love or beauty, or even of the value of money, do so in terms which engage not only the mind but the ear, the eye, and the sense of rhythm.

Let us consider one of the simpler examples of this group to see how Jonson shifts the symbolism from one of the actors to the king. *Love's Welcome at Bolsover* was written as a three-part welcome to Charles and Henrietta Maria at the house of the Earl of Newcastle in 1634. At a banquet they were entertained with a riddling song about love, sung not by mythological persons but by "two *Tenors*, and a *Base*." This was followed after the banquet by a comic dance of "Mechanicks" introduced by a surveyor, Iniquo Vitruvius, an obvious satire of Inigo Jones. The last part of the entertainment was a dialogue between Eros and Anteros with a final comment by Philalethes.

In the dialogue Anteros introduces himself to his brother Eros as "Love-again," who is necessary to the continued growth of "Love." And, indeed, when Eros accepts his brother he discovers that he has already grown three inches. They attribute these wonderful effects to the place,

> AN. The King, and Queenes Court, which is circular,
> And perfect. ER. The pure schoole that we live in,
> And is of purer Love, the Discipline. (136-8)

At this point Philalethes enters and in prose (contrasting with their heroic couplets) directs the Cupids' attention to the assembly in the great hall of Bolsover, which he calls "the divine Schoole of Love." "An Academie, or Court, where all the true lessons of Love are throughly read, and taught; the Reasons, the Proportions, and Harmonie, drawne forth in analytick Tables, and made demonstrable to the *Senses*" (144-7). Up to this point Eros and Anteros have been the symbols of love; in them could be read both the strife and the agreement with which lovers are familiar. But Philalethes in his next speech subtly shifts the spectators' attention from Eros and Anteros to other symbols:

> Returne to your selves (little Deities) and admire the Miracles you serve, this excellent *King*, and his unparallel'd *Queene*, who are the Canons, the Decretals, and whole Schoole-Divinitie of Love. Contemplate, and studie them. Here shall you read *Hymen*, having lighted two Torches, either of which enflame mutually, but waste not. One Love by the others aspect increasing, and both in the right lines of aspiring. The Fates spinning them round and even threds, and of their whitest wooll, without brack, or purle. Fortune, and Time fetter'd at their feet with Adamantine Chaines, their wings deplum'd, for starting from them. All amiablenesse in the richest dresse of delight and colours, courting the season to tarry by them, and make the *Idea* of their Felicitie perfect; together with the love, knowledge, and dutie of their Subjects perpetuall. So wisheth the glad, and gratefull Client, seated here, the over-joy'd Master of the house; and prayeth that the whole Region about him could speake but his language. Which is, that first the Peoples love would let that People know their owne happinesse, and that knowledge could confirme their duties, to an admiration of your sacred Persons; descended, one from the most

peacefull, the other the most warlike, both your pious, and just
progenitors; from whom, as out of Peace came Strength, and out
of the Strong came sweetnesse, so in you, joyn'd by holy marriage
in the flower and ripenesse of yeares, live the promise of a numerous Succession to your Scepters, and a strength to secure your
owne Ilands, with their owne Ocean, but more your owne Palme-
branches, the Types of perpetuall Victorie. To which, two words
be added, a zealous *Amen*, and ever rounded, with a Crowne of
Welcome. Welcome, Welcome. (159-90)

The movement of this speech from an address to the Cupids for their
edification, through a more general statement about the king and queen,
to a direct address in which Philalethes is speaking for their host and
the people of the region, gives it its impact; it effectively expands the
entertainment from a pleasantly philosophical discussion of the necessity
for mutual love before a perfect union is possible to a tribute to the
king and queen as symbols ("the Canons, the Decretals, and whole
Schoole-Divinitie") of ideal love and union. As perfect examples of
married love the king and queen control fortune and time, and thus are
happy; but their happiness is an example for the people, whose happiness in turn depends on their returning the love of the king so that
between them and the king there is a perfect union. The perfection is
symbolized again in the heredity of the monarchs, one the son of James
the peaceful and the other the daughter of the warlike Henry IV of
France. The idea is given the authority of Scripture in Jonson's reference to the paradox of strength and sweetness.[1] And finally the union
of the king and queen is expanded to refer to the political union of the
British Isles.

In an extremely simplified form *Love's Welcome* does the same thing
that *Hymenaei* does: first it sets up a mythological symbol for union,
developing its possibilities in several ways. In *Hymenaei* Juno, the
presiding goddess, through the anagram Unio, introduces a number of
varieties of union. In *Love's Welcome* Eros and Anteros introduce the
idea of union in love and marriage, and stand as symbols of love. Both
Juno and the Cupids are, however, limited symbols, not only in the
application of their attributes (e. g. Eros does not automatically symbolize the union of England and Scotland) but in the verbally tricky
way in which Jonson has used them and which Gordon deplores in the
anagram on Juno. But Jonson does not leave Juno or the Cupids
carrying the entire burden of the masques; they are no more than the

1. Jonson notes in the margin, "Alluding to the holy Riddle," that is, Samson's
riddle in Judges 14: 14.

means of introducing the theme and giving to it the sanction of antiquity. When it comes to filling out the theme and providing a symbol which can support the interlocking universal scheme which Gordon recognizes as Jonson's purpose in *Hymenaei*, the poet shifts to the king as his symbol.

To show how much a part of the Jonsonian masque the king-symbol is, it is necessary only to consider the exception to the statements made above—*Lovers Made Men*, which was performed as a part of the festivities to honor Henri, Baron de la Tour, the French ambassador, in 1617. His host was Lord Hay, once the English ambassador at the French court. This is the only one of Jonson's masques and entertainments not written for royalty.

The performance opens with Mercury leading a group of lovers to the river Lethe. He explains that they have been drowned in love's tempest; he has seen

one *throw his heart away,*
Another sighing, *vapour forth his soule,*
A third, to *melt himselfe in teares,* and say,

O Love, I now to salter water turne
  Then that I die in; then, a fourth, to crie
  Amid the surges, *oh! I burne, I burne*:
  A fift, laugh out, *it is my ghost, not I.*   (63-9)

The Fates, who are sitting near Lethe, say they have no record of the deaths and suggest that the lovers drink from the river. This they do, and as their metamorphosis is taking place they dance an antic dance, disappearing into a wood at the end. Almost immediately they reappear, changed into reformed lovers and the courtiers they are. Cupid appears and subtly tries to put them into their old state, but they are protected by Mercury, and at the end of the masque the dances symbolize the desirability of tempering love (Cupid) with wit (Mercury) to keep from falling into utter foolishness as it was represented in the beginning of the masque.

The first contrast between this masque and one written for the king is that the metamorphosis (a common device) is effected by Lethe's waters, not by the power of the king. The imagery of the masque, too, centers on water (Love's tempest, the river Lethe, lovers' tears) and on wounds (Love's weapons and the wounds they inflict), without the suggestion that the king is the Master of the Ocean or the King of Love. Furthermore the dances are " rites " not in honor of one of the spectators but (as Cupid takes it) in honor of Cupid, and they are danced to express the dangers of the love-game and the necessity of a controlling wit in love rather than to honor a king.

Lovers Made Men lacks the impact of the masques performed for the king because the audience and the masquers are peers and there is no real difference in rank which Jonson can turn into a symbol of some greater universal order. The difference between the king and his courtiers is the principal source of the effectiveness of the other masques, for in one way or another Jonson is constantly playing with the difference, now having a rustic character appear rude to the king, now having a nobleman bow to him, now making the king a supernatural power of heaven. Withdraw the king, and the major source of interest in the masque is gone. *Lovers Made Men* is an amusing fable illustrating pleasantly a commonplace about love; it lacks the emotional power that the presence of royalty gives to other masques.

It is just this quality which makes the Combats of Concepts more than plain allegory or plain debate. In most of these masques Jonson is dealing with two or more apparently acceptable standards of value and showing that the one the king stands for is the best. Since even the lower standards have some supporters, these masques occasionally question quite seriously the king's rights. For example, *Love Restored* opens with the presentation of the Puritan view toward masques: they are far too expensive and they are immoral. There is a great deal to be said on the Puritan side and Jonson lets Plutus say it. The conclusion of the masque is that the king ought to be a spectacle of magnificence and a master of munificence, and that these goals can be achieved through masques. The fact that at the time of the masque's performance James was in financial straits adds a special fillip to Jonson's theme.[2] James's power is also questioned in one of the earliest entertainments, the *Entertainment of the King and Queen at Theobalds* (1607), performed when the Earl of Salisbury turned over Theobalds, his family estate, to the king. Through the figure of the Genius of the House the problem of the king's right to dispossess one of his subjects (even though he reimbursed him) is raised. Similarly, in the masques of *Blackness* and *Beauty* and in the *Haddington Masque*, a debate about love or beauty is lifted above the level of abstract argument and into a sphere which engages the emotions, by Jonson's constant awareness of the presence of the king. In both *News from the New World* and *Love*

2. The only scenery for the masque appears to be a chariot in which Cupid enters. Furthermore, the price of the masque (£280. 8s. 9d. [H & S, 10, 533]) is far lower than the average (*Oberon*, the previous year, cost six times as much). James had been having a great deal of trouble with Parliament about his income. Shortly before the masque was performed negotiations with Parliament had ceased, and James was looking for other sources of money. Cf. Davies, *The Early Stuarts*, pp. 13-14, and Gardiner, *History of England*, 2, 63-87, 106-13.

Freed from Ignorance and Folly, in which the king is associated with light, the same device is used.

A particularly fine masque of this sort and one complex enough to require study in some detail is *Pleasure Reconciled to Virtue*. In it Jonson manages to arouse the spectators' emotions in terms of mythology and personification without resorting to the use of any "human" characters. As the title suggests, the masque deals with attitudes toward pleasure. Is all pleasure unvirtuous? Or is there some condition under which virtue and pleasure are not in conflict?

The opening scene represents the pleasure of gluttony in the fat figure of Comus,[3] whose drunken companion is Hercules' bowl-bearer. To please the Belly-god, as he describes Comus, the Bowl-bearer calls forth a drunken fancy, a dance of bottles and a tun. But the festivities are halted by Hercules, just come from his fight with Antaeus who represents "inhumanity" (bestiality). Hercules says:

> What rytes are these? breeds Earth more Monsters yet?
> *Antaeus* scarce is cold: what can beget
> this store? (& stay) such contraries upon her?
> Is Earth so fruitfull of hir owne dishonor?
> Or 'cause his vice was Inhumanitie
> hopes she, with vitious hospitalitie
> to work an expiation, first? and then
> (help Vertue) theis are Sponges, & not men.[4]

After pointing out that the bowl-bearer has dishonored his bowl, which was a prize for virtue, Hercules banishes Comus and his crew with these words:

> Burdens, & shames of nature, perish, dye,
> for yet you never liv'd; But in the stye
> of vice have wallow'd; & in that Swines strife
> byn buried under the offence of life.
> Goe, reele, & fall, under the load you make,
> till your swolne bowells burst with what they take.
> Can this be pleasure, to extinguish man?
> or so quyte change him in his figure? Can
> the Belly love his paine, and be content
> with no delight, but what's a punishment?

---

3. Jonson's treatment of Comus may be profitably compared with Milton's. See William Madsen's study in this volume.

4. Lines 87-94. In quoting from the text of this masque I have normalized words in which superscript letters appear and have standardized *u* and *v*. Herford and Simpson base their text on a manuscript rather than a printed version.

> Theis *Monsters* plague themselves: & fitly too,
> for they do suffer what, and all they doo.
> But here must be no shelter, nor no shrowd
> for such: Sinck *Grove*, or vanish into clowd.   (101-14)

The physical deformity of the fat god is only a token of the deformity
of his nature; it is unnatural for anyone to wish to plague himself, for
the belly to love his pain. But these "monsters" are easily driven
away, and with them their grove. In its place appears Mount Atlas,
the goddesses Pleasure and Virtue with the musicians at its feet.
Hercules, the servant of Virtue, is instructed to sleep after his labors
while a crown is made for his reward. While he sleeps, a group of
pygmies, "brothers" of Antaeus, come upon him. Thinking they have
him at their mercy, they dance an antic caper of celebration. But as
soon as he awakes they scurry away like rats. The appearance of the
pygmies is interpreted by Mercury, who descends from the mountain
to crown Hercules:

> Theis
> shold not disturb the peace of *Hercules*.
> *Earths* worms, & *Honors* dwarffs, at too great ods,
> prove, or provoke the issue of the gods.   (168-71)

These people are little—actually and figuratively—and their pleasure
at thinking themselves the equals of Hercules is self-delusion. In them
is represented a kind of pleasure which is not a deadly sin but merely
a despicable, unwarranted inflation of the ego, characteristic of "*Earths*
worms, & *Honors* dwarffs."

There is no question of the propriety of banishing gluttony and
smallness of spirit, since these "pleasures" are perverted ones. But
there are more important pleasures which it is not so easy to deal with,
those of love and beauty. Mercury announces that on this night
"Vertue, & her noted opposite, Pleasure" have decided to agree and
for the pleasure of Hesperus (King James) Virtue has brought

> twelve PRINCES [who] have byn bred
> in this rough *Mountaine*, & neere *Atlas* head,
> the *hill* of *knowledge*. One, & cheif of whom
> of the bright race of *Hesperus* is come,
> Who shall in time the same that He is, be,
> and now is only a lesse Light then He.   (202-7)

That is, the leader of the virtuous princes is Prince Charles.

> Theis now she trusts with *Pleasure*, & to theis
> she give⟨s⟩ an entraunce to the *Hesperides*,

> faire *Beuties garden[s]* : Neither can she feare
> they should grow soft, or wax effeminat here,
> Since in hir sight, & by hir charge all's don,
> *Pleasure* the Servant, *Vertue* looking on.   (208-13)

Those who follow pleasure, even in the court of Hesperus, are in some danger that they may " grow soft, or wax effeminat " unless they are watched over by Virtue. But the Chorus, calling them forth, sings :

> Ope, aged Atlas, open then thy lap
> and from thy beamy bosom, strike a light,
> that men may read in thy misterious map
> > all lines
> > and signes
> of roial education, and the right.
> > Se how they come, and show
> > that are but borne to know.
> > > Descend,
> > > descend,
> > though pleasure lead,
> > > feare not to follow :
> > they who are bred
> > > within the hill
> > > of skill,
> > may safely tread
> > > what path they will :
> no ground of good, is hollow.   (218-35)

In dealing with these new pleasures, Jonson presents the questions in terms of personifications (Pleasure and Virtue), mythology (Hercules, Mercury, Atlas), and invented fable (Virtue's twelve princes who have been trained in virtue), and visual symbol (the mountain, in whose " misterious map " may be read the " lines / and signes / of roial education, and the right "). It is time now to introduce the pleasures that the Princes will have to withstand. For this purpose Jonson brings in Daedalus, the artificer of the labyrinth at Crete, because the reconciliation between Pleasure and Virtue is to come about under the image of safely negotiating the labyrinths of love and beauty. Daedalus raises the question :

> Come on, come on ; and where you goe,
> > so enter-weave the curious knot
> as ev'n th'observer scarce may know
> > which lines are Pleasures, and which not.
> First, figure out the doubtfull way

> at which, a while all youth shold stay,
> where she and Vertue did contend
> which should have Hercules to frend.
> Then, as all actions of mankind
> are but a Laborinth, or maze,
> so let your Daunces be entwin'd,
> yet not perplex men, unto gaze.
> But measur'd, and so numerous too,
> as men may read each act you doo.
> And when they see the Graces meet,
> admire the wisdom of your feet.   (253-68)

To make sure that the spectators will watch the dancing closely, and the readers the descriptions of the dances, Daedalus adds:

> For Dauncing is an exercise
> not only shews the movers wit,
> But maketh the beholder wise,
> as he hath powre to rise to it.   (269-72)

The dances are to represent the ability of the virtuous to negotiate any labyrinth, and the first demonstrates generally that these princes are well trained. When it is done, Daedalus compliments them and professes himself to be greatly enlightened by their performance. They are now ready to try a real labyrinth:

> Begin, begin; for looke, the faire
> do longing listen, to what aire
> you forme your second touch,
> that they may vent their murmuring hymnes
> iust to the tune you move your limbes,
> and wish their owne were such.
> Make haste, make haste, for this
> the Laborinth of BEAUTIE is.   (288-95)

With this Jonson brings in the spectators as actors in his masque; the ladies who will take part in the next dance are now, as they sit eagerly on the sidelines, the representatives of beauty, the lures for the unwary. After the second dance is through, Daedalus instructs the Princes to take the ladies out in the "subtlest maze of all: that's LOVE."

> Goe choose among—But with a mind
> as gentle as the stroaking wind
> runs ore the gentler flowres.
> And so let all your actions smile,
> as if they meant not to beguile

> the Ladies, but the howres.
> Grace, Laughter, & discourse, may meet,
> and yet, the beautie not goe les:
> for what is noble, should be sweet,
> but not dissolv'd in wantonnes.
> Will you, that I give the law
> to all your sport, & some-it?
> It should be such shold envy draw,
> but ever overcome-it.   (303-16)

Except for fifteen lines dealing with Hesperus in Mercury's speech introducing the masquers, and the final song, the masque now stands before us complete: Comus as gluttony, the pygmies as honor's dwarfs, and now the Princes as virtue dancing a labyrinth of love and beauty with the ladies of Hesperus' court. This last action seems very limited in its application, for apparently it represents only the safe negotiation of an evening's flirtation. The dangers of this pleasure are not the damnation that goes with gluttony but rather softness and effeminacy. If this were all there is in the masque it would be a failure on the grounds that Gordon gives for *Hymenaei*: its symbols are weak.

In discussing this masque I have deliberately kept the king out of it so that the effect of his presence would appear the more striking when Mercury's speech was quoted. After he has explained the role of the pygmies, Mercury says:

> But now
> the time's arriv'd, that *Atlas* told thee of: How
> b⟨y⟩ 'un-alterd law, & working of the stars,
> there should be a cessation of all iars
> 'twixt VERTUE, & hir noted opposite,
> PLEASURE: that both shold meet here, in the sight
> of HESPERUS, the glory of the WEST,
> the brightest star, that from his burning Crest
> lights all on this side the *Atlantick seas*
> as far as to thy *Pillars Hercules*.
> Se where He shines: *Justice*, & *Wisdom* plac'd
> about his Throne & those with *Honor* grac'd,
> *Beautie*, & *Love*. It is not with his Brother
> bearing the world, but ruling such another
> in his renowne.   (186-200)

In the light of this passage the meaning of the Princes' dancing begins to be more comprehensive. Love and beauty are not confined to the flirtations of courtiers nor the beauties of the ladies, but are part of the adornments of the king's throne. And the king's throne (and here the expansion of the meaning starts in earnest) is not merely the "state" in the banqueting-house but also a constellation in which the king is Hesperus, surrounded by the lesser lights of justice, wisdom and honor, love and beauty. As a star the king is of course associated with heaven, which gives him a kind of divinity. Furthermore, through his brilliance his influence spreads over the western part of the world. He rules a world within a world. And, most important, as a star he is part of the "un-alterd law, & working of the stars" which causes the "cessation of all iars" between Pleasure and Virtue.

By association with the king, the love and beauty which appeared to be merely dalliance have taken on a cosmic significance. It remains only to raise the controlling power, Virtue, to the same eminence; for the virtue that kept the courtiers from seducing the ladies is not of a great enough magnitude to have much effect on the working of the stars. The last speech in the masque converts the courtiers' virtue to cosmic virtue. As the Princes leave, Mercury calls to them:

> An eye of looking back, were well,
>   or any murmur that wold tell
>   your thoughts, how you were sent,
>   and went,
> to walke with Pleasure, not to dwell.
> Theis, theis are howres, by Vertue spar'd
>   hirself, she being hir owne reward,
>   But she will have you know,
>   that though
> hir sports be soft, hir life is hard.
>   You must returne unto the Hill
>   and there advaunce
> with labour, and inhabit still
>   that height, and crowne,
>   from whence you ever may looke downe
>   upon triumphed Chaunce.
> She, she it is, in darknes shines.
>   'tis she that still hir-self refines,
>   by hir owne light, to everie eye,
> more seene, more knowne, when Vice stands by.
>   And though a stranger here on earth,
>   in heaven she hath hir right of birth.
>   There, there is Vertues seat.
> Strive to keepe hir your owne,
>   'tis only she, can make you great,
>   though place, here, make you knowne.   (323-48)

The speech is so important that it is "after repeated in Song, by 2. *trebles, 2. tenors, a base,* and the whole Chorus" as the Princes dance back into the mountain. By comparison with virtue, dancing and dalliance are "sports" and only occasionally permitted. The life of virtue is laborious, but it is associated with true greatness. At this point all the symbols of monarchy which have been used are brought together to emphasize the value of virtue: the Princes are by definition royal and they are to inhabit the *height* and *crowne* of the most eminent feature of the landscape, Mount Atlas. They will thus be superior to *Chance,* which is inferior only to divinity. Just as James is the crown, he is in one sense their instructor in virtue; and as he is Hesperus whose radiance lights up the western world, so Virtue "in darknes shines. / 'tis she that still hir-self refines, / by hir owne light, to everie eye." Both Virtue and James shine brighter in the presence of vice (gluttony and the pygmies). When Mercury reaches the last lines the Princes are prepared for the apparent denial of the king's omnipotence, and the resolution of this denial is to make the king's position even stronger. Heaven, not the court, is virtue's seat, and only virtue, not worldly rank, is of any value. That this seems to go against the usual current of court compliments (wringing from Herford and Simpson the tribute of a "high-toned close" [*10,* 590]) forces our attention on the fact that Jonson has already established heaven as the seat of Hesperus, and Hesperus as the superior of Virtue; he includes all virtue, justice, wisdom, honor, love, and beauty in his constellation. The last two lines allow Jonson to have his cake and eat it, for they are at once a salutary reminder to the king and at the same time a means of intensifying the idea of the monarchy as the embodiment of all good.

Without the king the masque is next to nothing. It is because Jonson can incorporate him into the masque, strike sparks against the crown, that the masque grows and expands. *Pleasure Reconciled to Virtue* is more than a warning not to eat too much, not to be presumptuous, and not to flirt beyond the bounds of decency; by virtue of the king's presence all existence becomes its sphere, for the king is justly the embodiment of all the goods in the universe. The principle on which Jonson's masques are based is clearly stated in the preface to Chapman's only surviving masque.

> I am enforced to affirm this: that as there is no poem nor oration so general, but hath his one particular proposition; nor no river so extravagantly ample, but hath his never-so-narrow fountain, worthy to be named; so all these courtly and honouring inventions (having poesy and oration in them, and a fountain to be expressed, from whence their rivers flow) should expressively arise out of the

places and persons for and by whom they are presented; without which limits they are luxurious and vain.[5]

To avoid luxury and vanity the masque must have a central idea growing out of the very circumstances of its performance: the dancing of the noble masquers, the splendor of the setting, and above all the presence of the king.

5. *The Plays and Poems of George Chapman*, ed. T. M. Parrott (2 vols. London, G. Routledge & Sons, 1910-14), *2*, 444. Jonson said to Drummond in 1619, "That next himself only Fletcher and Chapman could make a Mask" (H & S, *1*, 133).

Selected Bibliography

Allen, Don Cameron. " Ben Jonson and the Hieroglyphics," *PQ, 18* (1939), 290-300.

Baehrens, Cornelia Emilia. *The Origin of the Masque.* Groningen, 1929.

Baskerville, C. R. " The Sources of Jonson's *Masque of Christmas* and *Love's Welcome at Welbeck*," *MP, 6* (1908), 257-69.

Bayne, Rev. Ronald. " Masque and Pastoral," *Cambridge History of English Literature, 6* (1910), ch. 13, 370-420.

Bowden, William. *The English Dramatic Lyric, 1603-42,* Yale Studies in English, Vol. *118.* New Haven, 1951.

Brinkley, Roberta F. *Arthurian Legend in the Seventeenth Century,* Johns Hopkins Monographs in Literary History, No. 3. Baltimore, 1932.

Brotanek, Rudolph. *Die englischen Maskenspiele,* Wiener Beiträge zur englischen Philologie, 15. Vienna and Leipzig, 1902.

Campbell, Lily Bess. *Scenes and Machines on the English Stage.* Cambridge, 1923.

Castelain, Maurice. *Ben Jonson.* Paris and London, 1907.

Chambers, E. K. *The Elizabethan Stage.* 4 vols. Oxford, 1923.

——— *The Medieval Stage.* 2 vols. Oxford, 1903.

Chute, Marchette. *Ben Jonson of Westminster.* New York, 1953.

Cunningham, Dolora. " The Jonsonian Masque as a Literary Form," *ELH, 22* (1955), 108-24.

Cunningham, Peter. *Inigo Jones: A Life of the Architect,* Shakespeare Society Publications, No. 39. London, 1848.

Cutts, John P. " Original Music to Browne's Inner Temple Masque, and other Jacobean Masque Music," *N & Q,* n.s., *1* (1954), 194-5.

Dillon, Viscount. " Barriers and Foot Combats," *Archaeological Journal, 61* (1904), 276-308.

Duncan, E. H. " The Alchemy in Jonson's *Mercury Vindicated*," *SP, 39* (1942), 625-37.

Emslie, Macdonald. " Three Early Settings of Jonson," *N & Q, 198* (1953), 466-8.

Evans, Willa McClung. *Ben Jonson and Elizabethan Music.* Lancaster, Pa., 1929.

Feuillerat, Albert. *Documents Relating to the Office of the Revels in the Time of Elizabeth,* Bangs Materielen, No. 21. Louvain, 1908.

——— *Documents Relating to the Revels at Court in the Time of King Edward VI and Queen Mary,* Bangs Materielen, No. 44. Louvain, 1914.

Furniss, W. Todd. " Jonson, Camden, and the Black Prince's Plumes,"
    MLN, 69, 487-8.
——— " Jonson's Antimasques," Renaissance News, 7, 21-2.
——— " The Annotation of Jonson's Masqve of Qveenes," RES, N.S., 5,
    344-60.
Gilbert, Allan H. " The Function of the Masques in Cynthia's Revels,"
    PQ, 22 (1943), 211-30.
——— The Symbolic Persons in the Masques of Ben Jonson. Durham,
    N. C., 1948.
Gordon, D. J. " Ben Jonson's ' Haddington Masque ': the Story and the
    Fable," M.L.R., 42 (1947), 180-7.
——— " Hymenaei: Ben Jonson's Masque of Union," Journal of the
    Warburg and Courtauld Institutes, 8 (1945), 107-45.
——— " The Imagery of Ben Jonson's The Masque of Blacknesse and
    The Masque of Beautie," Journal of the Warburg and Courtauld Insti-
    tutes, 6 (1943), 122-41.
——— " Poet and Architect: The Intellectual Setting of the Quarrel
    between Ben Jonson and Inigo Jones," Journal of the Warburg and
    Courtauld Institutes, 12 (1949), 152-78.
Greg, W. W. A List of Masques, Pageants, &c. Supplementary to a List
    of English Plays. London, 1902.
Johnston, George Burke. Ben Jonson: Poet. New York, 1945.
Jonson, Ben. Works, ed. Peter Whalley. 7 vols. London, 1756.
——— Works, ed. W. Gifford. 9 vols. London, 1816.
——— Works, ed. C. H. Herford, Percy and Evelyn Simpson. 11 vols.
    Oxford, The Clarendon Press, 1925-52.
——— Jonson's Masque of Gipsies, ed. W. W. Greg. London, 1952.
——— Masques and Entertainments, ed. Henry Morley, Carisbrooke Li-
    brary, No. 9. London, 1890.
——— The Masque of Queenes by Ben: Jonson with the Designs of Inigo
    Jones, ed. G. Chapman. London, 1930.
Knights, L. C. Drama and Society in the Age of Jonson. London, 1937.
Nason, Arthur Huntington. Heralds and Heraldry in Ben Jonson's Plays,
    Masques and Entertainments. New York, 1907.
Nicoll, Allardyce. Stuart Masques and the Renaissance Stage. London,
    1937.
Palmer, John. Ben Jonson. London, 1934.
Parrott, T. M. " Comedy in the Court Masque: A Study of Jonson's
    Contributions," PQ, 20 (1941), 428-41.
Reyher, Paul. Les Masques anglais. Paris, 1909.
Sackton, A. H. Rhetoric as a Dramatic Language in Ben Jonson. New
    York, 1948.
Sibley, Gertrude M. The Lost Plays and Masques, 1500-1642. Ithaca,
    N. Y., and London, 1933.

Simpson, Percy. " The Castle of the Rosy Cross: Ben Jonson and Theophilus Schweighardt," *M.L.R.*, *41* (1946), 206-7.

———— and Bell, C. F. *Designs by Inigo Jones for Masques & Plays at Court*, The Walpole Society, No. 12. Oxford, 1924.

Steele, Mary S. *Plays & Masques at Court during the Reigns of Elizabeth, James and Charles*. New Haven and London, 1926.

Sullivan, Mary. *Court Masques of James I*. Lincoln, Neb., 1913.

Swinburne, A. C. *A Study of Ben Jonson*. London, 1889.

Symonds, John A. *Ben Jonson*. London, 1886.

Talbert, E. W. " The Classical Mythology and the Structure of *Cynthia's Revels*," PQ, *22* (1943), 193-210.

———— " Current Scholarly Works and the ' Erudition' of Jonson's *Masque of Augurs*," *SP, 44* (1947), 605-24.

———— " The Interpretation of Jonson's Courtly Spectacles," *PMLA, 41* (1946), 454-73.

Tannenbaum, Samuel A. *Ben Jonson (A Concise Bibliography)*, Scholars' Facsimiles and Reprints. New York, 1938.

———— and Tannenbaum, Dorothy R. *Supplement to a Bibliography of Ben Jonson*. New York, 1947.

Tiddy, R. J. E. *The Mummer's Play*. Oxford, 1923.

Welsford, Enid. *The Court Masque*. Cambridge, 1927.

Wheeler, Charles F. *Classical Mythology in the Plays, Masques, and Poems of Ben Jonson*. Princeton, 1938.

THE IDEA OF NATURE IN MILTON'S POETRY

by William G. Madsen

Preface

THE STUDY of the idea of nature in Milton s poetry is essentially a study of the idea of nature in *Comus* and *Paradise Lost*. Not only are all the major themes and motives present in these poems, but they are the only poems in which Milton makes extensive use of the idea of nature as an integral part of the poetic and intellectual structure. The minor poems, for example, have a good deal of nature symbolism but make little use of philosophical ideas of nature; *Paradise Regained*, on the other hand, uses the idea of nature but offers no conceptions or themes that are not already present in *Paradise Lost*. In my chapter on *Paradise Lost* I point out some of the significant parallels between the two poems.

In *The Christian Doctrine* Milton says that the word "Nature" means "either the essence of a thing, or that general law which is the origin of every thing, and under which every thing acts." These are undoubtedly the two principal denotations of the word, but they provide no hint of the range and complexity of connotation it has acquired in the course of twenty-five centuries. I have therefore found it necessary to glance from time to time at the rich heritage of cosmological, anthropological, and theological speculation that lies behind Milton's poetic use of the idea of nature. Thus in the chapter on *Comus* will be found a brief account of the libertine and classical-Christian conceptions of nature as an ethical norm, together with a definition of the Christian idea of the relation between nature and grace. In the chapter on *Paradise Lost* Milton's cosmology and anthropology are compared with those of various classical systems to which Milton is often said to be indebted. My aim, however, is not so much to define Milton's idea of nature in the abstract as to show how it is used as a controlling and organizing principle in the poetry itself.

All quotations from Milton's poetry follow the text of Merritt Y. Hughes, New York, The Odyssey Press, 1935-37. Quotations from the prose works are from *The Student's Milton*, ed. F. A. Patterson, New York, Crofts, 1941.

In its original form this essay was submitted as a dissertation for the degree of Doctor of Philosophy at Yale University. I am grateful to Cleanth Brooks, E. T. Donaldson, Maynard Mack, the late Stanley T. Williams, and A. M. Witherspoon, who read it in an earlier version and made helpful comments; to Benjamin C. Nangle, who has seen it through the press; to Davis P. Harding, who has been a patient and perceptive critic at every stage; and to Louis L. Martz, who as my dissertation director was a never-failing source of fruitful suggestions, valuable criticisms, and moral support. And finally I owe a debt of gratitude to my wife and parents for seeing me through many dark days.

WILLIAM G. MADSEN

Wayne State University
  March 1, 1957

1

Comus

Comus and the Libertine Idea of Nature

THE name of Comus, the god of feasts and revels, is derived from the Greek noun *kōmos*, which signifies a revel or carousal, or the band of revelers itself. As a personification Comus appears for the first time in the *Imagines* of Philostratus the Elder in the second or third century A.D. In this work he is described as a "youth . . . delicate and not yet full grown, flushed with wine." In the *imago* that Philostratus is describing Comus is asleep before the golden doors of a wedding chamber; his head, which is crowned with roses, is bent forward and his face is in the shade, the moral of this being, says Philostratus, "that persons of his age should not go revelling, except with heads veiled." Philostratus also describes the revelers: the men and women are wearing each other's clothes and aping each other's movements, and they are all dancing wildly and clapping their hands.[1]

In the Renaissance Comus was a well-known figure. The description of him in the *Fabularum Liber* of Augustus Hyginus, published at Basel in 1570, follows that of Philostratus almost word for word, except that Hyginus omits the moral. Neither Philostratus nor Hyginus gives Comus any parents, and Milton may have got the hint for making Bacchus his father from the *Historia de Deis Gentium* of L. G. Giraldus: "Comus, i. e., *kōmos*, was the god of feasts and revelling: some of the Greek writers linked him with Dionysius. His picture is described by Philostratus and a great many others: Philostratus represents him as crowned with a garland, and he cleverly adds a great many other pleasant things in this description." For the Italian humanists Comus became the personification of the reconciliation of pleasure and virtue. The cue for this interpretation was taken from a phrase in one of Cicero's letters: "virtute duce, comite fórtuna."[2] The pun was

1. Philostratus the Elder, *Imagines*, tr. Arthur Fairbanks, The Loeb Classical Library (London, William Heinemann, 1931), Bk. I, ch. 2.
2. *Epistolae ad familiares*, X. iii (Ad Plancum). Cited by Edgar Wind, *Bellini's Feast of the Gods. A Study in Venetian Humanism* (Cambridge, Mass., Harvard University Press, 1948), p. 46, n. 8.

irresistible. In Bellini's painting, "Comes virtutis," one sees, in the words of Wind, a companion of virtue "graciously offering the reward of pleasure, a Bacchus-like figure (for Comus was the son of Bacchus), comfortably riding on a chariot drawn by cupids and following on the heels of persevering Virtue: *virtute duce, comite fortuna.*" And in the grotto of Isabella d'Este, the largest picture of which was to be Lorenzo Costa's "The Gate of Comus," "Comus-Comes serves as a guardian spirit, a symbol of the reconciliation of Plato with Epicurus." [3] Further evidence that Comus was generally regarded as a "harmless Godlet of Revels" [4] is to be found in Richard Linche's *The Fovntaine of Ancient Fiction*, first published in London in 1599, which is an English translation of Cartari's *Le imagini de i dei de gli antichi*. In this work Comus is described in the section on Bacchus, and he is associated with mirth, joy, and "pleasance," or the good effects of wine.

In view of this general trend of interpretation, it is quite surprising that the two best-known works before Milton's in which Comus makes his appearance should present him as a gross belly-god on the one hand and a subtly vicious hedonist on the other. In Ben Jonson's mask *Pleasure Reconciled to Virtue*, which W. Todd Furniss discusses in detail at the conclusion of the preceding study, Comus appears as "ye god of *cheere*, or ye *belly*, riding in tryumph, his head crownd with roses, & other flowres; his haire curld." After a song, in which Comus is hailed as "ye bouncing belly, / first father of Sauce, & deuiser of gelly," the bowl-bearer praises the belly in a long prose speech. Then follows the first antimasque, danced by a tun and some bottles, after which Hercules appears, calls Comus and his revelers (among other things) "Burdens, & shames of nature," and proceeds to destroy the grove. The reconciliation of Pleasure and Virtue follows, and Comus has no part in it. [4a]

Jonson's mask, first presented at court in 1619, was not published until 1640, and Milton may or may not have seen it in manuscript. But there seems to be no question that he knew Erycius Puteanus' *Comus, sive Phagesiposi Cimmeria. Somnium*, first published in 1608, and published again at Oxford in the very year of Milton's mask. In this little fantasy, Comus becomes a typical "Renaissance naturalist." He is a sybarite whose parents are Venus and Mercury; he himself is a hermaphrodite who is able both to give and to receive pleasure. Pute-

3. Wind, p. 48. Bellini's "Comes virtutis" is reproduced by Wind, Plate 56.

4. The phrase is Hilaire Belloc's, in *Milton* (Philadelphia, Lippincott, 1935), p. 101.

4a. I quote from C. H. Herford and Percy and Evelyn Simpson, *Ben Jonson* (11 vols. Oxford, The Clarendon Press, 1925-52), Vol. 7.

anus even puts into his mouth the commonplace naturalistic "appeal to Nature."[5] Milton reinforces this naturalistic interpretation of Comus by making Circe his mother. Homer's enchantress, in one guise or another, had become one of the leading representatives of Renaissance naturalism.[6] In Natale Conti's *Mythologiae*, for example, Ulysses is equated with Reason and Circe with Nature: "I am inclined to believe that Ulysses is that part of our soul that partakes of reason, and that Circe is nature. The companions of Ulysses are those powers of the soul that conspire with the affections of the body and do not obey reason, and nature is the appetite for illegitimate things. For right law is the curb and rein of depraved minds, since it is fitting to think of those powers as beasts, but reason, which alone makes them like God, is unconquered and remains constant against those allurements of appetite."[7] Circe here represents the libertine Nature to which Comus constantly appeals and whose philosophical genealogy may be traced as far back as the Greek Sophists and Cynics.[8] This is the Nature

5. There is a detailed summary of this work, together with some interesting parallels between Milton and Puteanus, in Ralph H. Singleton, "Milton's *Comus* and the *Comus* of Erycius Puteanus," *PMLA*, *58* (1943), 949-57.

6. See Merritt Y. Hughes, "Spenser's Acrasia and the Circe of the Renaissance," *Journal of the History of Ideas*, *4* (1943), 381-99.

7. Natale Conti, *Mythologiae, sive explicationes fabularum, Libri decem* (Geneva, 1641), Bk. VI, ch. vi, p. 568. Davis P. Harding plausibly conjectures that "Milton's first contact with the allegorized version of Circe and Ulysses came through the pages of Renaissance commentary on the *Metamorphoses* or through the verbal exposition of one of his schoolmasters." *Milton and the Renaissance Ovid*, Ill. Stud. in Lang. and Lit., *30*, No. 4 (Urbana, University of Illinois Press, 1946), 60.

8. It is conjectured that the Greek word *physis*, which is our *nature*, first meant simply "birth" or "genesis." By the time of Homer it had come to mean "outward characteristics," and when the sixth-century Ionian scientists began to speculate about the universe, they gave to their investigations the name *Peri Physeos Panton*, "concerning the characteristics of all things." It was not the outward characteristics the Ionians were interested in, however, but the underlying reality, and in this fashion "nature" came to mean the inner characteristics of things, or things as they really are. At the same time the Ionians used expressions like *kata physin* and *para physin* to mean "in reality" or "according to the real nature of things" as opposed to erroneous popular conceptions. The Sophists, in their work of dissolving traditional religious and moral ideas, took over these expressions and opposed them not only to popular opinion but also to the religious and moral ideals embodied in the laws and customs of the state. This Sophistic opposition between Nature and Convention was adopted by the Cynics, for whom the natural life was the life furthest removed from the restraints of law, society, conventional morality, prevalent

of Jean de Meun, Théophile de Viau, Marlowe, Edmund in *Lear*, "Jack" Donne, Carew, and the whole band of dissolute court poets that many editors have thought Milton had in mind in his portrayal of Comus. In 1624 the Jesuit Père Garasse, in his *Doctrine curieuse des beaux-esprits de ce temps ou pretendus tels*, summarized the philosophy of Théophile and the French libertines in the following words: "Il n'y a point autre Divinité ny puissance souveraine au monde que la Nature, laquelle il faut contenter en toutes choses sans rien refuser à nostre corps, ou à nos sens, de ce qu'ils desirent de nous en l'exercise de leurs puissance et facultez naturelles." Garasse goes on to list what he considers the only three legitimate uses of the term "nature": 1) the order of second causes, 2) the nature or essence of a thing, and 3) the peculiar inclination of each thing.[9] Morality, he cautions, must not be based on this last "nature," but of course that is just what the libertines, French and English alike, were doing. Not only that, but they professed to find sanction for the indulgence of their appetites in the order of second causes itself. In Thomas Randolph's *The Muses Looking-Glass*, for instance, there is an appeal to Nature very similar to the one Milton gives Comus. Colax, a Flatterer, is praising Acolastus, a voluptuous Epicure:

> nature has been bountifull
> To provide pleasurs, and shall we be niggards
> At plentious boards? He's a discourteous guest
> That will observe a dyet at a feast.
> When nature thought the earth alone too little
> To finde us meat, and therefore stor'd the ayr
> With winged creaturs, not contented yet,
> She made the water fruitfull to delight us.
> Nay I believe the other Element too
> Doth nurse some curious dainty for mans food;
> If we would use the skill to catch the Salamander:
> Did she do this to have us eat with temperance?
>
> . . . when she bestow'd
> So powerfull faces, such commanding beauties
> On many glorious Nymphs, was it to say

opinion, and even ordinary decency. See J. W. Beardslee, Jr., *The Use of Physis in Fifth-Century Greek Literature* (Chicago, 1918), pp. 3, 12, 43, 61-3; and A. O. Lovejoy and G. Boas, *Primitivism and Related Ideas in Antiquity* (Baltimore, 1935), pp. 103-6, and p. 106, n. 12.

9. The quotations from Garasse are taken from George Boas, *The Happy Beast in French Thought of the Seventeenth Century* (Baltimore, The Johns Hopkins Press, 1933), pp. 66-8.

> Be chast and continet? not to enjoy
> All pleasures, and at full, were to make nature
> Guilty of that she ne're was guilty of,
> A vanity in her works.[1]   (II. 3)

This speech by no means represents the total meaning of Randolph's play, which is a dramatization of Aristotle's *Nicomachean Ethics* ending with a mask presided over by Mediocrity, in which all the virtues dance together. Some of Randolph's other poems would class him as a libertine poet, however. Here are two passages, one from " A Pastorall Courtship," the other from " Upon love fondly refus'd for conscience sake ":

> See everything that we espie
> Is fruitfull saving you and I :
> View all the fields, survey the bowers,
> The Buds, the blossoms, and the flowers,
> And say if they so rich could be
> In barren base Virginity.
> Earth's not so coy as you are now,
> But willingly admits the Plow.
> For how had man or beast been fed,
> If she had kept her maiden head?

> Nature, Creations law, is judg'd by sense,
>   Not by the Tyrant conscience,
> Then our commission gives us leave to do,
>   What youth and pleasure prompts us to :
> For we must question, else heavens great decree,
>   And tax it with a treachery ;
> If things made sweet to tempt our appetite
>   Should with a guilt stain the delight.

Sexual license was only one of the lessons drawn from Nature by Renaissance naturalists. In Sidney's *Arcadia* the wicked aunt Cecropia tries to make an atheist of Pamela by appealing in the best Epicurean manner to the self-sufficiency of Nature and the indifference of the gods to human concerns. Pamela denies that there is any such Nature as Cecropia appeals to. Nature, she says, is simply the aggregate of many individual " natures," contraries that are held together only because there is a heavenly Nature that bridles them.[2] Unlike Cecropia, Comus

---

1. Randolph's play was first performed in 1630 and first published in 1638. Henry J. Todd was the first editor to call attention to this parallel between Milton and Randolph in *Comus, A Mask* (Canterbury, 1798), note to line 710.

2. *Works*, ed. Albert Feuillerat (Cambridge, 1912), *1*, 406-10. In *Mythology*

does not make a direct attack on the Lady's faith, but she sees his drift well enough when she accuses him and his crew of neglecting the All-giver, and there is perhaps a subtle hint of his Epicurean atheism in the lines where the Lady says that if she should try to convince Comus of his error,

> the uncontrolled worth
> Of this pure cause would kindle my rapt spirits
> To such a flame of sacred vehemence,
> That dumb things would be mov'd to sympathize,
> And the brute Earth would lend her nerves, and shake,
> Till all thy magic structures rear'd so high,
> Were shatter'd into heaps o'er thy false head.   (793-9)

"Brute Earth," as Hughes points out, translates Horace's "bruta tellus" in the ode in which Horace professes to renounce Epicureanism because Jove has sent his thunder crashing through a clear sky, "whereby the brute earth and the wandering streams, whereby Styx and the dread seat of hated Taenarus, and the boundary where Atlas stands, were shaken."[3]   Whatever his philosophical creed, Comus is adept at pressing philosophy into the service of immorality. His scornful reference to "that same vaunted name Virginity" (738) recalls the thoroughgoing nominalism of Marlowe's Leander:

> This idol which you term virginity
> Is neither essence subject to the eye,
> No, nor to any one exterior sense,
> Nor hath it any place of residence,
> Nor is't of earth or mould celestial,
> Or capable of any form at all.   (I, 270-5)

But the Lady has already revealed herself as an equally thoroughgoing Platonic idealist:

> O welcome pure-ey'd Faith, white-handed Hope,
> Thou hov'ring Angel girt with golden wings,
> And thou unblemish't form of Chastity,
> I see ye visibly . . .   (213-16)

Her philosophic equipment is more than adequate to counter the all-dissolving skepticism of her tempter.

In Comus' very first song, the lyrical strain that has so ravished the

and the Renaissance Tradition in English Poetry, Minneapolis, 1932, Douglas Bush calls attention to this passage from the _Arcadia_, as well as to numerous other examples of Renaissance naturalism. See p. 135, n. 27, and p. 267, n. 46.

3. _Odes_, I. xxxiv, lines 9-12.

critics, Milton has carefully suggested the speciousness of Comus'
appeal to Nature by giving him some very unnatural practices, and
some very unnatural imagery also. He starts off innocently enough, as
any good tempter would, by referring to such natural phenomena as
the evening star and the sun and the " Sounds and Seas " which " with
all their finny drove / Now to the Moon in wavering morrice move "
(115-16). We cannot be sure about him for upwards of twenty-five
lines, so cleverly does he wind himself into our easy hearts with his
Horatian flowers and wine, his sly dig at old fuddy-duddies, his bold
claim to be of " purer fire," and his evocation of Merrie England with
its wakes and pastimes. Even the lines,

> What hath night to do with sleep?
> Night hath better sweets to prove,
> *Venus* now wakes, and wak'ns Love.
> Come let us our rites begin,
> 'Tis only day-light that makes Sin,   (122-6)

can be taken as playful hyperbole, although the not-so-easy-hearted
reader may note the inversion of the natural relation between night and
sleep and suspect that the party is getting rough.[4] In the very next
lines the mask is off and the trap is sprung:

> Hail Goddess of Nocturnal sport,
> Dark veil'd *Cotytto*, t'whom the secret flame
> Of mid-night Torches burns; mysterious Dame
> That ne'er art call'd, but when the Dragon womb
> Of Stygian darkness spets her thickest gloom,
> And makes one blot of all the air,
> Stay thy cloudy Ebon chair,
> Wherein thou rid'st with *Hecat'*, and befriend
> Us thy vow'd Priests, till utmost end
> Of all thy dues be done, and none left out,
> Ere the blabbing Eastern scout,
> The nice Morn on th' *Indian* steep,
> From her cabin'd loop-hole peep,
> And to the tell-tale Sun descry
> Our conceal'd Solemnity.   (128-42)

---

4. Cf. Clement of Alexandria: " O unblushing shamelessness! Once on a
time night was silent, a veil for the pleasure of temperate men; but now for the
initiated, the holy night is the tell-tale of the rites of licentiousness; and the
glare of torches reveals vicious indulgences." *Exhortation to the Heathen*, in
The Ante-Nicene Fathers, ed. Alexander Roberts and James Donaldson (Buffalo,
1885), *2*, 177.

Cotytto and Hecate are odd companions for pert fairies and dapper
elves, and one would hardly expect to find them at a merry wake or
pastime. It is difficult to see how anyone ever could have been taken
in by this imposter, but the ugly-headed monsters are there to prove it,
and there are not a few gullible critics too. It has been said that Milton
lost his sureness of touch in delineating Comus; that one side of the
poet's nature sympathized with Comus (which is no doubt true if
Comus is taken to represent merely the innocent pleasures of music and
the dance), and that this sympathy betrayed him into giving Comus a
"ravishing lyrical strain" against his better judgment. This is indeed
an odd charge to bring against a poet, that he has written poetry, but
it is an even odder idea of poetry that would limit it to "beauties"
of imagery and meter taken out of the total context of the poem. As
a matter of fact, neither the imagery nor the meter of the passage
quoted above strikes one as being the work of a master of ravishing
lyrical strains. The first nine lines, with their consonantal clusters, are
veritable jawbreakers, and Cotytto and Hecate and Dragon and Stygian
hardly call up visions of delight. We might notice also that the
"poetic" diction of "gilded Car of Day" and "glowing Axle" in the
opening lines of this insinuating song has given way at the end to the
saucy irreverence of "blabbing Eastern scout" and "tell-tale Sun."
Comus himself has described the technique which he here employs:

> I under fair pretence of friendly ends,
> And well plac't words of glozing courtesy,
> Baited with reasons not unplausible,
> Wind me into the easy-hearted man,
> And hug him into snares.   (160-4)

The extent to which Milton is in control of his material may be
illustrated by a comparison of his technique with that of Spenser in the
Bower of Bliss episode of *The Faerie Queene*.[4a] Spenser was con-
fronted with a similar problem of making vice alluring and at the same
time not letting Guyon seem frigid and bloodless. His attempt to do
this is both subtle and interesting. He begins by setting up in Book
II the same two opposing conceptions of Nature that we find in *Comus*:
the libertine and the Christian. Phaedria's Nature is in the libertine
tradition: After contrasting man's "toilsome paines" (II. vi. 15) and
"fruitlesse labors" (II: vi. 16) with Nature's "fruitfull lap" she asks,

> 'Why then doest thou, O man, that of them all
> Art lord, and eke of Nature soveraine,

4a. Quotations are from the Cambridge Edition, ed. R. E. Neil Dodge, Cambridge, Mass., Houghton Mifflin, 1936.

Wilfully make thy selfe a wretched thrall,
And waste thy joyous howres in needlesse paine
Seeking for daunger and adventures vaine?
What bootes it al to have, and nothing use?
Who shall him rew, that swimming in the maine
Will die for thirst, and water doth refuse?
Refuse such fruitlesse toile, and present pleasures chuse.'

(II. vi. 17)

In the very next canto Guyon's argument with Mammon provides us
with another idea of Nature:

'Indeede,' quoth he, 'through fowle intemperaunce,
Frayle men are oft captiv'd to covetise:
But would they thinke, with how small allowaunce
Untroubled nature doth her selfe suffise,
Such superfluities they would despise,
Which with sad cares empeach our native joyes:
At the well head the purest streames arise:
But mucky filth his braunching armes annoyes,
And with uncomely weedes the gentle wave accloyes.

'The antique world, in his first flowering youth,
Fownd no defect in his Creators grace,
But with glad thankes, and unreproved truth,
The guifts of soveraine bounty did embrace:
Like angels life was then mens happy cace:
But later ages pride, like corn-fed steed,
Abusd her plenty and fat swolne encreace
To all licentious lust, and gan exceed
The measure of her meane, and naturall first need.

(II. vii. 15-16)

Spenser then proceeds to describe the Bower of Bliss in terms which
suggest that it is the product of a libertine Nature made even more
wanton by Art. The theme is introduced in the very first view we get
of the Bower, when Atin goes to fetch Cymochles:

And over him, Art, stryving to compayre
With Nature, did an arber greene dispred,
Framed of wanton yvie . . .   (II. v. 29)

In the full-dress description of the Bower in Canto XII the idea is
further developed.

Thence passing forth, they shortly doe arryve
Whereas the Bowre of Blisse was situate;

> A place pickt out by choyce of best alyve,
> That Natures worke by art can imitate: (II. xii. 42)

> Thus being entred, they behold arownd
> A large and spacious plaine, on every side
> Strowed with pleasauns, whose fayre grassy grownd
> Mantled with greene, and goodly beautifide
> With all the ornaments of Floraes pride,
> Wherewith her mother Art, as halfe in scorne
> Of niggard Nature, like a pompous bride
> Did decke her, and too lavishly adorne,
> When forth from virgin bowre she comes in th' early morne.
>   (II. xii. 50)

> One would have thought, (so cunningly the rude
> And scorned partes were mingled with the fine,)
> That Nature had for wantonesse ensude
> Art, and that Art at Nature did repine;
> So striving each th' other to undermine,
> Each did the others worke more beautify;
> So diff'ring both in willes agreed in fine:
> So all agreed through sweete diversity,
> This gardin to adorne with all variety.   (II. xii. 59)

In the passage from Canto V, quoted above, the ivy appears to be real.
In Canto XII, however, it is artificial:

> And over all, of purest gold was spred
> A trayle of yvie in his native hew:
> For the rich metall was so coloured,
> That wight, who did not well avis'd it vew,
> Would surely deeme it to bee yvie trew: (II. xii. 61)

C. S. Lewis, who was the first to call attention to Spenser's use of this
device, has said that in *The Faerie Queene* Spenser consistently equates
art with evil.[5] This is misleading, however. In the description of the
Temple of Venus in Book IV, art cooperates with nature in a praise-
worthy way:

> 'For all that Nature by her mother wit
> Could frame in earth, and forme of substance base,

---

5. C. S. Lewis, *The Allegory of Love* (London, 1936), pp. 324 ff. For an able criticism of Lewis' view see N. S. Brooke, "C. S. Lewis and Spenser: Nature, Art, and the Bower of Bliss," *Cambridge Journal*, 2 (1948/9), 420-34.

> Was there, and all that Nature did omit,
> Art, playing second Natures part, supplyed it.'   (IV. x. 21)

In the Bower of Bliss, however, art does not strive to control and order nature, as it does in the Temple of Venus, but rather to outdo her in wantonness (II. xii. 59). Guyon, who knows that the lesson of Nature is temperance, ruthlessly destroys "all those pleasaunt bowres and pallace brave" (II. xii. 83), and he restores to their "naturall" forms the men who had been turned into beasts (II. xii. 86).

Now it is obvious that Spenser is trying to control the reader's attitude by an appeal to the central classical-Christian conception of Nature as an ethical norm, but he has succeeded only in putting into Guyon's mouth a statement to the effect that nature teaches temperance, while giving to Phaedria and Acrasia all the imagery of natural beauty and fertility. Phaedria's island was

> a chosen plott of fertile land,
> Emongst wide waves sett, like a litle nest,
> As if it had by Natures cunning hand
> Bene choycely picked out from all the rest,
> And laid forth for ensample of the best: (II. vi. 12)

In Acrasia's realm the air was "Gently attempred, and dispos'd so well, / That still it breathed forth sweet spirit and holesom smell" (II. xi. 51), more sweet and wholesome than "Eden selfe, if ought with Eden mote compayre" (II. xii. 52). When Guyon and the Palmer come near the Bower, they hear the "joyous birdes," who

> shrouded in chearefull shade,
> Their notes unto the voice attempred sweet:
> Th' angelicall soft trembling voyces made
> To th' instruments divine respondence meet: (II. xii. 71)

A. S. P. Woodhouse has ingeniously tried to explain the birds by suggesting that Spenser is saying that Nature unenlightened by grace is an unreliable guide,[6] but this would seem to contradict Guyon's statement that Nature teaches temperance. The trouble with the Bower of Bliss episode is that evil is given a natural as well as an artificial setting and hence is made to seem in accordance with nature to some degree, at least, and this is precisely what Guyon had said it was not. Guyon talks about Nature, but it is Phaedria and Acrasia who are associated with it. They have all the beauty, and he has all the virtue.

In *Comus*, on the other hand, it is the Tempter who talks about

6. A. S. P. Woodhouse, "Nature and Grace in the *Faerie Queene*," ELH, *16* (1949), 219.

Nature and beauty, but it is the Lady who is beautiful and who has the powers of nature and the poetry of nature on her side. The contrast between them is brought out in the opening speech of the Spirit, where it is said that Comus' abode is a

> drear Wood,
> The nodding horror of whose shady brows
> Threats the forlorn and wand'ring Passenger.   (37-9)

The Lady's Father, on the other hand, has as his charge the western front of one of the

> Sea-girt Isles
> That like to rich and various gems inlay
> The unadorned bosom of the Deep.   (21-3)

After Comus appears and invokes Cotytto and Hecate in his song, the Lady invokes

> Sweet Echo, sweetest Nymph that liv'st unseen
> Within thy airy shell
> By slow Meander's margent green,
> And in the violet embroider'd vale
> Where the love-lorn Nightingale
> Nightly to thee her sad Song mourneth well.   (230-5)

Comus himself admits the "Divine enchanting ravishment" (245) of this song, and it is not the Lady's chastity that freezes him to congealed stone but her beauty that takes him for a moment outside of himself (as Eve's beauty is later to affect Satan). Even in praising her song, however, Comus must needs mention Scylla and Charybdis (257-9). He then addresses the Lady in his falsely assumed natural guise of shepherd. He speaks of the "labour'd Ox" and the "swink't hedger" and the "green mantling vine," and promises to conduct the Lady to a "low / But loyal cottage" (291-321). But when we next see Comus he has thrown off the guise of shepherd, and his low cottage has become "a stately Palace, set out with all manner of deliciousness; soft Music, Tables spread with all dainties." He talks now of courts and feasts and solemnities, and the low cottage becomes a place for homely features to hide in. But the Lady knows that all his talk about Nature is "dear Wit and gay Rhetoric" (790) and that Nature herself will destroy his artificial palace:

> And the brute Earth would lend her nerves, and shake,
> Till all thy magic structures rear'd so high,
> Were shatter'd into heaps o'er thy false head.   (797-9)

Comus feels a "cold shudd'ring dew" dip him all over, "as when the wrath of *Jove* / Speaks thunder" (802-4).

An even more striking contrast to Comus is provided by the Attendant Spirit. Both "appear . . . as shepherds, preside over dances, celebrate the sensuous riches of nature, and use the tetrameter metre that Milton allots to no one else. As the powers of Comus seduce men to the level of brutes, the Attendant Spirit would persuade them to rise to the level of angels."[7] The Attendant Spirit thus reinforces imaginatively and poetically the doctrine of the Lady. Comus is skilled in the art of baleful herbs; the Spirit has the beneficent haemony. Comus celebrates youth and joy

> Meanwhile welcome Joy, and Feast   (102)
> Strict Age, and sour Severity,
> With their grave Saws in slumber lie   (109-10)

but the Spirit tells us that Youth and Joy are the offspring of the pure unspotted soul that enjoys heavenly love (1009-11). Comus claims to know each lane and every alley green of the wild wood (311-12), as indeed he does, and he assures the Lady "It were a journey like the path to Heav'n" to help her find her brothers (303-4), but the Spirit is the only "faithful guide" (944) to her Father's home. The Spirit represents the ordered and harmonious Nature of the heavenly bodies: his mansion is in one of the spheres, before the starry threshold of Jove's court, and in the Epilogue he says he is returning to the broad fields of the sky and that he can soar from the green earth's end "To the corners of the Moon" (1017). Comus, on the other hand, represents the chaotic Nature of waste fertility, and the only principle of control he knows is the "curious taste" of the pleasure-seeker.

Thus it is the Lady's Christian attitude toward Nature, not Comus' libertine attitude, that is supported by the poem's imagery. The wilderness of this world, through which the often misled and lonely traveler makes his way toward his Father's home, is transformed, for better or for worse, into a likeness of the human "natures" that inhabit it. For Comus it is a realm of Stygian darkness peopled with monstrous and unnatural forms. For the Lady it is a realm where

> does a sable cloud
> Turn forth her silver lining on the night,
> And casts a gleam over this tufted Grove.   (223-5)

---

7. *Milton*, ed. Maynard Mack (New York, Prentice-Hall, 1950), p. 8.

The Lady and the Christian Idea of Nature

If Comus is a disciple of the libertine Renaissance school of Nature, the Lady is squarely in the classical-Christian tradition of Plato, Aristotle, St. Augustine, St. Thomas, and Richard Hooker, all of whom are agreed that the dictates of nature are the dictates of reason and of God.

In the *Republic* and the *Laws* Plato rejected the Sophistic antinomy between Nature and Convention and asserted that the norms of conduct that had found expression in positive and customary law were themselves "natural" insofar as they reflected the activity of mind or could be brought under the rule of reason. The *locus classicus* of Plato's rehabilitation of the idea of Nature is to be found in Book X of the *Laws*. Some people, says the Athenian Stranger,

> would say that the Gods exist not by nature, but by art, and by the laws of states, which are different in different places, according to the agreement of those who make them; and that the honourable is one thing by nature and another thing by law, and that the principles of justice have no existence at all in nature, but that mankind are always disputing about them and altering them; and that the alterations which are made by art and by law have no basis in nature, but are of authority for the moment and at the time at which they are made.—These, my friends, are the sayings of wise men, poets and prose writers, which find a way into the minds of youth. They are told by them that the highest right is might, and in this way the young fall into impieties, under the idea that the Gods are not such as the law bids them imagine; and hence arise factions, these philosophers inviting them to lead a true life according to nature, that is, to live in real dominion over others, and not in legal subjection to them.

Cleinias agrees that the citizens ought to be persuaded that law and art "both alike exist by nature, and no less than nature, if they are the creations of mind in accordance with right reason," but admits that it will be difficult to convince the multitude of this, especially in view of the prevalence of impious discourses. But the Athenian thinks he has a convincing argument:

> Nearly all of them, my friends, seem to be ignorant of the nature and power of the soul, especially in what relates to her origin; they do not know that she is among the first of things, and before all bodies, and is the chief author of their changes and transpositions.

And if this is true, and if the soul is older than the body, must not the things which are of the soul's kindred be of necessity prior to those which appertain to the body?

Cleinias. Certainly.

Athenian. Then thought and attention and mind and art and law will be prior to that which is hard and soft and heavy and light; and the great and primitive works and actions will be works of art; they will be the first, and after them will come nature and works of nature, which however is a wrong term for men to apply to them; these will follow, and will be under the government of art and mind.

Cleinias. But why is the word 'nature' wrong?

Athenian. Because those who use the term mean to say that nature is the first creative power; but if the soul turn out to be the primeval element, and not fire or air, then in the truest sense and beyond other things the soul may be said to exist by nature; and this would be true if you proved that the soul is older than the body, but not otherwise.[8]

And Plato then undertakes to prove that the soul is prior to the four elements.

Unlike Plato, Aristotle made no attempt to integrate his ethical philosophy with his metaphysics; consequently he was under no compulsion to invoke the sanction of Nature. For Aristotle the moral virtues, which are habits of the appetitive part of the soul, are " engendered in us neither by nature nor yet in violation of nature; nature gives us the capacity to receive them, and this capacity is brought to maturity by habit." [9] Aristotle's virtuous man acts not according to nature but according to *orthos logos*, which can be translated " right reason " or " right principle." It is orthos logos that determines what is the mean to be observed in all actions, and in the moral sphere orthos logos is the virtue of Prudence or Practical Wisdom.[1]

Aristotle's right reason becomes associated with Nature in the ethical system of Stoicism. It was not at all difficult for Stoicism to equate the two terms, since in their natural philosophy Nature is Reason in

---

8. Book X (889-92). I use the translation of B. Jowett, *The Dialogues of Plato* (New York, Random House, 1937), 2, 631-4.

9. *Nicomachean Ethics*, II. i. 3 (1103a); tr. H. Rackham, The Loeb Classical Library, Cambridge, Mass., Harvard University Press, 1934.

1. *Nicomachean Ethics*, VI. v (1140a-b). For a fuller discussion of right reason see below, pp. 239-40.

the sense that the Divine Fire or Logos is immanent in the universe. Man participates in this principle in a special way, since man's soul is literally a part of the Divine Fire, and the good life for man consists in observing willingly the dictates of the rational law.

Cicero, as a lawyer and statesman, was especially interested in the Stoic equation of God, Nature, Reason, and Law. In the first book of *De Legibus* he lays a solid foundation for the philosophy of law that was later to be articulated by St. Thomas Aquinas and Richard Hooker. The most learned men, says Cicero, have defined law as "the highest reason, implanted in Nature, which commands what ought to be done and forbids the opposite. This reason, when firmly fixed and fully developed in the human mind, is Law. And so they believe that Law is intelligence, whose natural function it is to command right conduct and forbid wrongdoing." [2] Since all men are originally endowed with reason (though in some it is darkened by bad habit or false belief), all men are members with the gods of the commonwealth of the universe and hence all men share in Justice, which is thus seen to derive from Nature and not from opinion.[3] The following passage sums it up neatly: "For those creatures who have received the gift of reason from Nature have also received right reason, and therefore they have also received the gift of Law, which is right reason applied to command and prohibition. And if they have received Law, they have received Justice also. Now all men have received reason; therefore all men have received Justice." [4] Cicero performed the valuable service of rescuing the term "nature" from the Epicureans, as Plato had rescued it from the Sophists and Ionian materialists. He summed up in a persuasive context the principal meanings of "nature," and thus imparted to the word an added vitality it has not wholly lost in the course of two thousand years.

The appeal to Nature by no means disappeared with the advent of Christianity. St. Paul himself speaks of "that which is against nature" (Romans 1:26) and of the Gentiles who "do by nature the things contained in the law" (Romans 2:14). Most of the early Fathers were trained in classical modes of thought, and Clement of Alexandria and Tertullian, for example, constantly appeal to Nature. Clement says that we should not exceed in our desires the limits set by nature, nor go contrary to nature. Water, not wine, he says, is the "natural, temperate, and necessary beverage." He condemns not only sodomy and pederasty as unnatural, but even shaving, boring holes in the ear

---

2. *De legibus*, I. vi. 18; tr. Clinton Walker Keyes, The Loeb Classical Library, London, Heinemann, 1928.

3. Ibid., I. x. 29, I. vii. 23, and I. x. 28.

4. Ibid., I. xii. 33.

lobes, and using cosmetics.[5] Tertullian went so far as to call the wearing of floral crowns unnatural, a view that earned him the ridicule of Hooker.[6]

It is in St. Augustine that the Christian philosophy of the moral order of Nature first takes shape. For St. Augustine Nature is neither a closed system of strict determinism hostile to man's moral nature nor a monistic or pantheistic system in which man is wholly swallowed up, but a hierarchy of individual "natures" or essences, of which man is a part, and which has been freely created out of nothing by God and rationally ordered to ends ordained by Him. St. Augustine rejected the Manichean dualism of good and evil that he had adopted in his youth and embraced the Neoplatonic idea of evil as privation. Every nature, insofar as it is a nature, he says, is good, and it is only by means of free will that evil has been introduced into the universe.

> Vice cannot be in the highest good, and cannot be but in some good. Things solely good, therefore, can in some circumstances exist; things solely evil, never; for even those natures which are vitiated by an evil will, so far indeed as they are vitiated, are evil, but in so far as they are natures they are good.
> All natures, then, inasmuch as they are, and have therefore a rank and species of their own, and a kind of internal harmony are certainly good.[7]

God made the will good, and the first evil will "was rather a kind of falling away from the work of God to its own works than any positive work. . . . Moreover, the bad will, though it be not in harmony with, but opposed to nature, inasmuch as it is a vice or blemish, yet it is true of it as of all vice, that it cannot exist except in a nature. . . ."[8] St. Thomas Aquinas adopted St. Augustine's conception of the moral order of Nature and made it an integral part of his own more systematic philosophy. The special relevance of Aquinas to our discussion of Nature as an ethical norm lies in his elaboration of the Roman conception of the law of nature. Aquinas defines law as "a rule and measure of acts, whereby man is induced to act or is restrained from acting"; hence law is something pertaining to reason, which is the first principle of human acts. There are four kinds of law: the eternal, the natural, the

5. Clement of Alexandria, *The Miscellanies*, or *Stromata*, II. xix; *The Instructor*, or *Paedagogus*, II. ii, and passim, in *The Ante-Nicene Fathers*, ed. Roberts and Donaldson, Vol. 2.

6. Richard Hooker, *Of the Laws of Ecclesiastical Polity*, II. v. 7, in *Works*, ed. Rev. John Keble (3d ed. Oxford, 1845), *1*, 307.

7. *The City of God*, XII. 3, and XII. 5; tr. Marcus Dods, New York, 1950.

8. Ibid., XIV. 11

human, and the divine. That there is an eternal law is shown by the fact that the whole community of the universe is ruled by Divine Reason: the "very Idea of the government of things in God the Ruler of the universe has the nature of a law." This eternal law is nothing else than the type of Divine Wisdom, as it directs all actions and movements. All creatures in one way or another participate in the eternal law, either by way of knowledge or by way of actions and passions, and the participation of the rational creature in the eternal law is called the natural law. In its general principles the natural law is the same for all men, but as to details, although the majority of men agree on them, there may be differences of opinion owing to the fact that reason in man may be darkened by passion or by evil habit.[9]

The reader who views the intellectual debate between Comus and the Lady against the philosophical background I have briefly sketched will not, I think, be inclined to agree with Brooks and Hardy that the Lady "does not really refute Comus's arguments." "In attempting to refute him," they say,

> she argues from an implied basic premise so different from his that its introduction amounts almost to the dismissal of the disputed problem. Comus's argument depends upon the assumption that nature's fertility is of itself, even without the co-operation of man, inexhaustible, and that any rule of restraint placed upon Nature, or upon ourselves in our acceptance of her gifts, is not Nature's own law. The Lady does not attempt to impugn the evidence with which he supports this. She proceeds directly, rather, from another basic assumption—that Nature "*Means* her provision onely to the good, / That live according to her . . . holy dictate of spare Temperance." She grounds her argument for stability through a more equal distribution of goods only on this assumed intent. Some evidence might be adduced for the moral principle of order and reason that she supposes to be operative in Nature, as against Comus's idea of riotous profusion; but she does not present it.[1]

It is indeed true that the Lady presents no evidence for the moral principle of order and reason in Nature. Why should she? Milton and his audience, and perhaps the Lady also, knew that it had been presented again and again by the most respected philosophers of the Western

9. St. Thomas Aquinas, *Summa theologica*, literally translated by Fathers of the English Dominican Province, New York, 1947. Ia-IIae, Q. 90, A. 1; Q. 91, AA. 1, 2; Q. 93, AA. 1, 3-6; Q. 94, AA. 4, 6.

1. Cleanth Brooks and John Edward Hardy, *Poems of Mr. John Milton* (New York, Harcourt, Brace, 1951), p. 221.

world. To the passages already quoted may be added two dealing
specifically with temperance, one from the classical philosopher Cicero,
one from the Christian philosopher Hooker:

> Further, as to the duty which has its source in propriety, the
> first road on which it conducts us leads to harmony with Nature
> and the faithful observance of her laws. If we follow Nature as
> our guide, we shall never go astray, but we shall be pursuing that
> which is in its nature clear-sighted and penetrating (Wisdom),
> that which is adapted to promote and strengthen society (Justice),
> and that which is strong and courageous (Fortitude). But the
> very essence of propriety is found in the division of virtue now
> under discussion (Temperance). For it is only when they agree
> with Nature's laws that we should give our approval to the move-
> ments not only of the body, but still more of the spirit.[2]

> But when we come to consider of food, as of a benefit which
> God of his bounteous goodness hath provided for all things living;
> the law of Reason doth here require the duty of thankfulness at our
> hands, towards him at whose hands we have it. And lest appetite
> in the use of food should lead us beyond that which is meet, we owe
> in this case obedience to that law of Reason, which teacheth medi-
> ocrity in meats and drinks.[3]

Hooker speaks of the law of reason, but for him as for Thomas Aquinas
nature and reason bid the same:

> Laws of Reason have these marks to be known by. Such as
> keep them resemble most lively in their voluntary actions that very
> manner of working which Nature herself doth necessarily observe
> in the course of the whole world. The works of Nature are all
> behoveful, beautiful, without superfluity or defect; even so theirs,
> if they be framed according to that which the Law of Reason
> teacheth. . . . Law rational therefore, which men commonly use
> to call the Law of Nature, meaning thereby the Law which human
> Nature knoweth itself in reason universally bound unto, which also
> for that cause may be termed most fitly the Law of Reason; this
> Law, I say, comprehendeth all those things which men by the light
> of their natural understanding evidently know, or at leastwise may
> know, to be beseeming or unbeseeming, virtuous or vicious, good
> or evil for them to do.[4]

---

2. Cicero, *De officiis*, I. xxviii. 100; tr. Walter Miller, The Loeb Classical
Library, London, Heinemann, 1913.
3. Hooker, *Ecclesiastical Polity*, I. xvi. 7, in *Works*, *1*, 283.
4. Ibid., I. viii. 9, in *Works*, *1*, 233-4.

It is not true, however, that the Lady's premise is different from Comus'. On the contrary, they agree that Nature is abundantly fertile. From this premise they each draw two conclusions. Comus declares that Nature intends her fertility " to please and state the curious taste " (714), and that men should therefore indulge their appetites indiscriminately. The Lady declares that Nature intends her bounty only for the good, and that luxury in the midst of want is an affront to justice. Perhaps neither of these inferences as to Nature's intent will seem conclusive to the modern reader, but Milton's seventeenth-century reader would have realized that in seeking to distinguish between legitimate and illegitimate claims of nature on the basis of motive the Lady is squarely in the Christian tradition. Only the good can give good things, she says (702-3), and only the good can receive good things (764-5). " In all cases of this kind," says St. Augustine, " it is not the quality of the things we use, but our motive in using them and our way of striving for them, that causes our actions to be either commendable or reprehensible." [5] The Christian ethic does not repudiate the pagan virtue of temperance, but it puts the emphasis on right motive rather than on " hitting the mark." The important question is the one asked by St. Augustine: Whom do you love? If, like Comus, you love yourself and your own pleasure, you are a member of the City of Babylon; if, like the Lady, you love God and your neighbor, you are a member of the Heavenly City of Jerusalem.[6]

The Lady thus takes up the central position in the great philosophical dialogue on the idea of nature. Comus, however, would have us believe that she belongs on the far Right:

> O foolishness of men! that lend their ears
> To those budge doctors of the *Stoic* Fur,
> And fetch their precepts from the *Cynic* Tub,
> Praising the lean and sallow Abstinence.   (706-9)

This is his usual method, of course, deliberately to confuse the issue by perverting language as he perverts everything else. There is a grain of truth in what he says; otherwise the method would not work. Cicero had regarded the long-standing enmity between Stoics and Epicureans as a contest between Virtue and Pleasure,[7] and in Richard Brathwayt's

---

5. *De doctrina Christiana*, II. 12. 19, tr. John J. Gavigan, in *The Fathers of the Church: Writings of St. Augustine*, gen. ed. Ludwig Schopp, Vol. 4. Cf. Aquinas, *Summa theologica*, I, Q. 98, A. 2 ad 3, where it is said that the place of reason is not to lessen sensual pleasure, and that a sober person does not take less pleasure than a glutton in his food.

6. St. Augustine, *The City of God*, Bk. XIX, esp. chs. 17 and 24.

7. *De finibus*, II. xiv. 44, tr. H. Rackham, The Loeb Classical Library, London, Heinemann, 1914.

Natures Embassie, published in 1621, Pandora, the spokesman for Pleasure, inveighs against " Stoick and strict contemplation." [8] From this point of view the Lady takes her stand with Stoicism against the Epicureanism of Comus. Comus, however, would have us believe that the Lady follows Stoicism in its complete suppression of all pleasure and all desire. But this is not what she says. She has just spoken not of lack of appetite but of a " well-govern'd and wise appetite " (705), and in a moment she speaks of temperance (767), not abstinence. She does not deny that nature's gifts are bounteous; she merely says that if everyone observed the mean and were content with " a moderate and beseeming share," no just man would pine with want.

Most readers no doubt will grant this much, since nothing could be more obvious. But it has been alleged that the Lady's doctrine of virginity takes back what her doctrine of temperance grants, and that this contradiction reflects some basic indecision on Milton's part. The Lady's doctrine of temperance, it is said, suggests a reconciliation of the conflicting claims of the natural and the spiritual; her doctrine of virginity a repudiation of nature. [9]

The simplest way of meeting this charge is to deny that the Lady is talking about perpetual virginity, as J. C. Maxwell and William Haller have recently done. Maxwell, reminding us of the social setting of Milton's mask, suggests that the aristocratic audience at Bridgewater Castle would have assumed as a matter of course that this thirteen-year-old girl would one day marry; the question would not arise, and the Lady's praise of chastity and virginity would be taken as the pronouncements of an idealistic young girl resolved to maintain her purity. [1] Haller, reminding us of Milton's religious background, says that Milton's Puritan teachers " held up no conception of virginity as an end or good in itself, were not concerned with celibacy, associated chastity with marriage, and urged everybody for his or her soul's good to love and marry." He is strongly of the opinion that the Lady is talking about premarital chastity; otherwise, he says, we would be forced to conclude that " Milton, a convinced Protestant if every there was one, was letting his mind work, on this one occasion, in a manner directly contrary to the whole tenor of the religious and moral training

8. Richard Brathwayt, *Natures Embassie: or, The Wilde-Mans Measure: Danced naked by twelve Satyres, with sundry others continued in the next section* (1621), p. 7.

9. Arthur Barker, *Milton and the Puritan Dilemma* (Toronto, University of Toronto Press, 1942), pp. 8-11.

1. " The Pseudo-Problem of ' Comus,' " *Cambridge Journal*, 1 (1947/8), 380.

to which he had been subjected and to the ideas which he himself began to set forth so unequivocally in 1642." [2]

E. M. W. Tillyard, on the other hand, in his recent essay on " The Action of Comus," believes that the Lady advocates complete abstinence. " The Lady thinks herself cast for the part of Belphoebe or Parthenia; Comus would like to turn her into a Hellenore, a wanton." But " Comus and the Lady are both wrong, or, if right, in ways they did not perceive." Actually, he says, her role is that of marriage, a solution of the debate between Comus and the Lady that is obliquely presented in the Epilogue through the erotic symbolism of the Hesperian tree and the Garden of Adonis. " The play concerns chastity and the Lady is the heroine. Comus advocates incontinence, Acrasia; the Lady advocates abstinence. The Attendant Spirit gives the solution, advocating the Aristotelian middle course, which for the Lady is the right one; and it is marriage." [3]

I think that Tillyard has misinterpreted the Lady's doctrine of virginity by confusing it with that of the Elder Brother. Of the Lady he says that " she is extremely fierce, speaking of her rapt spirits being kindled to a flame of sacred vehemence. She is indeed Diana or Minerva in action. Chastity too is a mystery, able to give her votaries supernatural powers." The Lady does indeed speak of her rapt spirits being kindled to a flame of sacred vehemence, but the rest of this description has been imported from the Elder Brother's encomium on chastity, which, as we shall see, has little or nothing to do with the Christian interpretation of that virtue. The Lady is not fierce, and she is not Diana or Minerva in action, and her chastity has not given her supernatural powers. These are not Milton's ideas about chastity, nor are they the Lady's, as is commonly supposed. They are the Elder Brother's, into whose mouth they are put in the play.

For the Christian doctrine of virginity is a positive not a negative one, as Milton's reading of the praises of virginity by the Church Fathers probably showed him. There are several reasons why the young Milton should have imitated his tutor Thomas Young in going to the Fathers for spiritual and intellectual nourishment, but perhaps the most compelling is that in them he would have found that blend of Platonism and Christianity that is so characteristic of his early work, and especially of *Comus*. In Clement of Alexandria, in Gregory of Nyssa, and in St. Augustine, Milton found echoes of his own high ethical idealism, his admiration for the philosophy of divine Plato, his lively faith in Christianity, and his conviction that whatever was true

---

2. "Hail, Wedded Love," *ELH*, *13* (1946), 86, 88.
3. *Studies in Milton* (London, Chatto & Windus, 1951), pp. 94, 82, 94-5.

in pagan thought could be brought into harmony with the tenets of his faith. And not least he found warm and glowing tribute to that virtue that had come to have special significance for the young man who had dedicated himself to the high calling of poet and seer.

The most characteristic themes employed by the Fathers in their praises of virginity are

1. Virginity is above nature and hence is a gift of God.
2. For this reason pride in one's virginity is blasphemous.
3. Virginity without charity is unthinkable.
4. Purity of mind and heart must accompany purity of body.
5. Virginity (which implies charity and purity) is the means by which the soul begins its ascent to God.
6. Perpetual virginity is a better state than marriage for those who are called to it, but marriage in itself is a great good.[4]

What strikes the modern reader of these treatises is their positive tone. This is not a negative and self-regarding virtue that is being hymned, but the purity of mind and body and the charity of will that he must have who would be like the angels and see God. One feels that the role assigned to the purely physical state of virginity is a secondary one, and in Gregory of Nyssa, as a matter of fact, virginity soon becomes a symbol of Platonic detachment from earthly passions and desires:

> I venture to affirm that, to one who has cleansed all the powers of his being from every form of vice, the Beauty which is essential, the source of every beauty and every good, will become visible. The visual eye, purged from its blinding humour, can clearly discern objects even on the distant sky; so to the soul by virtue of

---

4. References for each of these six points are as follows:

1. St. Augustine, *De continentia*, 1; *Confessions*, VI. 11-20; St. Ambrose, *Concerning Virgins*, I. iii. 11; Cyprian, *On the Dress of Virgins*, 4; Gregory of Nyssa, *On Virginity*, 1.

2. St. Augustine, *De virginitate*, pp. 31 ff.

3. Ibid., pp. 54-6; *De doctrina Christiana*, III. 10. 15; *Enchiridion de fide, spe et caritate*, 32, par. 121.

4. St. Augustine, *De virginitate*, 8; *De continentia*, 4-5; Gregory of Nyssa, *On Virginity*, 14, 18, 21.

5. Gregory of Nyssa, *On Virginity*, 2, 5, 11; Clement of Alexandria, *The Miscellanies*, or *Stromata*, V. iv; Cyprian (?), *Of the Discipline and Advantage of Chastity*, 7.

6. St. Ambrose, *Concerning Virgins*, I. vii. 34; Gregory of Nyssa, *On Virginity*, 8.

her innocence there comes the power of taking in that Light; and
the real Virginity, the real zeal for chastity, ends in no other goal
than this, viz. the power thereby of seeing God.[5]

One returns to *Comus* from a reading of the Fathers with new eyes.
Most of the themes are there. The point most often insisted upon by
the Fathers is that virginity is a gift of God. But there are critics who
believe that in *Comus* Milton teaches the self-sufficiency of virtue and
the superfluousness of grace. The speech of the Elder Brother is
adduced in support of this theory:[6]

> *Second Brother.* What hidden strength,
> Unless the strength of Heav'n, if you mean that?
> *Elder Brother.* I mean that too, but yet a hidden strength
> Which if Heav'n gave it, may be term'd her own.   (416-19)

The Elder Brother has allowed himself to be carried away by his
enthusiasm for the divine philosophy of Plato, but there is no reason
to suppose that these lines reproduce Milton's own thought. This is
a drama, after all, and perhaps Milton has availed himself of the opportunity to represent several points of view. This little philosopher is
something of a prig, and no doubt the older members of Milton's
audience would have smiled at his earnest faith in the self-sufficiency
of philosophic virtue. The Lady at any rate knows better:

> O welcome pure-ey'd Faith, white-handed Hope,
> Thou hov'ring Angel girt with golden wings,
> And thou unblemish't form of Chastity,
> I see ye visibly, and now believe
> That he, the Supreme good, t' whom all things ill
> Are but as slavish officers of vengeance,
> Would send a glist'ring Guardian, if need were,
> To keep my life and honour unassail'd.   (213-20)

And again,

> Eye me blest Providence, and square my trial
> To my proportion'd strength.   (329-30)

---

5. Gregory of Nyssa, *On virginity*, 11, in *A Select Library of Nicene and
Post-Nicene Fathers* (New York, 1893), Vol. 5.

6. J. S. Harrison, *Platonism in English Poetry* (New York, 1903), p. 63;
M. A. Larson, " Milton's Essential Relationship to Puritanism and Stoicism,"
Philological Quarterly, 6 (1927), 212; Paul Morand, *De Comus à Satan* (Paris,
1939), pp. 61-2; Robert M. Adams, " Reading *Comus*," *Modern Philology*, 51
(1953), 27, 29-30.

This contrast between the Elder Brother and the Lady is subtly reinforced by Milton's use of light imagery. On this night of temptation in the wilderness the stars,

> That nature hung in Heav'n, and fill'd their Lamps
> With everlasting oil to give due light
> To the misled and lonely Traveller   (198-200)

are muffled, their influence "quite damm'd up / With black usurping mists" (336-7), and Chaos reigns in "double night of darkness and of shades." The Elder Brother hopes for the light of some human habitation, then bethinks himself of the pagan doctrine that

> Virtue could see to do what virtue would
> By her own radiant light, though Sun and Moon
> Were in the flat Sea sunk.   (373-5)

"He that has light within his own clear breast," he cries in an excess of enthusiasm, "may sit i' th' centre, and enjoy bright day" (381-2).[7] The Lady, in contrast, looks to heaven for her illumination:

> I did not err, there does a sable cloud
> Turn forth her silver lining on the night,
> And casts a gleam over this tufted Grove.   (223-5)

As for the Elder Brother's doctrine of chastity, his famous speech is a eulogy of the pagan, not the Christian virtue. What Herford says of the Lady's chastity is more true of the Brother's: that it is concerned to disable its foes, not to ennoble them:[8]

> 'Tis chastity, my brother, chastity:
> She that has that, is clad in complete steel,
> And like a quiver'd Nymph with Arrows keen
> May trace huge Forests and unharbour'd Heaths,
> Infamous Hills and sandy perilous wilds,
> Where through the sacred rays of Chastity,
> No savage fierce, Bandit, or mountaineer
> Will dare to soil her Virgin purity: (420-7)

> What was that snaky-headed *Gorgon* shield
> That wise *Minerva* wore, unconquer'd Virgin,
> Wherewith she freez'd her foes to congeal'd stone

---

7. Cf. the overconfident statement of the Red Cross Knight in *The Faerie Queene*, I. i. 12: "Vertue gives her selfe light, through darkenesse for to wade."

8. C. H. Herford, "Dante and Milton," *Bulletin of the John Rylands Library*, *8*, No. 1 (1924), 15.

> But rigid looks of Chaste austerity,
> And noble grace that dash't brute violence
> With sudden adoration, and blank awe?   (447-52)

The young scholar takes advantage of the occasion to practice the art of declamation and impress his younger brother with the range of his knowledge—mythological, literary, and philosophical. The patronizing tone, the superabundance of mythological reference, the irrelevance of all this to the Lady's situation, the diction itself, all suggest the imaginative but inexperienced schoolboy. "Huge Forests," "Infamous Hills and sandy perilous wilds," "savage fierce," "grots and caverns shagg'd with horrid shades," "Blue meagre Hag, or stubborn unlaid ghost," "goblin or swart Faery of the mine": these are literary landscapes peopled with the wicked characters that have thrilled children of all times. And the literary exercise ends with a free translation from the Greek of Plato's *Phaedo*. "How charming is divine Philosophy!" exclaims the younger brother. Both of them by now have quite forgotten about their lost sister.

Charming indeed, even eloquent, but not the sage and serious doctrine of virginity. What the Lady says is that the person who lives a life of temperance and purity will exercise charity toward God and his neighbor, giving to God the praise and thanks that are His due, and to his neighbor a fair share of God's bounteous gifts:

> If every just man that now pines with want
> Had but a moderate and beseeming share
> Of that which lewdly-pamper'd Luxury
> Now heaps upon some few with vast excess,
> Nature's full blessings would be well dispens't
> In unsuperfluous even proportion,
> And she no whit encumber'd with her store,
> And then the giver would be better thank't,
> His praise due paid, for swinish gluttony
> Ne'er looks to Heav'n amidst his gorgeous feast,
> But with besotted base ingratitude
> Crams, and blasphemes his feeder.   (768-79)

This is the lesson St. Augustine had inculcated when he opposed charity to lust:

> I define charity as a motion of the soul whose purpose is to enjoy God for His own sake and one's self and one's neighbor for the sake of God. Lust, on the other hand, is a motion of the soul bent upon enjoying one's self, one's neighbor, and any creature without reference to God. The action of unbridled lust in de-

moralizing one's own soul and body is called vice; what it does to harm another is called crime. These are the two classes of sin as a whole, but vices are first. When these have weakened the soul and brought it to a kind of destitution, it leaps into crimes in order to eliminate impediments to its vices or procure help for them. Likewise, what charity does for one's own benefit is utility; what it does for our neighbor's good is called kindness. In this case, utility leads the way, for no one can give another a benefit from a supply which he does not have. The more the power of lust is destroyed, the more the power of charity is strengthened.[9]

The connection between chastity and charity established by St. Augustine sheds new light on the Lady's apostrophe to Faith, Hope, and Chastity. The few critics who have not deplored this wicked substitution have explained it in Platonic terms. Milton, says Hughes in his note on this passage (212-20), " put Chastity in the place of the third Theological Virtue of Charity or Love because he thought of that virtue in Platonic terms, as the love of the Supreme Good which chastens all inferior passions." Hughes does not cite the well-known passage from the *Apology for Smectymnuus* at this point, but it is relevant:

> Thus, from the laureat fraternity of poets, riper years and the ceaseless round of study and reading led me to the shady spaces of philosophy; but chiefly to the divine volumes of Plato, and his equal Xenophon: where, if I should tell ye what I learn't of chastity and love, I mean that which is truly so, whose charming cup is only virtue, which she bears in her hand to those who are worthy; (the rest are cheated with a thick intoxicating potion, which a certain sorceress, the abuser of love's name, carries about;) and how the first and chiefest office of love begins and ends in the soul, producing those happy twins of her divine generation, knowledge and virtue.

We note the Platonic coupling of chastity and love, which surely gives us the clue to what Milton is up to. But he goes on to speak of Christianity in the same passage:

> Last of all, not in time, but as perfection is last, that care was ever had of me, with my earliest capacity, not to be negligently trained in the precepts of Christian religion: this that I have hitherto related, hath been to show, that though Christianity had been but slightly taught me, yet a certain reservedness of natural disposition, and moral discipline, learnt out of the noblest philoso-

---

9. *De doctrina Christiana*, III. 10. 16.

phy, was enough to keep me in disdain of far less incontinences than this of the bordello. But having had the doctrine of holy scripture unfolding those chaste and high mysteries, with timeliest care infused, that the ' body is for the Lord, and the Lord for the body; ' thus also I argued to myself, that if unchastity in a woman, whom St. Paul terms the glory of man, be such a scandal and dishonor, then certainly in a man, who is both the image and glory of God, it must, though commonly not so thought, be much more deflouring and dishonorable; in that he sins both against his own body, which is the perfecter sex, and his own glory, which is in the woman; and, that which is worst, against the image and glory of God, which is in himself. Nor did I slumber over that place expressing such high rewards of ever accompanying the Lamb with those celestial songs to others inapprehensible, but not to those who were not defiled with women, which doubtless means fornication; for marriage must not be called a defilement.[1]

Plato's "noblest philosophy" teaches "moral discipline," but it is only in Christianity that the high mystery of chastity is revealed. Chastity and charity are but two sides of the same coins: or better still, two stages ("due steps") in the ascent of the soul to God.

Even if we assume that the Lady's doctrine is one of perpetual virginity, which seems unlikely, there is no need to see an irreconcilable conflict between the claims of the spiritual and the claims of the natural. From the traditional Christian point of view virginity is in a sense not a denial of nature at all, but its fulfillment. For Milton, as for Christians before and since, man looks beyond nature for the satisfaction even of his natural desires. The human intellect, says St. Thomas, naturally desires knowledge, and the highest knowledge is God; the human will naturally desires the good, and the highest good is God.[2] Hooker's statement of this orthodox commonplace would perhaps have been definitive for Protestant Englishmen:

> Capable we are of God both by understanding and will: by understanding, as He is that sovereign Truth which comprehendeth the rich treasures of all wisdom; by will, as He is that sea of Goodness whereof whoso tasteth shall thirst no more.

---

1. *Apology for Smectymnuus*, in *The Student's Milton*, ed. F. A. Patterson (New York, F. S. Crofts, 1941), pp. 549-50. Hereafter cited as Patterson. Woodhouse convincingly demonstrates the close relationship of this passage to the argument of *Comus*, in "The Argument of Milton's *Comus*," *University of Toronto Quarterly*, *11* (1942), 50-1.

2. See Etienne Gilson, *The Spirit of Medieval Philosophy*, tr. A. H. C. Downes (New York, 1936), pp. 261-2, 274-5.

For although the beauties, riches, honours, sciences, virtues, and perfections of all men living, were in the present possession of one; yet somewhat beyond and above all this there would still be sought and earnestly thirsted for. So that Nature even in this life doth plainly claim and call for a more divine perfection than either of these two that have been mentioned.[3]

Man's desire for perfect happiness is natural, Hooker continues, but it can be satisfied only by supernatural means. It is one of the paradoxes of Christian thought that God has given man a natural desire for the supernatural. From this point of view virginity—even perpetual virginity—can be considered a mean: that is, if it is done from the rule of reason, according to God's commandment, and for the sake of eternal life. But if it is done for vainglory or out of superstition, it will be excessive.[4] And presumably it will be defective if it is not accompanied by charity.

We have not yet done with the doctrine of virginity, however. On the literal level it may be taken either as premarital chastity or as perpetual virginity, as the reader prefers. On a deeper level it is a symbol of Christian purity in the widest sense, the purity that prepares the soul for the ascent to God. On a still deeper—and perhaps the ultimate—level of meaning, virginity is a symbol of the transformation of the natural order by the operation of divine grace. It is here that the thought, action, and imagery of the poem are fused, as the following pages, I trust, will make clear.

Sabrina and the Christian Idea of Grace

We had occasion to suggest a few pages back that the Elder Brother's doctrine of virginity is not necessarily Milton's or the Lady's. Most if not all critics have assumed that it is, but the action of the play hardly bears them out.[5] For the Lady does not stalk through the woods armed like one of Dian's huntresses, nor do her rigid looks of chaste austerity freeze Comus to congealed stone. Furthermore, the Spirit himself mildly rebukes the Elder Brother for supposing that his type of weapon is sufficient to quell the might of hellish charm.

Even the Lady's resources are inadequate. Critics have complained that the outcome of the temptation scene is never in doubt, that the Lady is no more really tempted by Comus than Christ is by Satan in *Paradise Regained*. But isn't anyone surprised, after so much talk of

3. *Ecclesiastical Polity*, I. xi. 3-4.
4. Aquinas, *Summa theologica*, Ia-IIae, Q. 64, A. 1 ad 3.
5. Brooks and Hardy, p. 187.

the powers of virginity, conscience, and the virtuous mind, that the Lady still sits motionless, unable to continue the journey to her Father's home? She can sit in the centre and enjoy bright day the rest of her life for all the good it will do her. This is the crucial point of the action, and the appreciation of the role of Sabrina is essential to our understanding of the poem. And no one has better taught us the deeper implication of this, as of other aspects of the poem, than A. S. P. Woodhouse.

It is over ten years since Woodhouse's " The Argument of Milton's *Comus*" appeared in the *University of Toronto Quarterly*, and it would not be too much to say that it has been the most seminal influence on Milton criticism since Tillyard's *Milton* in 1930. We must read *Comus*, Woodhouse says, in the light of Milton's religious and philosophical frame of reference. Within this frame of reference, which is relevant to all works of art in Milton's time, man is regarded as existing both in the order of nature and in the order of grace. In the order of nature man's distinctive faculty is reason, his end is earthly happiness, and he attains his end through the institution of the State. In the order of grace his distinctive faculty is faith, his end is heavenly bliss, and he attains this end through the Church. The question of the relation between these two orders was much discussed in Milton's time, and several theories were current. One could segregate the two orders and embrace both simultaneously, perhaps by means of the double-truth theory; one could segregate them and embrace one to the (practical) exclusion of the other, as Hobbes embraced nature and Luther grace. Or one could follow the orthodox tradition of St. Thomas and Richard Hooker and attempt to integrate the two orders, holding that grace fulfills rather than destroys nature. This last is what Milton, as a Christian humanist, attempted to do in *Comus*.[6]

Woodhouse is on firm ground in distinguishing the orders of nature and grace and in stressing the fact that the central Christian tradition envisages an interpenetration of the two orders rather than a swallowing up of one by the other such as is found in naturalism on the one hand and in Lutheranism and Jansenism on the other. When it comes to applying these categories to the argument of *Comus*, however, he unaccountably finds it necessary to speak of three levels of ethical and religious experience: the level of nature, the level of grace, and a level common to both nature and grace. The level of nature, he says, is symbolized by the doctrine of temperance, which in the circumstances of the poem is necessarily a doctrine of continence. But this doctrine must be rendered secure and changed from a negative to a positive concept by the doctrine of chastity, which operates on a level common

6. Woodhouse, *UTQ*, *11*, 46-71.

to both nature and grace. It is grounded in nature, but is raised by the Platonic philosophy " to the point where it can be taken over by Christianity, which sanctions the natural virtues and, by the addition of grace, carries them on to a new plane." Of this new plane " the *doctrine of virginity* becomes in the poem the illustration and symbol (but not the complete synonym)." [7]

My objection to this classification is that it is fundamentally illogical: the three levels or orders do not have the same mode of existence. For if the supernatural order is defined as the natural order raised to a supernatural level and endowed with a supernatural mode of activity,[8] the idea of a level of pure grace will have no meaning, unless it is taken to refer to the interior life of God Himself. What Woodhouse calls the level common to nature and grace is what theologians call the order of grace or the supernatural order, and it is the level on which all true Christians and no doubt many non-Christians live. The alternative to life on this level (in theological language, being " in a state of grace ") is not simply life on the natural level but life in a state of sin. The distinction between the level of nature-grace, illustrated by chastity, and the " purely religious level " of grace, illustrated by virginity, is therefore an artificial one. All human actions (including premarital chastity and perpetual virginity) done according to the rule of right reason are good, and insofar as they are good they are " natural "; all good human actions done for the love of God, which is itself a gift of God's grace, are imprinted with a supernatural character and merit eternal life.

I would suggest that the difficulties inherent in Woodhouse's scheme of levels may be surmounted by adopting a restatement of his position such as the following: The action as well as the argument of *Comus* is designed to support the Christian view that nature (which includes the so-called natural virtues) is insufficient without grace, though good in itself. The Elder Brother's doctrine of chastity, which culminates in the Platonic fancy that the body may be transmuted into soul's essence, symbolizes the highest reach of pagan thought (nature) unenlightened by Christian revelation (grace). The inadequacy of " nature " is translated into the action of the poem when it is revealed that the Brothers are powerless to release the Lady. The Lady herself represents the Christian soul on its journey to its heavenly home. On the moral level her virginity represents Christian purity of mind and body; on the spiritual level it represents the penetration of the natural order by grace, exemplified in the action of the poem by the interven-

7. Ibid., 50.

8.See Matthias J. Scheeben, *The Mysteries of Christianity*, tr. Cyril Vollert (St. Louis, Mo., 1947), pp. 740-1.

tion of the martyred virgin Sabrina, now transformed into a river-goddess. The role of the Attendant Spirit is somewhat difficult o interpretation. His part in the action, where he is able to guide th Brothers and even the Lady but is not able to free her from hellish charm, would suggest that he represents not supernatural grace bu the higher potentialities of human nature, as Comus represents th lower; specifically perhaps the human soul. He represents the inter penetration of nature and grace from the point of view of nature Sabrina from the point of view of grace. He symbolizes the knowledg of right and wrong conferred by reason; she the power of doing righ conferred by grace.

The poetry surrounding Sabrina's appearance reflects the interpene tration of nature and grace, for though it is in the pastoral mode, i has unmistakable overtones of religious ritual:

> Thrice upon thy finger's tip,
> Thrice upon thy rubied lip;   (914-15)

and the address of the Attendant Spirit to Sabrina has the form of a litany with its repeated obsecrations " By the earth-shaking Neptune' mace . . . By hoary Nereus' wrinkled look," and the supplicatio " Listen and save," which appears twice. In the Spirit's address t the Lady following the exit of Sabrina, several of the poem's basi images are brought to focus.

> Come Lady, while Heaven lends us grace,
> Let us fly this cursed place,
> Lest the Sorcerer us entice
> With some other new device.
> Not a waste or needless sound
> Till we come to holier ground.
> I shall be your faithful guide
> Through this gloomy covert wide,
> And not many furlongs thence
> Is your Father's residence,
> Where this night are met in state
> Many a friend to gratulate
> His wish't presence, and beside
> All the Swains that there abide,
> With Jigs and rural dance resort.
> We shall catch them at their sport,
> And our sudden coming there
> Will double all their mirth and cheer;
> Come let us haste, the Stars grow high,
> But night sits monarch yet in the mid sky.   (938-57)

The image of the journey is given specific religious significance, if any were needed, in the reference to grace and to the "holier ground" of the "Father's residence." [9] The imagery of light, whose subtle modulations we have already observed, continues to reinforce the main theme of the poem. It may seem surprising that after the intervention of Divine Grace "night sits monarch yet in the mid sky." But this is the human condition: perfect illumination will be found only in our heavenly home. But the light of nature shines bright ("the Stars grow high") for those under the influence of grace.

The Epilogue, as Woodhouse has said, provides the final comment on the integration of nature and grace. The Spirit's dwellingplace, for example, represents neither Heaven nor life on the purely natural level, but nature raised to a supernatural level by grace: it is situated "in the broad *fields* of the *sky*" (my italics), and it is described in nature-imagery drawn from classical and biblical descriptions of the earthly paradise. Adonis represents human nature wounded not only by original sin [1] but also by the love of God. He has renounced his earthly love (Venus) and is waxing well of his wound, which will be healed (and he become unspotted) only after earth has been exchanged for Heaven.

In contrast to Venus and Adonis are Cupid and Psyche.

> *Iris* there with humid bow,
> Waters the odorous banks that blow
> Flowers of more mingled hue
> Than her purfl'd scarf can shew,
> And drenches with *Elysian* dew
> (List mortals, if your ears be true)
> Beds of *Hyacinth* and Roses
> Where young *Adonis* oft reposes,
> Waxing well of his deep wound
> In slumber soft, and on the ground
> Sadly sits th' *Assyrian* Queen;
> But far above in spangled sheen
> Celestial *Cupid* her fam'd son advanc't,
> Holds his dear *Psyche* sweet intranc't
> After her wand'ring labours long,

---

9. "*Comus*, with all its lovely reminiscence of the high poetry of the Renaissance, is the poet's version of that sermon of spiritual wayfaring which it would have been his part to preach if he had ever in fact mounted the pulpit." William Haller, *The Rise of Puritanism* (New York, Columbia University Press, 1938), p. 318.

1. *Milton*, ed. Mack, p. 8.

> Till free consent the gods among,
> Make her his eternal Bride,
> And from her fair unspotted side,
> Two blissful twins are to be born,
> Youth and Joy; so *Jove* hath sworn.   (992-1011)

Cupid is Venus' son, but he is far above her; Psyche's side is unspotted, while Adonis is wounded; Venus sits sadly, while the offspring of Cupid and Psyche will be Youth and Joy. Surely Hanford is right in saying that Milton here sings of heavenly love.[2] Psyche has won "the crown that Virtue gives / After this mortal change"; the Lady too will become the "eternal Bride" of the God of Love "After her wand'ring labours long" in the symbolic wilderness of this world, a wilderness transformed by grace into a place where

> eternal Summer dwells,
> And West winds with musky wing
> About the cedarn alleys fling
> *Nard*, and *Cassia's* balmy smells.

---

2. James Holly Hanford, "The Youth of Milton," in *Studies in Shakespeare, Milton and Donne*, Univ. of Mich. Pubs. Lang. and Lit., *1* (New York 1925), 152.

2

Paradise Lost

THE study of the idea of nature in *Paradise Lost* divides itself into three distinct but closely related topics: cosmology, or the nature of the universe; psychology, or the nature of man; and finally, the tension that is created first by the fall of Lucifer and then by the fall of Adam between the unfallen essence or nature of both angel and man and the facts of their fallen existence. This distinction between essence and existence is central to the structure of *Paradise Lost*, and it operates on all levels. On the rhetorical level it corresponds to the antithesis between nature and art which runs throughout the poem. On the narrative level it corresponds to the distinction between unfallen and fallen man. On the philosophical level it refers to the distinction between what a thing is, considered as an object of intelligibility, and the act of being (existence) of that thing.[1] We shall see as we proceed in our third section that the distinction between essence and existence as I have just stated it is far too simple and categorical to take account of the complexities of the poem. Indeed, one measure of Milton's success in justifying the ways of God to man may be the degree to which the poem succeeds in transcending the conflict between the nature of man in the Garden and the existence of man in the Wilderness of this world.

The Nature of the Universe

The cosmology of *Paradise Lost* is intimately related to the moral and artistic design of the poem. The great series of contrasts on which the poem is built—creation versus destruction, light versus darkness, order versus disorder—find their objective correlatives in the firm outlines of the Ptolemaic universe, which was "Won from the void and formless infinite" (III, 12), and whose limits were "circumscribe[d]"

---

1. Jacques Maritain, *An Introduction to Philosophy*, tr. E. I. Watkin (London, 1930), pp. 200-1. Strictly speaking, every created being is composed of essence and existence, and it is therefore not philosophically accurate to speak of the distinction between unfallen and fallen man in terms of essence and existence. I believe, however, that in the case of *Paradise Lost* it is illuminating to do so.

(VII, 266) by the Divine Architect. The poet begins, appropriately enough, by reminding his readers

> In the Beginning how the Heav'ns and Earth
> Rose out of *Chaos*,   (I, 9-10)

and in the very last book Adam compares the final redemptive process to the original creation:

> O goodness infinite, goodness immense!
> That all this good of evil shall produce,
> And evil turn to good; more wonderful
> Than that which by creation first brought forth
> Light out of darkness!   (XII, 469-73)

And throughout the poem the reader is never allowed to forget that just outside the limits of the created universe lies the wild kingdom of Chaos and Old Night, those fierce anarchs who are constantly striving to win back from the Creator the warring elements that His creative reason has fashioned into an ordered whole.

Recent scholarly studies of the idea of physical nature in *Paradise Lost* have tended to obscure the fact that the poem's cosmology, like its anthropology and psychology, is largely traditional. In spite of the work of McColley, Bush, and others, there are still critics who insist on finding all kinds of esoteric doctrines in the poem. It is necessary for a proper understanding of the poem, I think, to realize that its ideology is pretty squarely in the central tradition of Christian speculation. This is by no means a new idea, of course, but many claims for Neoplatonic, Hermetic, Stoic, and other kinds of "influence" have been allowed to go unchallenged.

To begin with the idea of matter, we know from *The Christian Doctrine* that Milton rejected the orthodox doctrine that God created matter *ex nihilo*, and adopted the view that matter is *ex Deo*, or an "efflux of the Deity."[2] Fortunately the critic of *Paradise Lost* need not determine whether philosophical or merely philological considerations compelled Milton to adopt this theory,[3] since the question of the origin of matter is left open in the poem itself. It is true that there are several passages that can be interpreted in such a way as to bring them into conformity with *The Christian Doctrine*, but these passages are also, I think, capable of another interpretation. The first is from the beginning of Raphael's famous "scale of nature" speech in Book V:

---

2. *The Christian Doctrine*, I, vii, in Patterson, p. 976.

3. It has been suggested that some at least of the heresies in *The Christian Doctrine* derive from Milton's philological exegesis of Scripture rather than from his philosophical studies. See George N. Conklin, *Biblical Criticism and Heresy in Milton* (New York, 1949).

> O *Adam*, one Almighty is, from whom
> All things proceed, and up to him return,
> If not deprav'd from good, created all
> Such to perfection, one first matter all,
> Indu'd with various forms, various degrees
> Of substance, and in things that live, of life;
> But more refin'd, more spiritous, and pure,
> As nearer to him plac't or nearer tending
> Each in thir several active Spheres assign'd,
> Till body up to spirit work, in bounds
> Proportion'd to each kind.   (V, 469-79)

In *The Christian Doctrine* we read:

> Matter, like the form and nature of the angels itself, proceeded incorruptible from God . . .
> For not even divine virtue and efficiency could produce bodies out of nothing, according to the commonly received opinion, unless there had been some bodily power in the substance of God; since no one can give to another what he does not himself possess.[4]

And Milton maintains that the Hebrew, Greek, and Latin words for "create" "uniformly signify to create out of matter," i. e. not out of nothing. But the reader of *Paradise Lost* cannot be expected to know what meaning Milton attached to the word "create" in *The Christian Doctrine*, and Raphael's words, when read in the context of the resounding Christian commonplaces of the poem, sound like an orthodox assertion that all things come from God. As for the notion of "one first matter all," it is, or can be construed as, the scholastic *prima materia* and as such is perfectly compatible with, though it need not imply, the theory of *creatio ex nihilo*.

The second passage which can bear either an orthodox or a heretical interpretation is from the speech of God the Father when He sends the Son to create the world.

> Boundless the Deep, because I am who fill
> Infinitude, nor vacuous the space.
> Though I uncircumscrib'd myself retire,
> And put not forth my goodness, which is free
> To act or not, Necessity and Chance
> Approach not mee, and what I will is Fate.
>   (VII, 168-73)

Denis Saurat has maintained that this passage .refers to the "retrac-

4. I, vii, in Patterson, pp. 976-7.

tion " theory of the Zohar.[5] According to this theory, God is infinitely extended, and in order to make room for other beings He must retract or withdraw part of his essence. But as C. S. Lewis has very cogently pointed out, the passage does not say that the space is vacuous because God has withdrawn, but that it is not vacuous although he has withdrawn.[6] Lewis adds that this may amount to saying that there is potentiality in God—a notion that is countenanced in *The Christian Doctrine* where it is said that matter may be considered as a " bodily power " of God or as a " virtue " " substantially inherent " in God,[7] but which is certainly not obtrusive in the poem.

Lewis, who has succeeded so well in defending the orthodoxy of *Paradise Lost*, has weakened his own case unnecessarily in allowing that the doctrine that matter is ex Deo " presumably appears in *Paradise Lost*, V, 403 and following—a fugitive colour on the poem which we detect only by the aid of external evidence from the *De Doctrina*." [8] The passage in question is the one in which Raphael explains to Adam that angels also require food:

> and food alike those pure
> Intelligential substances require
> As doth your Rational; and both contain
> Within them every lower faculty
> Of sense, whereby they hear, see, smell, touch, taste,
> Tasting concoct, digest, assimilate,
> And corporeal to incorporeal turn.   (V, 407-13)

It is difficult to see what this has to do with the doctrine that matter is substantially inherent in God, since Raphael here is speaking only of the angels. As a matter of fact, he specifically limits the application of this doctrine to created things:

> For know, whatever was created, needs
> To be sustain'd and fed . . :   (V, 414-15)

In *Paradise Lost*, then, matter is just there. It is nowhere stated that it was created out of nothing, nor is it said that it is an efflux of the Deity. The question, if it arises, is left unanswered, but of course for the orthodox Christian reader the question does not arise. He knows that matter was created ex nihilo, and it is not the purpose of a Christian epic poem to disturb settled beliefs.

5. *Milton: Man and Thinker* (London, 1944), pp. 102-4.
6. C. S. Lewis, *A Preface to Paradise Lost* (London, Oxford University Press, 1942), p. 86.
7. I, vii, in Patterson, p. 976.
8. Lewis, *Preface*, p. 88.

The actual creative process is described in VII, 216-557. This account, which closely follows Genesis, is preceded by a view of Chaos:

> the vast immeasurable Abyss
> Outrageous as a Sea, dark, wasteful, wild,
> Up from the bottom turn'd by furious winds
> And surging waves, as Mountains to assault
> Heav'n's highth, and with the Centre mix the Pole.
>
> (VII, 211-15)

The biblical warrant for the conception of Chaos is the second verse of Genesis: "And the earth was without form, and void; and darkness was upon the face of the deep." In the course of centuries Christian thought had enriched this simple statement with the aid of Platonic and Ovidian speculations about the original chaos, and by Milton's time it was customary to describe the Creation as the giving of forms to formless matter.[9] Ovid's contribution to the description of the creative process in *Paradise Lost* has been judiciously weighed by Davis P. Harding,[1] but Plato's has been vastly exaggerated by many critics. The cosmology of *Paradise Lost* is separated from that of Platonism, whether ancient or modern, by the same gulf that separates all classical from Christian cosmological systems.[2] Milton's cosmology envisages no conflict between reason and matter and draws no sharp distinction between the intelligible world and the sensible, as Plato's does. For Milton the universe is completely rational because it is the embodiment of an exemplar in the Mind of Omnipotent Deity: in this world nothing happens at random or by accident, because God's Providence is all-pervasive; evil is caused not by an Enemy co-eternal with God, and not by fluctuating matter, but by the will of an intelligent creature. And even the chaos of evil caused by man or angel the Almighty Maker can ordain " His dark materials to create more Worlds " (II, 916). For Plato, on the other hand, " the generation of this universe was a mixed result of the combination of Necessity and Reason," where Necessity refers to the irrational element of chance and blind physical causation. Reason "persuades" Necessity to guide "the *greatest part* of the things that become towards what is best,"[3] while in the Christian universe of *Paradise Lost* everything is for the best. Fifteen centuries of Christian speculation have intervened between Plato and Milton, and

9. George W. Whiting, *Milton's Literary Milieu* (Chapel Hill, N. C., 1939), pp. 17 ff.

1. *Milton and the Renaissance Ovid*, pp. 67-72.

2. See pp. 272-5, below.

3. *Timaeus*, 48A, tr. F. M. Cornford, *Plato's Cosmology* (London, Kegan Paul, 1937), p. 160.

for all the heterodoxy of *The Christian Doctrine, Paradise Lost* is closer in spirit to Aquinas than to Plato. Plato's universe is eternal and self-sufficient; Milton's was created in time and will be destroyed in time, and it depends for its existence at every moment on the active intervention of a personal God. For Plato the historical process is ultimately meaningless, since it is destined to be repeated again and again as the heavenly bodies return to their original positions and begin once more the Great Year of their revolutions. In *Paradise Lost* it is the classicist Satan who adopts this Platonic theory of the Great Year. He says that the angels are

> self-begot, self-rais'd
> By our own quick'ning power, when fatal course
> Had circl'd his full Orb, the birth mature
> Of this our native Heav'n, Ethereal Sons.   (V, 860-3)

For Milton, on the other hand, the historical process is charged with significance, and every human actor has his part to play in the drama of salvation, until at the end God shall raise

> New Heav'ns, new Earth, Ages of endless date
> Founded in righteousness and peace and love,
> To bring forth fruits Joy and eternal Bliss.
>   (XII, 549-51)

The Chaos of *Paradise Lost* is both like and unlike Plato's. For both Milton and Plato it represents the blind, purposeless activity of matter considered in abstraction from mind, but in Plato's universe this recalcitrant element is not completely subdued or "persuaded" by Reason: it is that part of the structure of the visible universe that cannot be understood. Milton's Chaos is a more subtle conception, and I think it is fair to say that it is a more important element in the poetic universe of *Paradise Lost* than in the physical universe. As a cosmological idea, it is "The Womb of nature and perhaps her Grave" (II, 911), but it has no part to play in the physical universe as it now exists. It is rather as a moral idea that it functions—as a symbol of what happens in the moral order when man rebels against God's law. Charles Williams and B. Rajan have both pointed out that with the Fall chaos comes into the microcosm: [4]

> They sat them down to weep, nor only Tears
> Rain'd at thir Eyes, but high Winds worse within

4. Charles Williams, Introduction to *The English Poems of John Milton*, The World's Classics, London, Oxford University Press, 1940, and B. Rajan, *Paradise Lost and the Seventeenth Century Reader* (London, Chatto & Windus, 1947), p. 74.

Began to rise, high Passions, Anger, Hate,
Mistrust, Suspicion, Discord, and shook sore
Thir inward State of Mind, calm Region once
And full of Peace, now toss't and turbulent:

(IX, 1121-6)

Chaos is mentioned at least eight times in Book X, and throughout the poem it is pictured as an ally of Satan, waiting with him its chance to wrest the world away from the powers of light and order.

Ruth Wallerstein has asked the question how far Milton's conception of creation in *Paradise Lost* can be considered Neoplatonic. She herself believes that one can at least say of Milton's conception of nature that it "belongs to that family of Platonic thought in which creation is the purely positive outflow of God's love."[5] No exception can be taken to this statement if it means no more than that Milton's God loves to create and loves His creation. But we should not go on to infer from this that the creation in *Paradise Lost* is a necessary outflow of God's love. A. O. Lovejoy has reminded us that the God of *Paradise Lost* is the self-sufficient Deity of Aristotle and not the source of Neoplatonic emanations.[6] As Adam tells God,

Thou in thyself art perfet, and in thee
Is no deficience found . . .
No need that thou
Shouldst propagate, already infinite;
And through all numbers absolute, though One.

(VIII, 415-16; 419-21)

The term "Neoplatonic" can hardly be applied to the conception of nature in *Paradise Lost* without being misleading, for the differences between the two systems are more important and more striking than the similarities. *Paradise Lost* and Neoplatonism have in common the hierarchical conception of reality and a sort of monism of matter and spirit, but they differ radically in their ideas of the creative process and in the mode of existence which each attributes to Nature. In Plotinus Nature or *physis* is the soul of the phenomenal world. In Proclus, whose system of triadic emanation is much more elaborate than that of Plotinus, Nature is the fourth in a series of five emanations ranging from the intelligible cause of things at the top to sensible things at the bottom. "Nature, therefore," he says,

---

5. *Seventeenth Century Poetic* (Madison, University of Wisconsin Press, 1951), p. 225.
6. *The Great Chain of Being* (Cambridge, Mass., 1936), pp. 160-1. Lovejoy cites the speech of Adam quoted in the text.

is the last of the causes which fabricate this corporeal-formed and sensible essence. She is also the boundary of the extent of incorporeal essences, and is full of reasons and powers through which she directs and governs mundane beings. And she is a Goddess indeed, in consequence of being deified, but she has not immediately the subsistence of a deity. For we call divine bodies Gods, as being the statues of Gods. But she governs the whole world by her powers, containing the heavens indeed in the summit of herself, but ruling over generation through the heavens; and every where weaving together partial natures with wholes.

Through Nature "the most inanimate beings participate of a certain soul, and such things as are corruptible, remain perpetually in the world, being held together by the causes of forms which she contains." Nature is "an incorporeal essence, inseparable from bodies, containing the reasons or productive principles of them, and incapable of perceiving itself." [7]

Marjorie Nicolson, in an influential article on Milton and Hobbes written some thirty years ago, maintained that Milton and the Cambridge Platonists adopted the Neoplatonic idea of a world-soul described above in order to offset the mechanical implications of the Cartesian philosophy.[8] One can readily agree that the conception of the "scale of Nature" found in *Paradise Lost* is directly opposed to the sharp dichotomy between matter and spirit contemplated by Descartes, but there does not appear to be any indication at all in the poem of a "spirit of Nature" such as Miss Nicolson speaks of. To Milton, she says, "the Spirit of Nature is a power less than God, yet part of him, incorporeal, pervading the matter of the universe, and by means of the direction of the power of God directing and ordering the parts of the universe in a way that is not mechanical." And again, "Nature is purposive . . . she is in some ways equivalent to God . . . and in the great hymn of Adam and Eve, it seems, indeed, as if Nature *were* God." [9] No such conception is presented in *Paradise Lost*, least of all in the hymn of Adam and Eve in Book V. It is not Nature as God, or God as Nature, that Adam celebrates, but Nature as the work of God, and God as the Creator of Nature:

> These are thy glorious works, Parent of good,
> Almighty, thine this universal Frame,
> Thus wondrous fair; thyself how wondrous then!

7. *The Commentaries of Proclus on the Timaeus of Plato*, tr. Thomas Taylor (London, 1820), *1*, 9-10.

8. "Milton and Hobbes," *Studies in Philology, 23* (1926), 422.

9. Ibid., pp. 422, 421.

Unspeakable, who sit'st above these Heavens
To us invisible or dimly seen
In these thy lowest works, yet these declare
Thy goodness beyond thought, and Power Divine:

(V, 153-9)

Nature is nowhere addressed in this hymn, and the word itself appears only once, in the phrase "Elements the eldest birth / Of Nature's Womb" (V, 180-1). The expression "Nature's Womb" apparently refers to Chaos, which had been described in Book II as "The Womb of nature and perhaps her Grave" (II, 911). And the word "Nature" refers to the sum total of "natures" or "essences," that is, to Nature as an abstraction, not to Nature as an entity.

Walter Clyde Curry, in a series of learned articles, has also tried to trace the cosmology of *Paradise Lost* to Neoplatonic sources. Not content with Hesiod, Plato, and Ovid as sources for Milton's "Chaos and Old Night," he maintains that "Chaos may be identified with the second divine principle of the 'intelligible triad,' and Night with the first or summit of the so-called 'intelligible and at the same time intellectual triad' of the Neoplatonic system."[1] Milton's description of Night as "eldest of things" (II, 962) is philosophically precise, says Curry, since in the Neoplatonic system the separation of essences into a multitude of beings—i. e. the production of *things*—takes place for the first time only when Mixture, the third hypostasis of the first triad, pours forth intelligible essences and powers into supercelestial place or Night. Hence Night really is eldest of *things*. Thus, concludes Curry, Milton has established "his imaginative structure upon a stable philosophical ground."[2] This is very ingenious, but it fails to take account of the fact that in describing the creation in Book VII Raphael speaks of "Light Ethereal" as "first of things" (VII, 243-4). Is there a philosophical distinction between "eldest of things" and "first of things?" I suspect not. When we read in the poem that Night is "eldest of things" I take it that we think of the darkness upon the face of the deep in the second verse of Genesis. And much later in the poem, when we read that light is "first of things," we think of the first creative act in the third verse of Genesis.

In another article Curry has brought his learning to bear on the "scale of Nature," but once again we must question the value of his results. For example, we are told to look to the *Fons Vitae* of the eleventh-century Jewish philosopher Avencebrol for the "ultimate" source of the Miltonic postulation of

---

1. "Milton's Chaos and Old Night," *Journal of English and Germanic Philology, 46* (1947), 39.
2. Ibid., p. 52.

> one first matter all,
> Indu'd with various forms, various degrees
> Of substance, and in things that live, of life;
> But more refin'd, more spiritous, and pure,
> As nearer to him plac't or nearer tending. (V, 472-6)

"But," he adds, "the channels through which these distinctive ideas were transmitted from Avencebrol to Milton are not clearly defined." [3] It is fair to ask, I think, just what relevance to *Paradise Lost* Avencebrol's "emanative and degenerative monism" [4] has. It is true that Avencebrol has a *materia universalis*, which may perhaps be equated with Raphael's "one first matter," but he also has a *forma universalis*, of which we hear nothing in *Paradise Lost*, which speaks only of "various forms, various degrees / Of substance" (V, 473-4). Surely it is going far afield to relate *Paradise Lost* to the Fons Vitae when all that need be said is that the conception of a first matter indued with various forms is common to all scholastic philosophies, Platonic and Aristotelian alike. What distinguishes Milton the theologian from the scholastics is that he regards this first matter not as a creatio ex nihilo but as an efflux of the Deity; we have already seen, however, that this is an idea that does not make its appearance in *Paradise Lost*. As for the doctrine that angels are composed of matter and form, it was the accepted theory of the Franciscan school as late as the sixteenth century. As a matter of fact, St. Bonaventure held that not only the angels but the soul of man as well were composed of both matter and form,[5] a theory that was vigorously attacked by St. Thomas Aquinas. It may be that St. Bonaventure is at more pains than Raphael to distinguish between "corporeal" matter and "spiritual" matter, but Raphael seems to be making this distinction when he says that the angels "corporeal to incorporeal turn" (V, 413). Curry knows all this, of course, and he himself has called attention to the "influence" of Avencebrol on the Franciscan school. Where he is vulnerable, I think, is in a tendency to overstress the esoteric nature of the cosmology of *Paradise Lost*. He says that Milton's conception of one first matter has a long and respectable history, but he fails to indicate just how respectable it is.

Woodhouse, the most recent investigator of Milton's views on the creation, suggests that Milton's rejection of the Platonic "hypothesis of an independently pre-existent matter" and of the Neoplatonic doc-

---

3. "Milton's Scale of Nature," in *Stanford Studies in Language and Literature 1941*, ed. Hardin Craig (Stanford University, 1941), p. 180.

4. Avencebrol's philosophy is so characterized by Maurice De Wulf, *History of Mediaeval Philosophy*, tr. E. C. Messenger (London, 1926), *I*, 228.

5. Anton Pegis, *St. Thomas and the Problem of the Soul in the Thirteenth Century* (Toronto, 1934), pp. 33-4.

trine of necessary emanation led him to construct a system that has certain affinities with "the tradition of theistic monism, of which the Stoics are the ancient representatives, and Spinoza the modern."[6] Woodhouse is too careful a scholar to fall into the trap of forcing all of Milton's thought into conformity with a philosophical system with which it has two or three doctrines in common, and he is therefore at pains to dissociate Milton from materialistic monism and from the strict determinism of Spinoza. It might be thought that the Stoic tradition, thus redefined, somewhat resembled *Hamlet* without the Prince of Denmark, but Woodhouse several pages later states that Milton turned from the avowed dualism of Platonism and the concealed dualism of Augustine "to a form of monism which adheres rather to the long tradition of thought extending from the Stoics to Spinoza" (p. 233). Rather than quibble over names, however, let us examine the specific doctrines that Woodhouse sees in *The Christian Doctrine* and *Paradise Lost*.

"Among the inescapable implications which Milton does not seek to evade is the admission of an element of corporeality in the Deity" (p. 222). Woodhouse cites the passage from *The Christian Doctrine* in which Milton says that there must be "some bodily power in the substance of God, since no one can give to another what he does not possess," and he remarks that "here the parallel is astonishingly close with Spinoza, who denies the immateriality of God because, if God's nature were essentially different from that of the world, he could not be its cause" (p. 223). But it is one thing to say that there is a bodily power in the substance of God, as Milton does, and another to say that body is "that mode which expresses in a certain determined manner the essence of God in so far as he is considered as an extended thing."[7] A necessary corollary of Spinoza's formulation is the eternality of matter; Milton, on the other hand, clearly postulates a creation in time which involved making actual what before was merely potential. The two conceptions are quite different.

This brings us to Woodhouse's second and third points, that Milton allows potentiality in God and disorder in "the presence of God" (pp. 223-4). Potentiality we may grant from the evidence of *The Christian Doctrine* without admitting that it is either explicit or implicit in *Paradise Lost*; as for disorder, we shall have to examine the proofs. Speaking of *The Christian Doctrine* Woodhouse says that Milton there "notices the objection that in its original state 'substance was imper-

6. "Notes on Milton's Views on the Creation: The Initial Phases," *Philological Quarterly*, 28 (1949), 222.

7. Spinoza, *Ethics*, Pt. II, Def. 1, tr. A. Boyle, Everyman's Library (New York, Dutton).

fect,' but can find no better answer than to retort that the difficulty
remains just as formidable if we suppose God to have 'produced it out
of nothing in an imperfect state,' which merely removes the reproach
from God as material, to God as efficient cause. In *Paradise Lost* [he
goes on to say] an answer has been found: the matter in its disordered
state is indeed in God's presence, but not in his *active* presence. He
has not chosen to put forth as yet his creative power, but, retired
within himself, has voluntarily left the matter a prey to necessity or
chance" (p. 226). But the fact of the matter is that in *The Christian
Doctrine* Milton did find an answer to the objection. Shortly after the
passage quoted by Woodhouse Milton says: "It is not true, however,
that matter was in its own nature originally imperfect; it merely received embellishment from the accession of forms, which are themselves
material."[8] What this passage demonstrates is that *The Christian
Doctrine* cannot be read as a gloss on *Paradise Lost*: the conception in
the treatise of a first matter which is in its own nature perfect and
requires merely the embellishment of forms is hardly compatible, to
say the least, with the conception in the poem of

> the vast immeasurable Abyss
> Outrageous as a Sea, dark, wasteful, wild,
> Up from the bottom turn'd by furious winds
> And surging waves, as Mountains to assault
> Heav'n's highth, and with the Centre mix the Pole.
>
> (VII, 211-15)

What did Milton "really" think? Of one thing we may be certain:
Paradise Lost is not *The Christian Doctrine* versified: Chaos has a
much more complex function in the poem than it has in the theological
treatise.

One further corollary of Milton's "monism" requires scrutiny: his
belief in "the inherent goodness of the matter."[9] This is clearly stated
in *The Christian Doctrine*, and it is, as Woodhouse points out, a staple
of the orthodox Christian tradition. But, like that of Chaos, the role
of matter in the poem is more complex than in the treatise. M. M.
Mahood, in her interesting discussion of Milton as a Baroque artist,
defines Milton's attitude toward matter in this way:

> Milton's humanism, however, is that of the seventeenth century,
> not of the sixteenth. Worldliness and otherworldliness are so
> joined in his nature, that he seeks to transcend physical limitations
> even while he asserts his faith in matter. The vitalising spirit with

8. *The Christian Doctrine*, I, vii, in Patterson, p. 976.
9. Woodhouse, *PQ, 28,* 228.

which his imagination imbues all matter is one means by which
he resolves the conflict. The same paradox is at the root of other
features in his poetry, and helps to explain one in particular which
baffles and even repels the present-day reader: the solidity of
Milton's Heaven and its denizens.[1]

Miss Mahood is right, I think, but only insofar as she is talking about
Milton's attitude toward matter per se; in the poem Milton frequently
uses physical nature to symbolize a state of mind or an attitude, and on
this symbolic level there is a decided antithesis between the material
and the spiritual, the literal and the metaphoric. The best-known
example of the antithesis is Milton's attitude toward religious worship;
here, indeed, the rejection of the material is quite literally intended:

> And chiefly Thou O Spirit, that dost prefer
> Before all Temples th' upright heart and pure   (I, 17-18)

> So Law appears imperfet, and but giv'n
> With purpose to resign them in full time
> Up to a better Cov'nant, disciplin'd
> From shadowy Types to Truth, from Flesh to Spirit,
> From imposition of strict Laws, to free
> Acceptance of large Grace, from servile fear
> To filial, works of Law to works of Faith.   (XII, 300-6)

A hostile critic would be entitled to ask, I think, why, if Milton thought
so highly of matter, he allowed it to play so little part in the worship
of his " corporeal " God. And the sympathetic critic could only answer
that on this point Milton's unrelenting Protestantism, felt to the very
depths of his being, had triumphed over his abstract belief in " the
inherent goodness of the matter."

Other examples, which hover between the literal and the symbolic,
are the destruction of Paradise by the Flood, which is paralleled by
the destruction of Satan's " perverted World " on the Last Day, and
the contrast between Eve's physical beauty and Adam's intellectual
beauty. For the most part, however, the antithesis is clearly intended
not to be taken on the literal level. A good example is the use of gold:

> *Mammon* led them on,
> *Mammon*, the least erected Spirit that fell
> From heav'n, for ev'n in heav'n his looks and thoughts
> Were always downward bent, admiring more
> The riches of Heav'n's pavement, trodd'n Gold,
> Than aught divine or holy else enjoy'd

---

1. *Poetry and Humanism* (New Haven, Yale University Press, 1950), p. 203.

> In vision beatific: by him first
> Men also, and by his suggestion taught,
> Ransack'd the Centre, and with impious hands
> Rifl'd the bowels of thir mother Earth
> For Treasures better hid. Soon had his crew
> Op'n'd into the Hill a spacious wound
> And digg'd out ribs of Gold. Let none admire
> That riches grow in Hell; that soil may best
> Deserve the precious bane.   (I, 678-92)

The rejection of gold is explicit, but at the same time we learn that it is found in Heaven. In Books III and IV we hear even more of it:

> Meanwhile
> The World shall burn, and from her ashes spring
> New Heav'n and Earth, wherein the just shall dwell
> And after all thir tribulations long
> See golden days, fruitful of golden deeds,
> With Joy and Love triumphing, and fair Truth.
>   (III, 333-8)

> With solemn adoration down they cast
> Thir Crowns inwove with Amarant and Gold, (III, 351-2)

> *Satan* from hence now on the lower stair
> That scal'd by steps of Gold to Heav'n Gate   (III, 540-1)

> And all amid them stood the Tree of Life,
> High eminent, blooming Ambrosial Fruit
> Of vegetable Gold;   (IV, 218-20)

>   half her swelling Breast
> Naked met his under the flowing Gold
> Of her loose tresses hid: (IV, 495-7)

It is not hard to see that the value of gold or any other material thing depends on one's attitude toward it:

> So little knows
> Any, but God alone, to value right
> The good before him, but perverts best things
> To worst abuse, or to thir meanest use.   (IV, 201-4)

This is precisely the view of St. Augustine, on whom Milton is supposed to have turned his back because of Augustine's alleged failure " really to rehabilitate the creature." [2] Here is a passage from *The City of God*: "Just as the covetous man forsakes justice and loves gold, the gold

2. Woodhouse, *PQ*, *28*, 232.

being not in fault but the man, even so is it in all other created things. They are all good, and may be loved well, or badly; well, when our love is moderate; badly, when it is inordinate" (XV.xxii). *Paradise Lost* does not deny the "inherent goodness" of matter; at the same time, the doctrine can hardly be said to be the touchstone of Milton's ethical and religious philosophy. Indeed, Milton's "faith in matter" is much less evident than his desire "to transcend physical limitations." There is a systematic progression in the epic from the material to the spiritual, from the literal to the metaphoric: from the abstract-made-concrete of Hell to the concrete-made-abstract of Heaven; from the literal seeds of the Garden to the metaphoric seeds of Grace; from the literal fruit of the Garden to the metaphoric fruits Joy and Love in Heaven; from the earthly Paradise itself to the metaphoric Paradise within. In the moral universe of *Paradise Lost* the inherent goodness of matter counts for little; as in *Comus*, it is the human attitude toward created things that is crucial, and it is in these terms that Milton portrays the Fall.[3]

It ought to be recognized once and for all that Milton is a poet, not a philosopher, and that the language of *Paradise Lost* is often called upon to carry more weight than it can bear from a philosophical point of view. We find a good example of the imprecision of the poem's philosophical vocabulary in the "scale of Nature" passage quoted earlier:

> O Adam, one Almighty is, from whom
> All things proceed, and up to him return,
> If not deprav'd from good, created all
> Such to perfection, one first matter all,
> Indu'd with various forms, . . .   (V, 469-73)

"Proceed" suggested Neoplatonic emanationism, and "created" the free activity of the Christian God. Curry points out that for Milton and other seventeenth-century Platonists the theory of emanation did not conflict with the idea of a historical creation. It was thought that matter and chaos were derived from God by an emanative process but that the ordering of the visible universe required a special volitional act of God.[4] In the lines just quoted, however, it is not said that "first matter" proceeds from God but that all "things" both "proceed" from God and are "created" by Him. It seems to be part of Raphael's strategy with Adam, and perhaps of Milton's strategy with us, to slur over vexed questions of science and metaphysics in order to concentrate on the great moral and theological truths:

> Solicit not thy thoughts with matters hid,
> Leave them to God above, him serve and fear . . .
>   (VIII, 167-8)

---

3. See below, pp. 246-9.   4. Curry, *JEGP*, *46*, 46, n. 49.

Even the dialogue on astronomy in Book VIII, which has often been cited as an example of Milton's complete familiarity with and sympathy for contemporary scientific theory, McColley has shown to be pretty old-fashioned in its ideas. Raphael does not even mention the Tychonic, or geoheliocentric theory, which, rather than the Ptolemaic, was the chief rival to Copernicanism; and in describing the Copernican theory he speaks of the three motions of the earth, an hypothesis that had long been superseded by the Keplerian theory of two motions.[5]

The truth of the matter is, as Basil Willey long ago said, that Milton "lived in a moral rather than a physical world."[6] Milton is more interested in human nature than in physical nature, and in *Paradise Lost* he is more concerned to construct a poetic universe than to philosophize about the universe in poetry. Like Plato in the *Timaeus*, he has his eye on the great ethical and religious doctrines, and the natural philosophy, such as it is, functions on the philosophical level as a buttress for the ethics, while on the poetic level it furnishes a vast array of symbols that can be manipulated so as to reinforce the total meaning of the poem. It is not surprising, therefore, that the natural philosophy of *Paradise Lost* should be, for the most part, traditional and orthodox, or at least not heretical, since the moral and religious values with which the poem concerns itself are themselves traditional, as we shall see. To speak of the poem's affinities with Platonism ancient and modern, Hermeticism, Cabbalism, Rosicrucianism, Behmenism, Stoicism, and whatnot is unnecessarily to obscure the analogical relationship between the various levels on which the great Christian epic moves. The question of where Milton actually derived his ideas is probably incapable of solution. Fortunately we need not know in order to read the poetry. The only relevant question is what function do the ideas have in the poem itself? And surely the answer to this is that their principal purpose is to reinforce the great moral and theological truths with which the poem is concerned, and to which we must now turn our attention.

The Nature of Man

In the hierarchy of natures envisaged by medieval philosophy, man occupied a unique position as a being who united in his human nature the sensitive nature of the creatures below him and the intellectual nature of the creatures above him in the scale. Man is thus poised between two worlds: earth, the home of the animals, with whom he

5. Grant McColley, "The Astronomy of *Paradise Lost*," *Studies in Philology*, 34 (1937), 209-47.

6. *The Seventeenth Century Background* (London, Chatto & Windus, 1934), p. 239.

shares his physical body and his nutritive and sensitive powers; and heaven, the home of the angels, with whom he shares his intellectual powers. Corresponding to this twofold (though unified) nature is a double good prepared for man by God: a visible good and an invisible good, a temporal and an eternal.[7] And man has been endowed with freedom of choice and hence the ability to prefer the lesser good to the higher, Nature to God.

The position of man in *Paradise Lost* is essentially the same as his position in the medieval world-picture. Spirit may be only a subtle form of matter, and angels may have their sexless loves, but there is a distinction, and man is different from both rocks and angels.

> So from the root
> Springs lighter the green stalk, from thence the leaves
> More aery, last the bright consummate flow'r
> Spirits odorous breathes: flow'rs and thir fruit
> Man's nourishment, by gradual scale sublim'd
> To vital Spirits aspire, to animal,
> To intellectual, give both life and sense,
> Fancy and understanding, whence the Soul
> Reason receives, and reason is her being,
> Discursive, or Intuitive; discourse
> Is oftest yours, the latter most is ours,
> Differing but in degree, of kind the same.   (V, 479-90)

But the lines that follow these have been misinterpreted by many commentators:

> time may come when men
> With Angels may participate, and find
> No inconvenient Diet, nor too light Fare:
> And from these corporal nutriments perhaps
> Your bodies may at last turn all to Spirit,
> Improv'd by tract of time, and wing'd ascend
> Ethereal, as wee, or may at choice
> Here or in Heav'nly Paradises dwell;
> If ye be found obedient, and retain
> Unalterably firm his love entire
> Whose progeny you are.   (V, 493-503)

Critics have associated these lines with the Elder Brother's schoolboy translation of the *Phaedo* in *Comus* (459-75) where he says that heavenly converse can turn the body into soul's essence and that lust

---

7. St. Bonaventure, *Breviloquium*, tr. E. E. Nemmers (St. Louis, Mo., 1946), Pt. II, ch. 11, pp. 73-4.

" imbodies " and " imbrutes " the soul and makes her lose " The divine property of her first being." But Raphael is merely speculating. What he says is that *if* Adam remains obedient (which of course he does not), he and his descendants *may* one day become like the angels. There is no indication that the process will be automatic, nor is the corollary of the doctrine stated, as it is in *Comus*, that man's body will become more gross by sinning. Raphael is holding out the hope of a reward to Adam, not describing the nature of things, and what he says is perfectly in keeping with patristic and medieval speculation about the ultimate destiny of unfallen man.[8]

Curry further confuses the issue by trying to find the source of this " Miltonic " doctrine in the speculations of various Neoplatonic schools. From Porphyry he would derive the doctrine of the dynamic power of the soul to determine the state of its body. This doctrine, he says, was later combined with the idea of " one first matter all " until in Milton's contemporary Henry More we have the belief that the human soul " may fashion for itself in successive states of existence a terrestrial, an aerial, and a celestial body." [9] Doubtless there are affinities between Neoplatonism and the passage from *Paradise Lost*, but there is also a radical difference that makes all efforts to assimilate them rather pointless. For in *Paradise Lost* it is not the business of man to try to spiritualize his body and rise in the scale of nature but rather to accept the human condition: to learn what his nature is and be true to it. One of the central concerns of *Paradise Lost* is to establish man's place in the hierarchy of natures and to explore the consequences of his failure to keep it. In a typical Renaissance Neoplatonist like Pico, on the other hand, man becomes detached from the hierarchy.[1] In Pico's *Oration on the Dignity of Man*, for instance, God addresses man in this fashion : " We have made thee neither of heaven nor of earth, neither mortal nor immortal, so that with freedom of choice and with honor, as though the maker and molder of thyself, thou mayest fashion thyself in whatever shape thou shalt prefer. Thou shalt have the power to degenerate into the lower forms of life, which are brutish. Thou shalt have the power, out of thy soul's judgment, to be reborn into the higher forms, which are divine." [2] *Paradise Lost* makes use of this theme, but as a

---

8. In the opinion of St. Thomas Aquinas, Adam, if he had not sinned, would have remained in Paradise for his animal life and then would have been transferred to Heaven for his spiritual life. *Summa theologica*, I, Q. 102, A. 4. For the destiny of fallen man in *Paradise Lost* see below, pp. 265-6 and n. 4.

9. Curry, " Milton's Scale of Nature," p. 185.

1. Paul O. Kristeller, " Ficino and Pomponazzi on the Place of Man in the Universe," *Journal of the History of Ideas*, 5 (1944), 226.

2. Tr. Elizabeth L. Forbes, in *The Renaissance Philosophy of Man*, ed. Ernst Cassirer et al. (Chicago, University of Chicago Press, 1948), p. 225.

symbol, not a philosophical doctrine. Vice, for instance, is "brutish" (XI, 518), and the perverters of Christ's teachings are "Wolves" (XII, 508). The best-known example is of course the fate of Satan. After transgressing the hierarchy by assuming the form of a serpent and giving it the rational power of speech, he is punished by being greeted on his return to Hell with hissing instead of words of praise, and once each year he and his followers are changed into the form of the animal which had subverted Eve. But this is not a "change of essence" in Satan, it is a symbolic *tour de force*.[3]

Corresponding to the hierarchy of natures in which man finds his place is a psychological hierarchy within man. This is a traditional conception, deriving ultimately from Plato, which Milton has adopted in its Christian form. It is quite true, as Herbert Agar has said,[4] that Plato and Milton both have a tripartite division of the soul, but it is misleading to call the doctrine of the soul in *Paradise Lost* "Platonic." In the first place, Plato had no conception of the Will, to which St. Augustine once and for all gave a central position in Christian psychology.[5] In the second place, Plato regarded the union of soul and body as accidental and as harmful to the soul. It is the business of the philosopher, says Socrates in the *Phaedo*, to be concerned with the soul and not with the body, and to get away from the body so far as he is able. The knowledge given by the senses is not only inferior to knowledge derived from the soul, it is untrustworthy in itself and is rather to be regarded as opinion than knowledge. The soul is imprisoned in the body and longs to return to its heavenly home. It need hardly be pointed out that the intimate union of body and soul contemplated in *Paradise Lost* is anything but Platonic.

Nevertheless, Plato does insist that the rational part of the soul rule over the spirited and appetitive parts, and it is this aspect of his doctrine that practically every ethical philosophy, including that of *Paradise Lost*, has adopted. In the *Phaedrus* Plato describes the soul in the metaphor of the charioteer and the two horses, one obedient and one unruly. The charioteer is Reason, the obedient horse the spirited part of the soul, and the unruly one the appetitive part. In the Timaeus these three parts of the soul are said to inhabit the head, the heart and lungs, and the belly and liver respectively, and in the *Republic* they are said to correspond to the three classes of Guardians, Warriors, and Artisans. Aristotle adopted Plato's basic distinction between the rational and irrational parts, further subdividing each part into two: the rational

3. Tillyard, *Studies in Milton*, p. 35.
4. *Milton and Plato* (Princeton, 1928), p. 13.
5. Paul O. Kristeller, *The Philosophy of Marsilio Ficino* (New York, 1943), p. 257.

into the speculative and the practical intellect, and the irrational into the appetitive and the vegetative. Aquinas elaborates on the Aristotelian division by distinguishing the rational appetite (will) from the sense appetite, and he subdivides the sense appetite into the irascible and the concupiscible emotions, which seem to correspond to Plato's spirited soul and appetitive soul respectively.[6] Raphael is in the Aristotelian-Thomistic tradition when, in explaining the scale of Nature, he describes the parts of the soul as "vital," "animal," and "intellectual" (*P. L.*, V, 484-5). Elsewhere in *Paradise Lost* we have the familiar division into Reason, Will, and Appetite or Passion, which are the three aspects of the soul that have to do with moral choice, the movements of the vegetative soul (in Aquinas, at least) being instinctive and hence nonmoral.

> For Understanding rul'd not, and the Will
> Heard not her lore, both in subjection now
> To sensual Appetite, who from beneath
> Usurping over sovran Reason claim'd
> Superior sway: (IX, 1127-31)

We have here the Platonic doctrine of the supremacy of reason, but also the Christian doctrine of the Will. In the ethical thought of St. Thomas the moral act typically involves the cooperation of Reason, Will, and Appetite. Sense appetite, as in Aristotle, supplies the material basis of the act; reason judges whether or not the sense appetite is to be indulged and to what extent (the doctrine of the mean); and the will, having received the judgment of the reason, moves to act. Like Plato and Aristotle before him, St. Thomas envisages a hierarchy of the faculties or powers of the soul with reason at the top and the emotions at the bottom. But his ethical thought, like that of St. Augustine and Milton, is specifically Christian in that he makes will an equal cooperator with reason in the moral act. Indeed, it is precisely because reason and will cooperate that man can be said to have freedom:

> The root of liberty is the will as the subject thereof; but it is the reason as its cause. For the will can tend freely towards various objects, precisely because the reason can have various perceptions of good. Hence philosophers define the free-will as being *a free judgment arising from reason*, implying that reason is the root of liberty.[7]

---

6. On the division of the sense appetite into the irascible and the concupiscible see *Summa theologica*, I, Q. 81, A. 2. On the will as appetite see I, Q. 82, A. 5. Cf. Edward Reynolds, *A Treatise of the Passions and Faculties of the Soul of Man* (London, 1650), p. 102, and Hooker, *Ecclesiastical Polity*, I. vii. 3.

7. *Summa theologica*, Ia-IIae, Q. 17, A. 1 ad 2.

Hooker is in the Thomistic tradition:

> To choose is to will one thing before another. And to will is
> to bend our souls to the having or doing of that which they see
> to be good. Goodness is seen with the eye of the understanding.
> And the light of that eye, is reason. So that two principal foun-
> tains there are of human action, Knowledge and Will; which Will,
> in things tending towards any end, is termed Choice.[8]

Compare Adam's statement to Eve:

> But God left free the Will, for what obeys
> Reason, is free, and Reason he made right, . . .
>
> (IX, 351-2)

Michael says much the same thing in the last book when he explains
to Adam the necessity of tyranny, reminding him that "true Liberty
. . . always with right Reason dwells / Twinn'd, and from her hath no
dividual being" (XII, 83-5).

What is this "right reason" to which Adam and Michael refer?
Douglas Bush, who sees in right reason one of the essential doctrines
of Christian humanism, tells us that it "is not merely reason in our
sense of the word; it is not a dry light, a nonmoral instrument of
inquiry. Neither it is simply the religious conscience. It is a kind of
rational and philosophic conscience which distinguishes man from the
beasts and which links man with man and with God. This faculty was
implanted by God in all men, Christian and heathen alike, as a guide
to truth and conduct."[9] Merritt Hughes, after reminding us that it is
"a Stoic conception, ultimately deriving from Plato's ethics," contents
himself with a quotation from Robert Greville, Lord Brooke, to the
effect that right reason is "the Candle of God, which He hath lighted
in Man, lest man groping in the Darke should stumble, and fall."[1]
Not even Lord Brooke, however, can tell us what right reason is. "But
who shall tell us what is Recta Ratio?" he asks. "I answere, Recta
Ratio."[2]

But there need be nothing mysterious about the conception if we
keep in mind the fact that right reason is not a faculty distinct from

8. *Ecclesiastical Polity*, I. vii. 2.

9. Douglas Bush, *Paradise Lost in Our Time* (Ithaca, N. Y., Cornell University Press, 1945), p. 37.

1. Robert Greville, Lord Brooke, *A Discourse . . . of . . . Episcopacy* (London, 1641), p. 27, cited by Merritt Y. Hughes, Introduction to *John Milton,
Prose Selections* (New York, The Odyssey Press, 1947), p. lxxxiv.

2. Greville, *Episcopacy*, p. 14, cited by Barker, *Milton and the Puritan
Dilemma*, p. 57.

reason itself but is rather a mode of the operation of reason. It is
"reason rectified," to employ Lord Brooke's own synonym; it is reason
made right, or reason properly exercised, or reason from which the
mists of passion and prejudice have been cleared away. To satisfy
ourselves that this is so we need go no further than Hooker's *Ecclesiastical Polity*, that bible of Christian humanism, in which it is said that
in all men except innocents and madmen "there is that light of Reason,
whereby good may be known from evil, and which discovering the same
rightly is termed right."[3] This view derives from Book VI of the
Nicomachean Ethics where Aristotle asks what it means to say that an
action is in accordance with right reason and answers that right reason
in moral questions is Prudence or Practical Wisdom.[4] To clinch the
matter, this is also the view of Michael, who seems to equate "right
reason" and "free Reason" (XII, 92) and to contrast both to reason
that is obscured or subservient to passion. This is also what Adam
says in the passage quoted above, and it is the view implied by God the
Father when he describes the rebel angels as those "who reason for
thir Law refuse, / Right reason for thir Law" (VI, 41-2).

The view that right reason is some sort of special truth-giving
faculty distinct from reason may have arisen because the Cambridge
Platonists, who popularized the conception, were for the most part
men who believed that the natural reason was possessed of innate ideas
which made it an infallible judge of truth and error, right and wrong.[5]
In short, theirs was the Platonic-Augustinian conception of reason as
intuition or recollection or illumination rather than the Aristotelian-
Thomistic conception of reason as "a principle of action, a power or
faculty by which truth was discovered in the sensibles, an aptitude for
discovering it . . ."[6] On this question Hobbes is found in the Aristotelian camp with Hooker. "Reason it selfe is alwayes Right Reason
. . ." he says in the *Leviathan*. "But," he adds, "no one mans Reason,
nor the Reason of any one number of men, makes the certaintie." And
in *The Elements of Law* he observes that "commonly they that call for
right reason to decide any controversy, do mean their own," and he
denies that there is any such thing "to be found or known *in rerum
natura*."[7]

3. I. vii. 4.

4. VI. xiii (1144b).

5. For a lucid exposition, fully documented, see Sterling P. Lamprecht,
"Innate Ideas in the Cambridge Platonists," *Philosophical Review*, 35 (1926),
553-73.

6. Perry Miller, *The New England Mind* (New York, Macmillan, 1939),
p. 190.

7. Hobbes, *Leviathan*, I. v (Cambridge, 1904), p. 22. *The Elements of Law*,
Pt. II, ch. 10, par. 8 (Cambridge, 1928), p. 150.

We are still left with the question of whether reason—that is to say "right reason"—in *Paradise Lost* is a Platonic or an Aristotelian conception. To this question a variety of answers has been given. Basil Willey says that by this term Milton, like the Cambridge Platonists, means "the principle of moral control rather than of intellectual enlightenment," which seems to me a fairly dubious distinction. According to Marjorie Nicolson, it is "a faculty innate, shared by man with God, an infallible judge of right and wrong, which directs and orders the will, the instincts, and the appetites . . ." B. Rajan conjectures that reason and understanding are perhaps regarded by Milton as the active and passive aspects of the same faculty, and he goes on to say that Milton seems to follow the Renaissance version of the Aristotelian psychology rather than the Platonic psychology. Irene Samuel, on the other hand, identifies right reason with the inner light.[8] An examination of the relevant passages from *Paradise Lost* will, I believe, support Rajan's contention that we are dealing with an Aristotelian rather than a Platonic conception, although there is nothing to support his suggestion—and it was offered only as a suggestion—that reason and understanding are to be distinguished from each other.

Rajan himself cites *Paradise Lost*, IX, 112-13: "Of Creatures animate with gradual life / Of Growth, Sense, Reason, all summ'd up in Man," which refers to the Aristotelian distinction between the nutritive, sensitive, and rational souls, as we have already remarked. There is also the passage in which Raphael speaks of the difference between man and angel:

> whence the Soul
> Reason receives, and reason is her being,
> Discursive, or Intuitive; discourse
> Is oftest yours, the latter most is ours,
> Differing but in degree, of kind the same. (V, 486-90)

That man's reason is not naturally intuitive is suggested by the passage in which Adam says that he understood the natures of the animals because "with such knowledge God endu'd / My sudden apprehension" (VIII, 353-4). Adam's knowledge here is not natural, but infused by God. Elsewhere in the poem understanding seems to be used as a synonym for reason:

> For Understanding rul'd not, and the Will
> Heard not her lore, both in subjection now
> To sensual Appetite, who from beneath

---

8. Willey, *The Seventeenth Century Background*, p. 242; Nicolson, *SP, 23*, 419; Rajan, *Paradise Lost*, p. 150; Samuel, "Milton on Learning and Wisdom," *PMLA, 64* (1949), 717, n. 15.

> Usurping over sovran Reason claim'd
> Superior sway: (IX, 1127-31)

Reason is the godlike faculty in man:

> There wanted yet the Master work, the end
> Of all yet done; a Creature who not prone
> And Brute as other Creatures, but endu'd
> With Sanctity of Reason . . .   (VII, 505-8)

But even in unfallen man it is possible for reason to err, as Adam warns Eve:

> But God left free the Will, for what obeys
> Reason, is free, and Reason he made right,
> But bid her well beware, and still erect,
> Lest by some fair appearing good surpris'd
> She dictate false, and misinform the Will
> To do what God expressly hath forbid.
>
> .   .   .   .   .
>
> Firm we subsist, yet possible to swerve,
> Since Reason not impossibly may meet
> Some specious object by the Foe suborn'd,
> And fall into deception unaware,
> Not keeping strictest watch, as she was warn'd.
>
> (IX, 351-6; 359-63)

The concepts presented here seem clearly to fall into an Aristotelian rather than a Platonic frame of reference. But, again, it is not so important to label Milton's conception of reason as it is to grasp the fact that reason is right only when it is used rightly.

As for the passions, almost all Christian thinkers, Catholic and Protestant alike, agreed that they were natural to man. Indeed, one of the principal objections to Stoicism in seventeenth-century England was its celebrated doctrine of apathy,[9] and even Puritans joined in the general chorus of condemnation:

> And in this consideration [i. e. that the passions are the natural movements of the soul] (so it be alwayes *Motion Naturall*, governed and dependant on right *Reason*) I find not any *Corruption*, though I finde an *Error* and abuse; that I meane, which maketh *Passion* in generall to be *Aegritudo Animi*, a Sicknesse and Perturbation, and would therefore reduce the mind to a senselesse *Apathie*, condemning all life of *Passion*, as *Waves* which serve

---

9. Henry W. Sams, "Anti-Stoicism in Seventeenth- and Early Eighteenth-Century England," *Studies in Philology, 41* (1944), 65-78.

onely to tosse and trouble *Reason.* An Opinion, which while it goeth about to give unto Man an absolute government over him-selfe, leaveth scarce any thing in him, which he may command and governe.

> . . . the agitations of Passion, as long as they serve onely to drive forward, but not to drown Vertue; as long as they keep their dependance on Reason, and run onely in that Chanel where-with they are thereby bounded, are of excellent service, in all the travell of mans life, and such as without which, the growth, suc-cesse, and dispatch of Vertue would be much impaired.[1]

This had been the general position of Aristotle, for whom the passions were the material element of the moral life, and reason the formal element or soul,[2] and it is also the view of Aquinas and Hooker, as might be expected.

There was not, however, general agreement as to the role of those passions that go by the name of concupiscence—in other words, the lusts of the flesh. The Reformation attitude stems from St. Augustine, for whom concupiscence is not simply a consequence of original sin but the material element of original sin: it is the concupiscence of the parents that transmits original sin to the children.[3] Calvin goes even further than his master: " Those who have called [original sin] *con-cupiscence* have used an expression not improper, if it were only added, which is far from being conceded by most persons, that every thing in man, the understanding and will, the soul and body, is polluted and engrossed by this concupiscence; or, to express it more briefly, that man is of himself nothing else but concupiscence."[4] John Weemes, author of *The Pourtraiture of the Image of God in Man,* expressly states that before the Fall Adam had no natural concupiscence.[5] In St. Thomas Aquinas, on the other hand, concupiscence is natural to man, and Adam was able to control it perfectly by his reason only because he had been endowed with supernatural graces.[6] Now it is not

1. Reynolds, *A Treatise,* pp. 47, 60

2. J. A. Stewart, *Notes on the Nicomachean Ethics of Aristotle* (Oxford, 1892), *2,* 107-8.

3. Rev. P. Pourrat, *Christian Spirituality* (London, 1922), *1,* 180.

4. John Calvin, *Institutes of the Christian Religion,* tr. John Allen (London, 1838), II. I. viii. Cf. III. III. xii., where Calvin says that " all the desires of [fallen] man are evil."

5. London, 1627, pp. 291-9. The difference between Weemes's view and that of Aquinas may be one of terminology only, since by concupiscence Weemes appears to mean inordinate desire. For Aquinas it is a neutral term. Weemes makes a point of his difference with the Catholic interpretation, however.

6. *Summa theologica,* I, Q. 95. Roy M. Battenhouse, " The Doctrine of Man

clear whether it is by natural or by supernatural means that Adam in
Paradise Lost is able to control his concupiscence, but there is no doubt
at all about the presence of concupiscence in his nature. So great is his
passion for Eve, Adam tells Raphael, that he fears Nature may have

>   left some part
> Not proof enough such Object to sustain,
> Or from my side subducting, took perhaps
> More than enough; at least on her bestow'd
> Too much of Ornament, in outward show
> Elaborate, of inward less exact.   (VIII, 534-9)

He understands that " in the prime end / Of Nature " Eve is inferior
to him, yet

> All higher knowledge in her presence falls
> Degraded, Wisdom in discourse with her
> Loses discount'nanc't, and like folly shows;
> Authority and Reason on her wait, . . .   (VIII, 551-4)

Raphael, who understands better than Adam that God and Nature bid
the same, warns him to " Accuse not Nature, she hath done her part "
(VIII, 561). True love, he says, has his seat

> In Reason, and is judicious, is the scale
> By which to heav'nly Love thou may'st ascend,
> Not sunk in carnal pleasure, for which cause
> Among the Beasts no Mate for thee was found.
>   (VIII, 591-4)

Appetite is "natural" in the sense that it is part of man's nature, but
it is "unnatural" to exalt it over reason, which is superior to appetite
in the psychological hierarchy and which ought to rule it—not suppress
it—at all times.

The Garden is "the great imaginative image of perfection"[7] in
Paradise Lost, and in its luxuriance on the one hand and its need of
cultivation on the other we may see, I think, an analogy to the relation
of passion and reason in the mind of man. Adam himself invites us
to make the analogy when he says that each tree in the Garden " Load'n
with fairest Fruit, that hung to the Eye / Tempting, stirr'd in me
sudden appetite / To pluck and eat" (VIII, 306-9). The luxuriance
is stressed again and again. "Nature's whole wealth" (IV, 207) is

in Calvin and in Renaissance Platonism," *Journal of the History of Ideas, 9*
(1948), 447-71, calls attention to the difference between Aquinas and Calvin in
this regard.
    7. Mack, Introduction to *Milton* p. 20.

in the Garden; its ground is "fertile"; the "crisped Brooks" run nectar "With mazy error under pendant shades" and feed "Flow'rs worthy of Paradise which not nice Art / In Beds and curious Knots, but Nature boon / Pour'd forth profuse on Hill and Dale and Plain" (IV, 241-3). But the Garden is also one of restraint, limitation, and order. Having told us that the Garden has been showered profusely not by "nice Art" but by "Nature boon," the poet goes on to describe the nuptial bower of Adam and Eve in terms which suggest that it is a work of art: It was a place "Chos'n by the sovran Planter"; the flowers "wrought / Mosaic," and "Broider'd the ground" with "rich inlay," "more colour'd than with stone / Of costliest Emblem" (IV, 691-703). Adam reminds Eve that in the morning they must be at their work of cultivating and pruning:

> Tomorrow ere fresh Morning streak the East
> With first approach of light, we must be ris'n,
> And at our pleasant labour, to reform
> Yon flow'ry Arbours, yonder Alleys green,
> Our walk at noon, with branches overgrown,
> That mock our scant manuring, and require
> More hands than ours to lop thir wanton growth:
> Those Blossoms also, and those dropping Gums,
> That lie bestrown unsightly and unsmooth,
> Ask riddance, if we mean to tread with ease;
> Meanwhile, as Nature wills, Night bids us rest.
>
> (IV, 623-33)

And Eve, on the fateful day of her temptation, speaks of the same necessity of curbing the luxuriance of the Garden, "Tending to wild" (IX, 212).

It was such passages as these that led critics in the past to distinguish between Milton the Poet, luxuriant and unrestrained, and Milton the Puritan, crabbed and restrictive. Today, I believe, most critics would agree with Rajan that "reason is not restrictive. On the contrary, it liberates those powers of fecundity which are otherwise mangled and suppressed in chaos." [8] Nature herself, we learn, teaches the virtue of temperance, which may be defined as the government of the passions by the rule of right reason. Adam calls Nature "wise and frugal" (VIII, 26), and Michael says that men who serve "ungovern'd appetite" pervert "Nature's healthful rules / To loathsome sickness" (XI, 517-24). One reason why the earth is so bountiful is "that temperance may be tri'd" (XI, 804-5). Nature even enforces her laws of tem-

---

8. B. Rajan, "Simple, Sensuous, and Passionate," *Review of English Studies,* *21* (1945), 297.

perance by rewarding those who observe them with a "natural" death
and punishing those who disobey them with "Convulsions, Epilepsies,
fierce Catarrhs, / Intestine Stone and Ulcer, Colic pangs" (XI, 483-4).
We might observe that there is a temperance of intellectual desire as
well as of sensual desire:

> But Knowledge is as food, and needs no less
> Her Temperance over Appetite, to know
> In measure what the mind may well contain, (VII, 126-8)

which is symbolized in Nature by the fact that

> God to remove his ways from human sense,
> Plac'd Heav'n from Earth, so far, that earthly sight,
> If it presume, might err in things too high,
> And no advantage gain.   (VIII, 119-22)

What happens when man does not exercise restraint is amply demonstrated in the description of the effects of the Fall.

It is misleading, however, to restrict the ethical content of *Paradise
Lost* to a history of the conflict between reason and passion, of which
the Fall is regarded as the first episode. To say that Milton regarded
virtue as knowledge and wickedness as uncontrolled passion [9] is wrongly
to limit *Paradise Lost* to classical modes of thought, which were
unable to rise above this simple antithesis.[1] Christian ethical thought
as early as St. Augustine was able to attain an integrated view of human
nature in which morality no longer consisted in the suppression of the
passions by reason or in the nice calculation of "individual or social
utility"[2] but in the turning of the whole man either to God or to self.
Not that Christianity abandoned the notion of a conflict: it could hardly
do that in the face of human experience. But the whole question was
put in a different context by being oriented to the idea of God rather
than to the idea of a purely natural good for man. In other words,
wrongdoing becomes not a question of "missing one's mark," as in
Aristotle, but of an offence against the divinely established nature of
things, against an order that man has knowledge of by means of his
reason. It also becomes a question not of preferring evil to good,
since in the Christian universe nothing is evil in and of itself, but of
preferring a lesser good to a higher. "For there was never sin com-

9. Agar, *Milton and Plato*, p. 11; Hughes, *Paradise Lost*, p. 340 (note to X,
718); A. J. A. Waldock, *Paradise Lost and Its Critics* (Cambridge, 1947), p. 23.

1. Charles Norris Cochrane, *Christianity and Classical Culture* (Oxford, The
Clarendon Press, 1940), p. 507. I am indebted to Cochrane's brilliant work
for my point of view in this paragraph, and for many other insights as well.

2. Ibid., p. 507.

mitted," says Hooker, "wherein a less good was not preferred before a greater, and that wilfully; which cannot be done without the singular disgrace of Nature, and the utter disturbance of that divine order, whereby the preeminence of chiefest acceptation is by the best things worthily challenged. There is not that good which concerneth us, but it hath evidence enough for itself, if Reason were diligent to search it out." [3] St. Bonaventure, quoting from St. Augustine, says the same thing: "Sin is not an appetite for things evil, but a rejection of the better." [4]

We can thus see that it is not quite accurate to say, as Rajan does, that "Eve sins because her faculty of reason is deceived while Adam sins by surrendering his will to his passions." [5] It is more accurate to say, I think, that in each case the whole person sins, and that in each case all the elements of the complex human act are present, though in different degrees. Eve's reason is deceived, but her appetite is also involved:

> Fixt on the Fruit she gaz'd, which to behold
> Might tempt alone, and in her ears the sound
> Yet rung of his persuasive words, impregn'd
> With Reason, to her seeming, and with Truth;
> Meanwhile the hour of Noon drew on, and wak'd
> An eager appetite, rais'd by the smell
> So savoury of that Fruit, which with desire,
> Inclinable now grown to touch or taste,
> Solicited her longing eye; . . .   (IX, 735-43)

This is not mere sleight of hand designed to lend plausibility on the dramatic level to Eve's rash act. It does serve this purpose, of course, but it operates even more significantly on the symbolic level, where it has been prepared for by the analogy that the poem has set up between the external or landscape Nature of the Garden and the essential nature of the human soul.

The emphasis is no doubt different in Adam's case, but the same elements are there. Adam deliberately chooses a lesser good, with full knowledge of his reason and full consent of his will. I do not deny that Adam's passion for Eve is aroused. He would be a stone, not a man, if it were not. But I do deny that it is any more fully aroused than Eve's passion for the fruit.

---

3. *Ecclesiastical Polity*, I. vii. 7.
4. *Breviloquium*, III. i. 5. J. S. Diekhoff's analysis of the Fall in *Paradise Lost* is one of the few I know of that make use of these traditional Christian concepts. *Milton's Paradise Lost* (New York, 1946), p. 104.
5. Rajan, *Paradise Lost*, p. 69.

> How can I live without thee, how forgo
> Thy sweet Converse and Love so dearly join'd?
>
> (IX, 908-9)

he asks. After the hymn to wedded love in Book IV there can be no
doubt that Adam here is choosing a good, and if it were not for the
fact that in so choosing he is also disobeying God, no one would accuse
him of letting passion rule his will.

Having made his decision, he proceeds to call in the aid of reason.
Then realizing that it is futile to try to deceive himself, he returns to
his first statement:

> However I with thee have fixt my Lot,
> Certain to undergo like doom . . .   (IX, 952-3)

And he completes the " mortal Sin / Original ":

> he scrupl'd not to eat
> Against his better knowledge, not deceiv'd,
> But fondly overcome with Female charm.   (IX, 997-9)

The last line must be read in the light of what has preceded it. Female
charm certainly refers to all those " Relations dear " and " Domestic
sweets " (IV, 756 and 760) that have been praised in the hymn to
wedded love. It is not surrendering to passion to value these things,
but it is a mortal sin to prefer them to God. What makes Adam's sin
so heinous is the fact that he was neither deceived nor overcome by
passion, but that deliberately, and after having taken counsel with
himself, and with the full cooperation of his reason and will, he chose
a lesser good. We may say if we like that Adam surrendered his will
to his passions, but surrendering to passion is not necessarily sinful,
unless by passion is meant inordinate passion. The love of God is a
passion, and we have it on the word of the Puritan Edward Reynolds
that God " is to be *loved*, not with a divided, but a *Whole Heart*. To
love any Creature either *without God*, or *above God*, is *Cupiditas, Lust*,
(which is the *formale* of every sinne, whereby we turne from God to
other things) but to *love* the *Creatures under God*, in their right *order*:
and *for God*, to their right *end*, (for hee made all things for himselfe)
this is *Charitas*, true and regular *Love*." [6] The soul, he says, should
yield itself up to God and conform " all its Affections and Actions to
his Will." The Augustinian conception of love as the " weight " of the
soul, which is here echoed by Reynolds, transcends the classical dichotomy between reason and passion. Whom do you love? was the
question asked by Augustine. When put to the test, Adam, like Satan,

6. *A Treatise*, p. 83. The quotation following is from p. 82.

shows that he loves himself more than God. On the dramatic level Adam's love of self is presented as love for Eve, but here, as elsewhere in the poem, we can see a deeper significance. Eve was made from Adam's rib, and he speaks of her as of another self:

> Flesh of Flesh,
> Bone of my Bone thou art, and from thy State
> Mine never shall be parted, bliss or woe. (IX, 914-16)

> So forcible within my heart I feel
> The Bond of Nature draw me to my own,
> My own in thee, for what thou art is mine;
> Our State cannot be sever'd, we are one,
> One Flesh; to lose thee were to lose myself. (IX, 955-9)

The conflict between reason and passion in the human soul is certainly a very real one, as moralists of all ages have testified and as we learn in the last two books of *Paradise Lost*, but we shall not understand Milton's conception of the Fall unless we realize that for him, as for Christian thought generally, the basic conflict is the conflict between love of self, which is pride, and the love of God, which is charity.

Essence and Existence

It is the tragedy of man that the facts of his fallen existence often appear to belie the theoretical truths of his nature or essence. Before the Fall man was true to his human nature, and this internal harmony is reflected in the harmony that obtains between man and the whole world of external nature, both animal and vegetable. This harmony is not sustained automatically, however, for, as we have seen, the Garden requires cultivation lest it run to excess, just as the soul needs to be vigilant against the wiles of the Enemy. Moreover, Nature herself holds dangers for man: he can abuse the freedom inherent in his human nature by disobeying God, and he can misuse external Nature by preferring it to God and using it for his own selfish purposes. At first, Adam's relationship with Nature was everything it ought to be. When he awoke in Eden, after his creation by God, he looked " straight toward Heav'n " (VIII, 257), and gazed for a while at the "ample Sky." Then suddenly and instinctively he sprang up and stood erect. Looking around him, he saw

> Hill, Dale, and shady Woods, and sunny Plains,
> And liquid Lapse of murmuring Streams; by these,
> Creatures that liv'd, and mov'd, and walk'd, or flew,
> Birds on the branches warbling   (VIII, 262-5)

He then looked at himself but did not know who he was or where he had come from. He addressed the sun and the earth and the animals, as he tells Raphael, and asked them to " Tell, if ye saw, how came I thus, how here?" (VIII, 277) And answering his own question, he says " Not of myself; by some great Maker then, / In goodness and in power preeminent" (VIII, 278-9). God then appeared to Adam, and after warning him not to eat the fatal fruit, brought all the animals before him. " I nam'd them," Adam says,

> as they pass'd, and understood
> Thir Nature, with such knowledge God endu'd
> My sudden apprehension.   (VIII, 352-4)

But Adam does not always read the book of Nature correctly. Before the Fall he had told Raphael he realized that in the " prime end / Of Nature" (VIII, 540-1) Eve was inferior to him, but when he is determining to eat the fruit with Eve he makes a specious appeal to Nature to justify his action: " no no, I feel / The Link of Nature draw me" (IX, 913-14). And he makes the same appeal in telling Eve of his decision: " So forcible within my heart I feel / The Bond of Nature draw me to my own" (IX, 955-6). Nature herself gives the lie to Adam's reasoning:

> Earth trembl'd from her entrails, as again
> In pangs, and Nature gave a second groan,
> Sky low'r'd, and muttering Thunder, some sad drops
> Wept at completing of the mortal Sin
> Original.   (IX, 1000-4)

After the Fall Adam persists in his partial view of Nature, and he draws from Michael a reproof as severe as Raphael's earlier one. Michael has just shown Adam the vision of the fair women and the sons of God:

> Such happy interview and fair event
> Of love and youth not lost, Songs, Garlands, Flow'rs,
> And charming Symphonies attach'd the heart
> Of *Adam*, soon inclin'd to admit delight,
> The bent of Nature; which he thus express'd.
>   True opener of mine eyes, prime Angel blest,
> Much better seems this Vision, and more hope
> Of peaceful days portends, than those two past;
> Those were of hate and death, or pain much worse,
> Here Nature seems fulfill'd in all her ends.
>   To whom thus *Michael*. Judge not what is best
> By pleasure, though to Nature seeming meet,

> Created, as thou art, to nobler end
> Holy and pure, conformity divine. (XI, 593-606)

I do not think that the poet, in the lines in which he speaks in his own person, is condemning pleasure and delight as the bent of *fallen* nature. We have already seen that concupiscence is natural to Adam in his unfallen state, and in the hymn to wedded love the delights of the marriage bed are praised, not condemned. It is not pleasure in itself that is wrong, but inordinate or immoderate pleasure. Michael himself does not say that pleasure is wrong; he says that it is not best, even though Adam, with his now limited and fallen view of Nature, might think it so. Adam can no longer understand the lessons that Nature, which is the work of God, has to teach him, because in turning from God to Nature, instead of from Nature to God, he has rejected the Divine Reason and with it the principle that makes Nature intelligible.

The fallen angels also make frequent appeals to a Nature they either do not understand or pretend not to understand. "For who can yet believe," asks Satan in Hell,

> though after loss,
> That all these puissant Legions, whose exile
> Hath emptied Heav'n, shall fail to re-ascend
> Self-rais'd, and repossess thir native seat? (I, 631-4)

Moloch appears to have the same confidence in the nature of the angels:

> But perhaps
> The way seems difficult and steep to scale
> With upright wing against a higher foe.
> Let such bethink them, if the sleepy drench
> Of that forgetful Lake benumb not still,
> That in our proper motion we ascend
> Up to our native seat: descent and fall
> To us is adverse. Who but felt of late
> When the fierce Foe hung on our brok'n Rear
> Insulting, and pursu'd us through the Deep,
> With what compulsion and laborious flight
> We sunk thus low? Th' ascent is easy then; . . .
> (II, 70-81)

It is true that Heaven is "thir happy Native seat," as Raphael tells Adam later (VI, 226), but what they seem to forget is that they have lost Heaven by laws of Nature which they themselves have set in motion. "How hast thou disturb'd / Heav'n's blessed peace," says Michael to Satan,

> and into Nature brought
> Misery, uncreated till the crime
> Of thy Rebellion? how hast thou instill'd
> Thy malice into thousands, once upright
> And faithful, now prov'd false. But think not here
> To trouble Holy Rest; Heav'n casts thee out
> From all her Confines. Heav'n the seat of bliss
> Brooks not the works of violence and War. (VI, 267-74)

Among the fallen angels it is Belial, the intellectual, who best compre-
hends the realities of the situation:

> Or could we break our way
> By force, and at our heels all Hell should rise
> With blackest Insurrection, to confound
> Heav'n's purest Light, yet our great Enemy
> All incorruptible would on his Throne
> Sit unpolluted, and the Ethereal mould
> Incapable of stain would soon expel
> Her mischief, and purge off the baser fire
> Victorious.   (II, 134-42)

Satan never did understand the nature of things, at least not after he
began his revolt, or if he did he found it expedient to lie about it. For
in his debate with Abdiel he denies that he is a creature who derives
his being from God, in a passage that forms a striking contrast to
Adam's views on awakening from creation:

> who saw
> When this creation was? remember'st thou
> Thy making, while the Maker gave thee being?
> We know no time when we were not as now;
> Know none before us, self-begot, self-rais'd
> By our own quick'ning power, when fatal course
> Had circl'd his full Orb, the birth mature
> Of this our native Heav'n, Ethereal Sons.
> Our puissance is our own, our own right hand
> Shall teach us highest deeds, by proof to try
> Who is our equal: (V, 856-66)

In speaking of "fatal course" Satan appeals to a nature of things that
is presumably above God, and he boasts that Heaven is "native" to the
rebel angels, by which he means not only that it is their birthplace but
also that it belongs to them "by nature." Here and elsewhere, as we
shall see, Milton associates "native" and "natural" through their

common derivation from the Latin *nasci*. Satan again appeals to Nature in addressing his followers after the first day of battle:

> True is, less firmly arm'd,
> Some disadvantage we endur'd and pain,
> Till now not known, but known as soon contemn'd,
> Since now we find this our Empyreal form
> Incapable of mortal injury
> Imperishable, and though pierc'd with wound,
> Soon closing, and by native vigor heal'd.
> Of evil then so small as easy think
> The remedy; perhaps more valid Arms,
> Weapons more violent, when next we meet,
> May serve to better us, and worse our foes,
> Or equal what between us made the odds,
> In Nature none: if other hidden cause
> Left them Superior, while we can preserve
> Unhurt our minds, and understanding sound,
> Due search and consultation will disclose. (VI, 430-45)

It is ironical that Satan should think his mind unhurt when he is appealing to a Nature whose laws he deliberately chooses to misunderstand. "God and Nature bid the same," Abdiel had said (VI, 176), but Satan is determined to prove him wrong by exploring external nature to its depths and using it for his own purposes. This, I take it, is one of the symbolic meanings of the invention of gunpowder (VI, 472-831). Satan foolishly turns to external Nature for proof of his contention that he is equal to God " In Nature" or essence, to find that in attempting to separate Nature from God he only succeeds in creating his own Hell. He knows that these materials are " dark and crude" until "toucht / With Heav'n's ray," but he persists in bringing to abortive birth the "infernal flame." Created good by essence, he and his followers freely choose to live out their evil existence in Hell, "thir fit habitation" (VI, 876),

> A Universe of death, which God by curse
> Created evil, for evil only good,
> Where all life dies, death lives, and Nature breeds,
> Perverse, all monstrous, all prodigious things. (II, 622-5)

Satan was without excuse. As an angel gifted with intuitive reason he should have known that in appealing from God to Nature he was indulging in the sheerest nonsense. Adam too will be without excuse. All of that long recital of Raphael's—the description of the creation of the world out of chaos and of the hierarchic scale of nature, the account of the war in Heaven and the fall of Satan—is designed to

acquaint Adam with the nature of reality so that he cannot plead
ignorance should he fail to exercise his freedom of choice properly.
But Adam, like Satan, deliberately chooses to misread the book of
Nature, and he is expelled from Paradise by law of nature similar to
the one which expelled the fallen angels from Heaven:

> To whom the Father, without Cloud, serene.
> All thy request for Man, accepted Son,
> Obtain, all thy request was my Decree:
> But longer in that Paradise to dwell,
> The Law I gave to Nature him forbids:
> Those pure immortal Elements that know
> No gross, no unharmonious mixture foul,
> Eject him tainted now, and purge him off . . .
>   (XI, 45-52)

Adam, again like Satan, takes refuge in a limited view of Nature.
Before the Fall he had seen God in the book of Nature; now he appeals
to Nature to hide God from him and him from God:

> O might I here
> In solitude live savage, in some glade
> Obscur'd, where highest Woods impenetrable
> To Star or Sun-light, spread thir umbrage broad,
> And brown as Evening: Cover me ye Pines,
> Ye Cedars, with innumerable boughs
> Hide me, where I may never see them more.
>   (IX, 1084-90)

Adam and Eve use Nature for their own selfish purposes. They go
"Into the thickest Wood" (IX, 1100) and cover their nakedness with
the leaves of the banyan tree, and later when Christ comes to judge them
they hide "themselves among / The thickest Trees" (X, 100-1).
Realizing the futility of this, Adam thinks he sees another way out in
the natural law of death. "For dust thou art," Christ had said to Adam,
"and shalt to dust return" (X, 208). The thought of his native dust
brings comfort to Adam, but he is plagued by one doubt: what if not
all of him shall die? What if "that pure breath of Life, the Spirit of
Man / Which God inspir'd" should die a "living Death" (X, 784-8)?
The thought is too horrible, and he again appeals to Nature's law:

> Will he draw out,
> For anger's sake, finite to infinite
> In punisht man, to satisfy his rigour
> Satisfi'd never; that were to extend
> His Sentence beyond dust and Nature's Law, . . .
>   (X, 801-5)

After his reconciliation with Eve, he tells her that with the help of God's grace they may

> pass commodiously this life, sustain'd
> By him with many comforts, till we end
> In dust, our final rest and native home.[7]   (X, 1083-5)

Adam does not yet know that the Son of God will come to lead man "Safe to eternal Paradise of rest" (XII, 314). He and Eve are content to find their rest in the "Native Soil" (XI, 270) of their earthly Paradise, and when Michael comes to tell them that they must be taken from the Garden to "fitter Soil" (XI, 262), Eve cries

> O unexpected stroke, worse than of Death!
> Must I thus leave thee Paradise? thus leave
> Thee Native Soil . . . ?   (XI, 268-70)

But Paradise is "native" to man only in the sense that Heaven was "native" to Satan, and Michael, who understands the nature of things better than Eve, tells her that she is bound to follow her husband: "Where he abides, think there thy native soil" (XI, 292). Adam, too, must learn that where God abides, there is his native soil. He tells Michael that what most afflicts him in leaving Paradise is the thought that he will not be able to raise altars on the grassy turf where he talked with God, that he will not be able to tell his sons that he saw God under this tree and heard His voice among these pines. But Michael tells him that God is everywhere:

> Yet doubt not but in Valley and in Plain
> God is as here, and will be found alike
> Present.   (XI, 349-51)

But it will be different. The Mount of Paradise is ruthlessly destroyed by the Flood, and in its place is "an Island salt bare, / The haunt of Seals and Orcs, and Sea-mews' clang" (XI, 834-5). Man, who has been false to his created nature, is condemned to drag out his weary existence in the moral wilderness of fallen nature.

Of that wilderness we get more than an adequate account in the vision of human history that is granted Adam in the last two books. Adam is appalled by what he sees: "Piety . . . and pure Devotion paid" by fratricide; the Lazar-house of disease, "Of ghastly Spasm, or racking torture, qualms / Of heart-sick Agony, all feverous kinds, /

7. The possible echo of *Aeneid* VII. 122 ("hic domus, haec patria est") in Adam's many references to "native home" and "native soil" reminds us that in one of its dimensions *Paradise Lost* is a systematic attack on the classical idea of the destiny of man. Dust is not Adam's "final rest and native home."

Convulsions, Epilepsies, fierce Catarrhs"; sons of God fast caught
"in the amorous Net."; war and bloodshed and "Sword-Law"; the
destruction by Flood of a "world perverse"; Nimrod, the hunter of
men, who destroyed "Concord and law of Nature" and who tried to
reach Heaven by building an earthly city; the captivity of the Chosen
People, first in Egypt and then in Babylon; the superstition and venality
of those who claim to represent Christ. "So shall the World go on,"
says Michael, "To good malignant, to bad men benign, / Under her
own weight groaning . . ." (XII, 537-9). Adam now has a different
idea of death. "Is this the way / I must return to native dust?" he
asks after witnessing the murder of Abel. This is but one way, replies
Michael. There are many forms of violent death, the worst being those
brought on by the monstrous disease caused by man's intemperance.
"But is there yet no other way," pleads Adam, "besides / These painful
passages, how we may come / To Death, and mix with our connatural
dust?"

> There is, said *Michael*, if thou well observe
> The rule of not too much, by temperance taught,
> In what thou eat'st and drink'st, seeking from thence
> Due nourishment, not gluttonous delight,
> Till many years over thy head return:
> So may'st thou live, till like ripe Fruit thou drop
> Into thy Mother's lap, or be with ease
> Gather'd, not harshly pluckt, for death mature:
>
> (XI, 530-7)

But even here is no comfort, for in old age

> thou must outlive
> Thy youth, thy strength, thy beauty, which will change
> To wither'd weak and gray; thy Senses then
> Obtuse, all taste of pleasure must forgo,
> To what thou hast, and for the Air of youth
> Hopeful and cheerful, in thy blood will reign
> A melancholy damp of cold and dry
> To weigh thy Spirits down, and last consume
> The Balm of Life.   (XI, 538-46)

Michael's vision of history in the last two books of *Paradise Lost*
has been severely condemned by the critics on both philosophical and
poetic grounds. C. S. Lewis finds these books an "untransmuted lump
of futurity," and he brands the writing as "curiously bad,"[8] though
he offers no concrete examples of its badness. Tillyard, in his 1930

8. *Preface*, p. 125.

Milton, went so far as to complain that not only the last two books but the last four or five were somehow more pessimistic and less energetic than the first four, and he explained this change of tone by saying that "Milton himself had altered during the writing of the poem." [9] In his latest work on Milton, however, he has written very acutely and appreciatively of the ninth and tenth books, and he even has some kind words for the eleventh and twelfth. He singles out for praise ("The only righteous in a World perverse") the lines on Christian liberty (XII, 285-306) and those on the world's decay (XII, 507-51). Of the former passage he says that "the legalistic side of the doctrine [of Redemption] is successfully fused with the ardour with which Milton describes the state of filial liberty." [1] For blame he singles out the following lengthy passage, which I should like to quote entire in order to make discussion possible. I shall quote sixteen more lines than Tillyard does for reasons which I hope will become clear.

> To whom thus *Michael*. Dream not of thir fight,
> As of a Duel, or the local wounds
> Of head or heel: not therefore joins the Son
> Manhood to Godhead, with more strength to foil
> Thy enemy; nor so is overcome
> *Satan*, whose fall from Heav'n, a deadlier bruise,
> Disabl'd not to give thee thy death's wound:
> Which hee, who comes thy Saviour, shall recure,
> Not by destroying *Satan*, but his works
> In thee and in thy Seed: nor can this be,
> But by fulfilling that which thou didst want,
> Obedience to the Law of God, impos'd
> On penalty of death, and suffering death,
> The penalty to thy transgression due,
> And due to theirs which out of thine will grow:
> So only can high Justice rest appaid.
> The Law of God exact he shall fulfil
> Both by obedience and by love, though love
> Alone fulfill the Law; thy punishment
> He shall endure by coming in the Flesh
> To a reproachful life and cursed death,
> Proclaiming Life to all who shall believe
> In his redemption, and that his obedience
> Imputed becomes theirs by Faith, his merits
> To save them, not thir own, though legal works.   410

---

9. *Milton* (London, Chatto & Windus, 1930), p. 291.
1. *Studies in Milton*, p. 166.

For this he shall live hated, be blasphem'd,
Seiz'd on by force, judg'd, and to death condemn'd
A shameful and accurst, nail'd to the Cross
By his own Nation, slain for bringing Life;
But to the Cross he nails thy Enemies,
The Law that is against thee, and the sins
Of all mankind, with him there crucifi'd,
Never to hurt them more who rightly trust
In this his satisfaction; so he dies,
But soon revives, Death over him no power
Shall long usurp; ere the third dawning light
Return, the Stars of Morn shall see him rise
Out of his grave, fresh as the dawning light,
Thy ransom paid, which Man from death redeems,
His death for Man, as many as offer'd Life
Neglect not, and the benefit embrace
By Faith not void of works: this God-like act
Annuls thy doom, the death thou shouldst have di'd,
In sin for ever lost from life; this act
Shall bruise the head of *Satan*, crush his strength
Defeating Sin and Death, his two main arms,
And fix far deeper in his head thir stings
Than temporal death shall bruise the Victor's heel,
Or theirs whom he redeems, a death like sleep,
A gentle wafting to immortal Life.   (XII, 386-435)

Of these lines Tillyard says,

> What is surprising is that he recounts this, the culminating scene
> in the great Puritan drama, with so comparatively little energy
> and passion. As passionate writing, the lines on Christian liberty
> a little before and the lines on the world's decay a little after quite
> overshadow the account of the Redemption. On the other hand
> Milton insists, with an emphasis he could have avoided had he
> wished, on the legalism of the transaction. Had not Milton written
> more passionately in nearby places, it could be argued that he was
> for some reason tired. Ingenuity could find many explanations,
> but a possible one is that Milton was powerless either to free
> himself from, or to impassion, the legalism that then for all Chris-
> tians, but especially for the Puritans, was inseparable from the
> doctrine of the Redemption.[2]

But Michael is not describing the "culminating scene in the great
Puritan drama"; he is expounding a doctrine. These lines have their

2. Ibid., pp. 163-4.

own kind of intellectual energy, and their very compression (which no doubt descends into crabbedness in 407-10) is a virtue rather than a fault. The passage lacks the heroic energy of the first two books because Milton is here writing " Of Patience and Heroic Martyrdom " (IX, 32). The contrast between Satan's "heroism" and Christ's runs throughout the passage, and the Satanic ideology of physical force is here revealed in all its futility. Michael begins by reminding us of the War in Heaven, where the forces that were ignorantly unleashed by the rebel angels were turned to the rebels' own destruction by the mighty Word (Reason) of God. Now once again the powers of Hell resort to force. But by seizing Christ, Satan frees man; by condemning Christ to death, he wins eternal Life for man; and in nailing Christ to the Cross, he nails there the Law and the sins that bind man to him. The meter is appropriate to the thought. The rhythm of " slain for bringing Life " in line 414 gives a sense of finality which is as illusory as the death itself, and the verse paragraph continues for another twenty-one lines. The rhythmical regularity of the last line, " A gentle wafting to immortal Life," reinforces the contrast between the violent agony of the Crucifixion and the gentleness of this death that is like sleep; and death itself, which is mentioned at least eight times in these twenty-one lines, receives its final negation in " immortal Life."

Rajan has tried to rehabilitate the last two books by placing them in the seventeenth-century religious milieu, but his cure is perhaps worse than the disease. He thinks that these books are " bleak and barren, and that the discipline they preach is an insurance against sin rather than a basis for virtue," and he tries to explain if not to justify this bleakness by showing that the pessimism of Michael's account derives from a " background of assent " to the typical seventeenth-century view of fallen man as a " loathsome," " wild," " corrupt," " degenerate," " vain," and " worthless " creature.[3] But then he goes on to say that the notes of pessimism and despair in the last two books are " not part and parcel of Milton's poetic design. They are intrusions in that design, forgivable, unavoidable, the clenched, spasmodic despair of the man who will one day write *Samson Agonistes*, but intrusions nevertheless which are in no way evidence of Milton's epic intention." [4] This, however, is to do an injustice to the poem as a whole, for I think it can be shown that the last two books are not an intrusion in the epic design but rather an integral part of the poetic and intellectual structure.

It is C. S. Lewis who gives us the clue to a proper understanding of them. " A fallen man *is* very like a fallen angel," he remarks.[5] The

3. *Paradise Lost*, pp. 79-82.
4. Ibid., p. 84.
5. *Preface*, p. 99.

significance of this dictum is that it enables us to see that the vision of
the last two books is implicit in the first two, especially in the building
of Pandemonium and in the heroic games of the devils.

> Others more mild,
> Retreated in a silent valley, sing
> With notes Angelical to many a Harp
> Thir own Heroic deeds and hapless fall
> By doom of Battle; and complain that Fate
> Free Virtue should enthrall to Force or Chance.
>
> (II, 546-51)

> In discourse more sweet
> (For Eloquence the Soul, Song charms the Sense,)
> Others apart sat on a Hill retir'd,
> In thoughts more elevate, and reason'd high
> Of Providence, Foreknowledge, Will, and Fate,
> Fixt Fate, free will, foreknowledge absolute,
> And found no end, in wand'ring mazes lost.
> Of good and evil much they argu'd then,
> Of happiness and final misery,
> Passion and Apathy, and glory and shame,
> Vain wisdom all, and false Philosophie: (II, 555-65)

Still others devote their time to exploring "That dismal World" (II,
572). "Thus roving on / In confus'd march forlorn, th' advent'rous
Bands . . . found / No rest" (II, 614-15; 617-18). These are *human*
activities—and not ignoble ones—that are thus described in even more
unflattering terms than Christ employs in *Paradise Regained*, and we
meet some of them again in the last books. Adam after the Fall
indulges in "evasions vain / And reasonings, though through Mazes"
(X, 829-30), and he can "find no way" out of the "Abyss of fears /
And horrors" to which his conscience has driven him (X, 842-4).
The race of Cain appear studious "Of Arts that polish Life, Inventors
rare" (XI, 610), but like the fallen angels they are "Unmindful of
thir Maker" (XI, 611). Fallen man admires only might and calls it
"Valour and Heroic Virtue" (XI, 690). And Nimrod, unconscious
of how man's "greatest Monuments of Fame, / And Strength and
Art are easily outdone / By Spirits reprobate" (I, 695-7), builds the
city of Babel, a ridiculous effort compared with the city of Pandemonium. Thus the vision of angel without God in the first two books
of the epic is paralleled by the vision of man without God in the last
two. The "arts" of fallen angel and fallen man are set against their
divinely created "natures."

We are now in a position to understand the significance of the contrast that Bush has noted between "natural simplicity, goodness, love, light, and life on the one hand and artificial luxury, evil, hate, darkness, and death on the other."[6] This antithesis, which he rightly says is "a religious and philosophic as well as artistic principle,"[7] operates in a number of different contexts. There is the parallel between human and diabolic art, which we observe in the preceding paragraph and which is expressly stated in the following passage:

> And here let those
> Who boast in mortal things, and wond'ring tell
> Of *Babel*, and the works of *Memphian* Kings,
> Learn how thir greatest Monuments of Fame,
> And Strength and Art are easily outdone
> By Spirits reprobate, and in an hour
> What in an age they with incessant toil
> And hands innumerable scarce perform.   (I, 692-9)

The "works of Memphian Kings" reappear in Book V as "the tedious pomp that waits / On Princes" in a passage which contrasts natural and artificial hierarchy:

> Meanwhile our Primitive great Sire, to meet
> His god-like Guest, walks forth, without more train
> Accompani'd than with his own complete
> Perfections, in himself was all his state,
> More solemn than the tedious pomp that waits
> On Princes, when thir rich Retinue long
> Of Horses led, and Grooms besmear'd with Gold
> Dazzles the crowd, and sets them all agape.
> Nearer his presence *Adam* though not aw'd,
> Yet with submiss approach and reverence meek,
> As to a superior Nature, bowing low,
>   Thus said.   (V, 350-61)

The princes of this earth have transgressed the natural hierarchy by arrogating to themselves power that belongs to God alone. Nimrod, Michael tells Adam,

> Will arrogate Dominion undeserv'd
> Over his brethren, and quite dispossess
> Concord and law of Nature from the Earth. (XII, 27-9)

Such tyranny, though unnatural, is God's just punishment. Because

6. *English Literature in the Earlier Seventeenth Century* (Oxford, The Clarendon Press, 1945), p. 385.
7. *Paradise Lost in Our Time*, p. 97.

man allows "upstart Passions [to] catch the Government / From Reason" (XII, 88-9), "God in Judgment just / Subjects him from without to violent Lords" (XII, 92-3). As Christ tells Satan in *Paradise Regained*, their outward slavery is both a punishment for and a symbol of their inward slavery.

Another example of the antithesis is the contrast between the natural love of Adam and Eve in the Bower, lulled to sleep by the spontaneous song of the nightingale, and the artificialities of the Petrarchan love tradition:

> Here Love his golden shafts imploys, here lights
> His constant Lamp, and waves his purple wings,
> Reigns here and revels; not in the bought smile
> Of Harlots, loveless, joyless, unindear'd,
> Casual fruition, nor in Court Amours,
> Mixt Dance, or wanton Mask, or Midnight Ball,
> Or Serenate, which the starv'd Lover sings
> To his proud fair, best quitted with disdain.
> These lull'd by Nightingales imbracing slept,
> And on thir naked limbs the flow'ry roof
> Show'r'd Roses, which the Morn repair'd. (IV, 763-73)

And in Book XI we have the further contrast with the "Gems and wanton dress" and "Soft amorous Ditties" by means of which the "Bevy of fair Women" seduce the Sons of God (XI, 582-4). In keeping with the purity and simplicity of Adam and Eve's love-making is their "adoration pure" (IV, 737), which may be contrasted with the "outward Rites and specious forms" (XII, 534) and "gay Religions full of Pomp and Gold" (I, 372) of fallen man.

Finally, one of the most familiar examples of the contrast is the passage in Book IX where the feelings of Satan on viewing Eve in the Garden are compared to those of a city-dweller visiting the country:

> As one who long in populous City pent,
> Where Houses thick and Sewers annoy the Air,
> Forth issuing on a Summer's Morn to breathe
> Among the pleasant Villages and Farms
> Adjoin'd, from each thing met conceives delight, . . .
>   (IX, 445-9)

Milton's use of "art" as a symbol of fallen existence, both angelic and human, has led some critics to regard him as an enemy of human civilization. Hugh Kenner, for example, calls him a "destroyer of cities." The only city that is built in Milton's poetry, he says, is Pandemonium, while the supreme act of Milton's hero Samson is the destruction of a city. Wordsworth's rejection of the city for the country, he goes on to say, owes its valid symbolism to Milton, and he implies—moving with ease from the symbolic to the literal level—that the slums of eighteenth- and nineteenth-century London owe their origin to *Paradise Lost*. "Between Prospero and the heroes of Pound," he concludes, "the cult of factive intelligence is dormant."[8] In short, Kenner seems to be accusing Milton of having made it possible for later poets to exalt the primitive over the civilized, instinct over reason, simplicity over sophistication, the "natural" over the "artificial." If this is so, however, it is only because *Paradise Lost* has been misread and not because the cult of factive intelligence is dormant in Milton. We have already seen that Adam and Eve's bower is a work of art as much as it is a work of nature, and we have also seen that man's art of cultivation and pruning is required to keep the garden in a proper condition. Reason, too, is exalted over instinct in the psychological hierarchy, just as the factive intelligence of God is exalted over the destructive will of Satan and the blind forces of Chaos. The antithesis is more complex than Kenner imagines. The "natural" is superior to the "artificial," but "nature" in the Garden would be unsightly were it not for the "art" of cultivation. It is not "nature" as the primitive or instinctive or irrational that we are dealing with—those terms better describe Chaos; it is "nature" as the divinely ordained hierarchy of essences. And it is not "art" as such that is condemned but art as the symbol of existence, human and angelic, without God.

It is of course true that as part of the larger nature-art antithesis Milton frequently opposes the Garden to the City, but he is at pains to distinguish the true Garden and the true City from the false ones. Although Heaven in *Paradise Lost* is usually presented as a metaphoric Garden, it is also imaged as a City with its turrets and pavements and is thus opposed to the false cities of Pandemonium and Babel.[9] In *Paradise Regained*, where the nature-art antithesis reinforces the basic contrast between the truth of Christ and the falsehood of Satan, the Garden-City antithesis is more elaborately worked out. The "holy City" of Jerusalem (*P. R.*, IV, 545) which is a type of Heaven, may be contrasted to the "Imperial City" of Rome, which is described as the product of human art and artifice (IV, 33-60). The spiritual Eden that Christ comes to raise in the waste wilderness and to which he is carried

8. Hugh Kenner, "New Subtlety of Eyes," in *An Examination of Ezra Pound*, ed. Peter Russell (Norfolk, Conn., New Directions, 1950), pp. 97-8. Cf. G. Wilson Knight, *Chariot of Wrath* (London, 1942), p. 137, and R. J. Werblowsky, *Lucifer and Prometheus* (London, 1952), p. 89.

9. Cleanth Brooks suggests that Eden may be considered "a garden poised between two cities, Pandemonium and the City of God." "Milton and Critical Re-estimates," *PMLA*, 66 (1951), 1047.

by the angels in IV, 586-90, may be contrasted both to the artificial garden engineered by Satan in the banquet scene in Book II and to Athens, which, though it is a city, is described in garden imagery, for example when the " Mellifluous streams " that issue from the mouth of Socrates are contrasted to the true "fountain of Light" (IV, 276-90). Poised between the true city and the false city, the true garden and the false garden, is the Wilderness, which is a more complex symbol in *Paradise Regained* than it is in *Paradise Lost*. It suggests, as Tillyard and Bush have said, the loneliness of Christ. It is also the place of trial and temptation, as in the *Morte d'Arthur* and countless folk tales. It is the state of mind of which Clement of Alexandria speaks when he says, " For thoroughly a stranger and sojourner in the whole of life is every such one, who, inhabiting the city, despises the things in the city which are admired by others, and lives in the city as in a desert, so that the place may not compel him, but his mode of life show him to be just." [1] It is also quite simply, as in *Paradise Lost*, the fallen human condition, the " world's wilderness " through which Joshua-Jesus will bring " long wander'd man / Safe to eternal Paradise of rest " (*P. L.*, XII, 313-4).

Can this antithesis between essence and existence be transcended? We know that we cannot return to the condition of our first parents when " art " and " nature " were in perfect harmony; we know also that God has promised that man shall not be condemned to an existence like that of the fallen angels, whose hellish arts are nothing more than a sterile mockery of divine creation. The question is relevant to *Paradise Lost* both as a work of art and as an attempt to justify the ways of God to man. How, one might ask, is Milton's epic to be distinguished from the "notes Angelical" of the fallen angels? The answer, of course, is that " Thir song was partial " (II, 552) because it was the product of their own darkened minds, while Milton's is the inspired work of divinely redeemed human " nature " rather than unredeemed human " art ":

> If answerable style I can obtain
> Of my Celestial Patroness, who deigns
> Her nightly visitation unimplor'd,
> And dictates to me slumb'ring, or inspires
> Easy my unpremeditated Verse:
> Since first this Subject for Heroic Song
> Pleas'd me long choosing, and beginning late;
> Not sedulous by Nature to indite
> Wars, hitherto the only Argument
> Heroic deem'd, chief maistry to dissect
> With long and tedious havoc fabl'd Knights

---

1. *Stromata*, VII. xii.

> In Battles feign'd; the better fortitude
> Of Patience and Heroic Martyrdom
> Unsung; or to describe Races and Games,
> Or tilting Furniture, emblazon'd Shields,
> Impreses quaint, Caparisons and Steeds;
> Bases and tinsel Trappings, gorgeous Knights
> At Joust and Tournament; then marshall'd Feast
> Serv'd up in Hall with Sewers, and Seneschals;
> The skill of Artifice or Office mean,
> Not that which justly gives Heroic name
> To Person or to Poem. Mee of these
> Nor skill'd nor studious, higher Argument
> Remains, sufficient of itself to raise
> That name, unless an age too late, or cold
> Climate, or Years damp my intended wing
> Deprest, and much they may, if all be mine,
> Not Hers who brings it nightly to my Ear. (IX, 20-47)

The symbolic significance of the contrast between the "skill of Artifice" and "my unpremeditated Verse," which appears also in *Paradise Regained* in the contrast between the "swelling Epithets thick laid" of Greek literature and the "majestic unaffected style" of the Bible (*P. R.*, IV, 343, 359), is clear: we have seen it running all through the poem. And if we need some intellectual justification for Milton's claim we can find it in the Puritan doctrine of the inspiration of the Elect and in the following passage from the *Apology for Smectymnuus*: ". . . that indeed according to art is most eloquent, which returns and approaches nearest to nature, from whence it came; and they express nature best, who in their lives least wander from her safe leading, which may be called regenerate reason."[2] It is thus that human art is restored to God.

Human nature also is restored to God by the divine art of regeneration. This is the doctrine by which Michael seeks to justify the ways of God to man. Regeneration is the work not of Nature but of Grace:

> Thus they in lowliest plight repentant stood
> Praying, for from the Mercy-seat above
> Prevenient Grace descending had remov'd
> The stony from thir hearts, and made new flesh
> Regenerate grow instead, . . .   (XI, 1-5)

Michael's dismal recital of human history thus becomes an object lesson in the struggle between "supernal Grace" and "sinfulness of Men"

---

2. Patterson, p. 543. See below, pp. 279-81.

(XI, 359-60).[3] The theological foundation has been laid in Book III, where God the Father says that because man was not self-tempted but was deceived by Satan, he "therefore shall find grace" (III, 131).

> Man shall not quite be lost, but sav'd who will,
> Yet not of will in him, but grace in me
> Freely voutsaf't; once more I will renew
> His lapsed powers.   (III, 173-6)

Grace will restore Nature, and it too will have its fruits. "See Father," says Christ when the prayers of Adam and Eve ascend to Heaven,

> See Father, what first fruits on Earth are sprung
> From thy implanted Grace in Man, these Sighs
> And Prayers, which in this Golden Censer, mixt
> With Incense, I thy Priest before thee bring,
> Fruits of more pleasing savour from thy seed
> Sown with contrition in his heart, than those
> Which his own hand manuring all the Trees
> Of Paradise could have produc't, ere fall'n
> From innocence.   (XI, 22-30)

But alas! the seeds of grace will more often than not fall on stony soil, and the fruits, though of more pleasing savor, seem scanty enough compared to the bounty of the Garden. Enoch is "The only righteous in a World perverse" (XI, 701), Noah the "only Son of light / In a dark Age" (XI, 808-9), "The one just Man alive (XI, 818), and Abraham the "one faithful man" from whom the "one peculiar Nation" will spring (XII, 111-13). Even with the coming of Christ and the reign of Grace (XII, 305), the faithful shall be few, "left among th' unfaithful herd, / The enemies of truth" (XII, 480-1). Nevertheless Adam sees reason to rejoice. The wicked deserve no better than they get, and for the good there is the prospect not only that Nature will be restored by Grace but that it will be raised to a supernatural level.[4] Christ, whom God has commanded to join man's nature to His (III, 282), will come at the last day

> to dissolve
> *Satan* with his perverted World, then raise
> From the conflagrant mass, purg'd and refin'd,
> New Heav'ns, new Earth, Ages of endless date

---

3. Rajan, *Paradise Lost*, p. 81, points out that this is the central phrase of Michael's speech to Adam.

4. The destiny of fallen man is thus (O felix culpa!) higher than the hypothetical destiny of unfallen man envisaged by Raphael in V, 493-503. See above, pp. 235-6.

> Founded in righteousness and peace and love,
> To bring forth fruits Joy and eternal Bliss.
>
> (XII, 546-51)

Michael's vision of history is presented in the terms of the massive contrasts that have been set up in the poem: God and Satan, Heaven and Hell, creation and destruction, light and darkness, grace and sin, nature and existence; and through it all, as we have seen, runs the deadly parallel between fallen angel and fallen man, carrying us back to the first two books of the epic. These are, no doubt, the categories in which Christian thought must ultimately express itself, and it is fitting that a poem which concerns itself with the nature of reality should employ them. But Michael, one feels, is too hasty in applying them to the concrete realm of human existence. We miss the accent of sympathy for frail, erring humanity. We hear it once in the lines in which he tells Adam how Christ shall

> bring back
> Through the world's wilderness long wander'd man
> Safe to eternal Paradise of rest. (XII, 312-14)

But for the most part the accents are harsh, the contrasts violent. This is too blinding a vision for our human eyes. We do not want to be told that in every age the faithful, like Abdiel, Enoch, and Moses, are few. It hardly seems to us that Michael has succeeded in justifying God's ways.

But Michael's vision is not the only one. There is also the drama of Adam and Eve as it unfolds before our eyes, and in that drama, as in *Samson Agonistes* later, there is evidence not only of human frailty but of human dignity too. In a brilliant essay E. E. Stoll has shown how in the last four books of the poem " epic grandeur . . . give[s] place to drama." " There is . . . an appropriate decrease in the magnitude, and increase in the complexity, of both the emotions and the expression, as we proceed through the great poem to its close." [5] The twilight mood in which the poem closes, he shows, is foreshadowed in the description of the evening which ends Adam and Eve's first day on earth, and it is reflected in such phrases as " though sorrowing, yet in peace " (XI, 117), " though in fall'n state, content " (XI, 180), " Quiet though sad " (XI, 272), and in the last lines of the poem.[6] It is here,

---

5. " From the Superhuman to the Human in *Paradise Lost*," in *Milton Criticism*, ed. James Thorpe (London, 1951), pp. 219, 224.

6. Stoll has not pointed out that the same pattern of expression is found in the first two books: " Confounded though immortal " (I, 53); " So spake th' Apostate Angel, though in pain, / Vaunting aloud, but rackt with deep despair " (I, 125-6); " To reign is worth ambition, though in Hell " (I, 262); " yet

in the poetry and in the human drama, that the doctrine of regeneration is justified and the reconciliation of opposites achieved. In a perceptive analysis of the crisis of *Paradise Lost* Tillyard shows that it is by the "simple effusion of decent human feeling" in Adam and Eve's reconciliation that God overcomes evil with good, "by things deem'd weak / Subverting worldly strong, and worldly wise / By simply meek" (XII, 567-9).[7] We see before our very eyes their stony hearts made regenerate. We also see—and Tillyard has not pointed this out, I believe—that the relationship between Adam and Eve both before and after the Fall is analogous to the relationship between God and Adam, and that the human drama of disobedience, estrangement, and reconciliation provides the dramatic justification of God's ways to man.[8] Adam has often been criticized for letting Eve go off to work alone on the day of temptation; but if the doctrine of freedom means anything, surely Adam is justified in saying "Go; for thy stay, not free, absents thee more" (IX, 372). So too God made Adam free:

> What pleasure I from such obedience paid,
> When Will and Reason (Reason also is choice)
> Useless and vain, of freedom both despoil'd,
> Made passive both, had serv'd necessity,
> Not mee.   (III, 107-11)

It is quite true that the poet makes us feel that Eve never should have left Adam:

> O much deceiv'd, much failing, hapless *Eve*,
> Of thy presum'd return! event perverse!
> Thou never from that hour in Paradise
> Found'st either sweet repast, or sound repose; . . .
>   (IX, 404-7)

Nevertheless Adam was right to give Eve her freedom, just as God gave Adam his. Eve was wrong proudly to turn away from Adam, just as Adam was wrong to follow her in her sin and turn away from God.

---

faithful how they stood, / Thir Glory wither'd" (I, 611-12); "Majestic though in ruin" (II, 305). This is but another of the parallels between fallen angel and fallen man.

7. *Studies in Milton*, pp. 43-4 .

8. Most critics, I think, would deny that there is any dramatic justification of God's ways in *Paradise Lost*. Grierson, for example, says that "the justification of God's ways to men begins and ends in the arguments put into God's mouth in Book III—viz., Adam's entire freedom." *Cross Currents in English Literature of the Seventeenth Century* (London, Chatto & Windus, 1929), p. 266.

After the sad event, the human pair are estranged, and Adam up-
braids Eve in words that God might very well have used with him:

> what could I more?
> I warn'd thee, I admonish'd thee, foretold
> The danger, and the lurking Enemy
> That lay in wait; beyond this had been force,
> And force upon free Will hath here no place.
>
> (IX, 1170-4)

God pardons Adam much more readily than Adam pardons Eve.
Christ, Who judges man, is also man's Intercessor (X, 96), and after
sentencing Adam to the human existence that we all know, He takes
pity on him and clothes his nakedness. God's ways are more easily
justified than man's: Adam is relentless toward Eve. In the agony of
his high reasonings " Of Providence, Foreknowledge, Will, and Fate, /
Fixt Fate, free will, foreknowledge absolute " (II, 559-60), Adam is
approached by " sad *Eve* " who " Soft words to his fierce passion . . .
assay'd " (X, 865). " Out of my sight, thou Serpent," he cries, and
he questions the wisdom of God in creating "this fair defect / Of
Nature " instead of filling the world with men (X, 891-3). The irony
of this situation, as Tillyard observes,[9] is that after Adam's denunciation of woman, Eve should begin the process of regeneration by restor-
ing the hierarchy she had destroyed when she aspired above her station:
she falls humble at Adam's feet, as Adam has not yet fallen humble at
the feet of God. Adam relents and loses his anger. Let us strive, he
says, " In offices of Love, how we may light'n / Each other's burden in
our share of woe " (X, 960-1). But Adam is not yet ready to make his
peace with God; he puts off his own act of reconciliation with the
subterfuge that prayer cannot alter high decrees (X, 952-3). But the
seeds of implanted grace are slowly bearing fruit, and Adam finally
realizes that prayer can, in a sense, alter high decrees after all. He tells
Eve that they can do no better

> than to the place
> Repairing where he judg'd us, prostrate fall
> Before him reverent, and there confess
> Humbly our faults, and pardon beg, with tears
> Watering the ground, and with our sighs the Air
> Frequenting, sent from hearts contrite, in sign
> Of sorrow unfeign'd, and humiliation meek.
> Undoubtedly he will relent and turn
> From his displeasure; in whose look serene,
> When angry most he seem'd and most severe,
> What else but favour, grace, and mercy shone?
>
> (X, 1086-96)

---

9. *Studies in Milton*, p. 40.

What more could the poet do to bring down to the level of our human experience the great doctrines of Sin and Redemption?

But Michael's vision of history remains, and the lurid flames of his eschatological fire may blind us to the more neutral shades of the human drama: the strident tone of his denunciation of sin may deafen our ears to the tearful sighs of repentance. Are the two visions irreconcilable? Have we succeeded in integrating Michael's vision with the early books of the poem only to discover, perhaps gratuitously, another kind of disunity? Is there a dichotomy between Michael's intellectual statement of the doctrine of regeneration and the poetic presentation of the process of regeneration in the human drama of Adam and Eve?

This is no doubt a question that every reader will wish to answer for himself. I should like to suggest, however, that if Michael's vision is thought to be irreconcilable with the vision of the ninth and tenth books, the explanation for this is not that the last two books are the anguished cry of a man disillusioned by the restoration of King Charles II, but that in the ninth and tenth books Milton has managed to rise above the abstract categories of Puritan thought. But I do not think that it is necessary to see an irreconcilable conflict. We must remember that Michael's vision of (fallen) human existence is an angelic one and hence abstract, and that it must be tempered by the human or concrete vision of human existence in the drama of the Fall and Regeneration that we have just analyzed. Nor are these two the only visions. There is also an abstract vision of (unfallen) human nature in the speeches of Raphael, and a concrete vision of human nature in the scenes between Adam and Eve and in the speeches of Adam before the Fall. The angelic visions, it will be noted, are at the two extremes of this spectrum, Raphael being perhaps too optimistic about the nature of man, Michael too pessimistic about his fallen existence, while the human visions lie fairly close together somewhere in between, a circumstance that may help to explain why Adam and Eve, as many critics have said, seem "already fallen" before they eat the apple. Each of these visions is inadequate taken by itself. The human vision is more limited in a sense than the angelic, but it is also more complex. Raphael knows more about the hierarchy in nature and in man than Adam, but he knows much less about passion, in spite of his blushes. Michael knows more about the historical battle between Grace and Sin, but his view is oversimplified and didactic, and he knows nothing of the struggle between faith and distrust that has been waged in Adam's heart. It is perhaps one of the measures of the greatness of *Paradise Lost* that it manages to hold in suspension all of these visions in one complex vision of the nature and destiny of man.

The final vision is the human, not the angelic one. In the last lines of the poem we leave the angels in the Garden of Essences and descend with the human pair to the Wilderness of Existence, though not quite as Michael sees it. In this "last shadowy scene of exile," as Stoll so finely says, is that "mingled web, good and ill together, that complex of thoughts and emotions which . . . represents human experience ever since" the Fall.[1]

> They looking back, all th' Eastern side beheld
> Of Paradise, so late thir happy seat,
> Wav'd over by that flaming Brand, the Gate
> With dreadful Faces throng'd and fiery Arms:
> Some natural tears they dropp'd, but wip'd them soon;
> The World was all before them, where to choose
> Thir place of rest, and Providence thir guide:
> They hand in hand with wand'ring steps and slow,
> Through *Eden* took thir solitary way.

"Quiet though sad," "though sorrowing, yet in peace," "though in fall'n state, content." The same pattern of thought, though not of expression, is in these last lines: though homeless, yet seeking their place of rest; though solitary and wandering, yet hand in hand and guided by Providence. This is human existence as we know it, and the "fiery Arms" and "dreadful Faces" are there to remind us that in this life we, unlike the blind Poet, can never return to the state of nature.

1. *Milton Criticism*, ed. Thorpe, pp. 222, 224.

3

Conclusion: Christianity and Classicism

Nature, Man, and God

FOR Milton, as for most Christians, classical ideas of Nature failed to achieve a satisfactory synthesis of Nature, Man, and God. In Platonism the physical world is, in a sense, unreal. Plato does not, like Parmenides, deny the existence of the World of Becoming, but he does deny that it is fully intelligible. The real world, the intelligible world, is the world of Ideas and Forms, which are unchanging and eternal. Neoplatonism pushed to the utmost limit this Platonic dichotomy between the ideal and the sensible.[1] Indeed, so much does Plotinus insist on the transcendence and incomprehensibility of God that all he can say of Him is that He is Good. For the rest, He is beyond all thought and all being, and no positive attributes can be ascribed to Him. Iamblichus, who was a disciple of Porphyry, even went so far as to posit a One beyond Plotinus' One, apparently feeling that even Goodness should not be attributed to God.[2] Both Plato and Plotinus are of two minds about matter.[3] On the one hand Plotinus praises the beauty and harmony of the cosmos and opposes Manichean dualism. On the other hand, he can say that " The bodily Kind, in that it partakes of Matter is an evil thing."[4] This same theme reappears in the *Hermetica*, where it is said that the Kosmos is good " in respect of its function of making things. But in all other respects the Kosmos is not good; for it is subject to perturbation, and the things which it makes are subject to perturbation. It is impossible then for things in this world to be pure from evil; and that which is good in this world is that which has the smallest share of evil; for in this world the good

1. Edward Caird, *The Evolution of Theology in the Greek Philosophers* (Glasgow, J. MacLehose and Sons, 1904), 2, 267.

2. Frederick Copleston, *A History of Philosophy*, *1* (Westminster, Md., The Newman Press, 1948), 476.

3. Caird, *Evolution*, *1*, 226.

4. Plotinus, *Enneads*, I. 6. 2. and I. 8. 4., tr. S. McKenna and B. S. Page, London, 1917-30.

becomes evil."[5] Even Aristotle, whose doctrine of immanent form sought to bridge the Platonic *chorismos* or gap between the realm of being and the realm of becoming, posited a Nature in which things move toward ends of which they are ignorant and which have not been ordained for them by a superior intellect. He has no Divine Being who may be said to order the processes of Nature as man orders the processes of his different arts. His Eternal Mover has no connection with the universe except as the object of desire, in which capacity it is the final (not the efficient) cause of the motions of the intelligences of the spheres.[6] Like the medieval scholastics Aristotle allows Chance and Fortune to play a large role in the sublunary world, but he does not view these concepts under the larger notion of Divine Providence, as Milton and the scholastics were able to do.

> Much of the Soul they talk, but all awry,
> And in themselves seek virtue, and to themselves
> All glory arrogate, to God give none,
> Rather accuse him under usual names,
> Fortune and Fate, as one regardless quite
> Of mortal things.   (*P. R.*, IV, 313-18)

As for man, classical systems find it difficult to give him a place in Nature without destroying what Christianity regards as his essential humanity. In Platonism and Neoplatonism he is an " unnatural " composite of matter and spirit who longs to escape from the prison of his body and return to his heavenly home. In Stoicism, on the other hand, man is simply a part of a closed deterministic system from which there is no escape. In many popular pagan theologies he is the sport of Fortune or Chance or blind Necessity.[7] Aristotle himself, though he managed to safeguard the substantial unity of the human composite with his doctrine of the soul as the form of the body, failed to define satisfactorily man's place in Nature. He agreed with Plato that man's intellect is in some sense a divine element, but he was no more able to integrate this divine element with his view of human nature than he was able to integrate his Eternal Mover with the physical universe. Just as he defines the activity of his Supreme Being as " a thinking on thinking,"[8] so he defines the supreme happiness of man as contempla-

---

5. *Hermetica*, ed. Walter Scott (Oxford, The Clarendon Press, 1924), *I*, 167, 169.

6. W. D. Ross, *Aristotle's Metaphysics* (Oxford, The Clarendon Press, 1924), *I*, cxxxvi, cli-ii.

7. Martin P. Nilsson, *Greek Piety*, tr. H. J. Rose (Oxford, 1948), pp. 92-185.

8. *Metaphysics*, XI. ix. 4 (1074b), tr. Hugh Tredennick, The Loeb Classical Library, London, Heinemann, 1933-5.

tion pure and simple. The life of contemplation, he says in Book X of the *Nicomachean Ethics,*

> will be higher than the human level: not in virtue of his humanity will a man achieve it, but in virtue of something within him that is divine; and by as much as this something is superior to his composite nature, by so much is its activity superior to the exercise of the other forms of virtue. If then the intellect is something divine in comparison with man, so is the life of the intellect divine in comparison with human life. Nor ought we to obey those who enjoin that a man should have man's thoughts and a mortal the thoughts of mortality, but we ought so far as possible to achieve immortality, and do all that man may to live in accordance with the highest thing in him; for though this be small in bulk, in power and value it far surpasses all the rest.[9]

In spite of J. A. Stewart's[1] attempt to prove that Aristotle doesn't mean what he says, Edward Caird's judgment would seem to be justified:

> The sharp division which Aristotle makes between the two lives which man can live, makes it difficult for him to say where the central principle of man's being is to be placed, and what, strictly speaking, constitutes the *self* or *Ego* to which everything else in him is to be referred. . . . The rift that runs through the philosophy of Plato seems here to have widened till it rends human nature asunder.[2]

For a Christian like Milton, on the other hand, the doctrines of voluntary creation and the Incarnation made it possible to reject the dichotomies between man and nature and nature and God that classical philosophy had regarded as rooted in the nature of things.[3] For Milton matter in itself implies no tendency to disorder; involvement in matter is not involvement in evil; and matter does not offer resistance to the forms that seek to impose themselves on it. As created by God, matter is good and is completely subservient to His purposes. The disorder in the world, far from being caused by matter, is the result of a spiritual disorder—the sin of the first man. Similarly the doctrine of the Incarnation conferred new dignity on matter and especially on the human body. For Milton, as for Christian thought generally, the Platonic and Neoplatonic dichotomy between the intelligible world and the sensible

9. X. vii. 8 (1177b-78a).
1. *Nicomachean Ethics of Aristotle,* 2, 249, 443-5, 448.
2. *Evolution,* 1, 313.
3. See Cochrane, *Christianity and Classical Culture,* esp. ch. 11.

world is replaced by the Christian distinction between God and His creation. Milton viewed the universe not merely as an image or reflection of the eternal Ideas, not as the playground of blind Chance and Necessity, not as the body of God, but as a free creation consisting of concrete, individual natures rationally ordered in a hierarchical scale ranging from inert matter at the bottom to intelligences at the top, with man occupying a middle position as the link between matter and spirit. The intellectual structure of *Paradise Lost* is what it is because Christianity had rescued God from the pantheistic universe to which the Stoics had confined Him, had rescued nature from the shadowy realm to which Plato had assigned it, and had rescued man from the various cults of futility to which he had been condemned by pagan theologies.

Nature and Grace

Milton's idea of nature as an ethical norm does not so much repudiate the central classical tradition of Plato, Aristotle, and Cicero as extend and qualify it in the light of the Christian conception of the nature and destiny of man. Milton's attitude toward the so-called natural virtues— justice, temperance, and the rest—is clear enough: he does not repudiate them, but like St. Augustine he puts the emphasis on right motive rather than on " hitting the mark." When it comes to the relationship between nature and grace, however, Milton's position is not so easy to define. Perhaps it will be best understood against the background of scholastic and reformation speculation.

There was no one orthodox view of the relationship between nature and grace in the Middle Ages. For St. Augustine, some of whose doctrines were later taken up by the Protestant reformers, nature tended to be swallowed up by grace.[4] The nature of man is not completely destroyed by the Fall in Augustine's thought, but it is so depraved as to be almost unrecognizable: " Thus, then, matters stood. Lying prostrate and wallowing in wretchedness, the condemned mass of the human race was being thrown from evils to new evils; joined by those of the angels who had sinned, it suffered punishments altogether deserved by its impious rebellion. Whatever the evil freely do through blind and unbridled concupiscence, and whatever they unwillingly suffer in punishments manifest or concealed, pertain to the just wrath of God."[5] For Aquinas, on the other hand, fallen man is deprived of the supernatural gift of integrity enjoyed by Adam, but not depraved

---

4. Gilson, *Spirit*, pp. 133-4.
5. *Enchiridion de fide, spe et caritate*, ch. 8, par. 27, tr. Bernard M. Peebles, in *The Fathers of the Church*, Vol. 4.

in nature. In his analysis of the Fall Aquinas tells us that there is a threefold good residing in human nature. First, there is human nature itself with its principles and properties such as the powers of the soul. This good was neither destroyed nor diminished by the Fall. Second, there is man's inclination to virtue. This good was diminished by original sin, since every sin results in a disposition to commit others. Third, there was the gift of original justice or integrity, by which all man's powers were in perfect subordination to reason so long as reason remained subject to God. This third good, not being a part of human nature at all, was totally destroyed by the Fall.[6] Aquinas believes that fallen man is still able, by virtue of his natural endowment, to do some particular goods, though not all the goods that are natural to him, but of course he cannot hope to attain the Beatific Vision without the aid of God's grace any more than Adam could, since the Beatific Vision is above nature.[7] Fallen man is restored to God's grace by means of the Sacrament of Baptism, the effect of which is to remove the guilt of original sin though not the effects. Hence concupiscence, which is natural to man, still rebels against reason to a certain extent, and it is difficult—though not impossible—for reason to control it.[8]

There are several important distinctions to be made between the Catholic doctrine of grace and that of evangelical Protestantism. Catholics believe that grace, which is defined as a supernatural quality infused into the soul by God, actually washes away the stain of sin and transforms the soul. Luther, on the other hand, defined grace simply as the favor or friendliness of God toward man, and for him the action of grace is to cover up and hide the deformity caused by sin without in any way cleansing or transforming the soul. It is this latter conception which apparently lies behind the image in stanza 2 of Milton's "Nativity Hymn":

> Only with speeches fair
> She [Nature] woos the gentle Air
>   To hide her guilty front with innocent Snow,
> And on her naked shame,
> Pollute with sinful blame,
>   The Saintly Veil of Maiden white to throw,
> Confounded, that her Maker's eyes
> Should look so near upon her foul deformities.

In *Comus*, however, with its imagery of a transformed nature, Milton had moved nearer to the Catholic view.

6. *Summa theologica*, Ia-IIae, Q. 85, A. 1. See Gilson, *Spirit*, p. 124.
7. Ibid., Ia-IIae, Q. 109, AA. 2, 5.
8. Ibid., Ia-IIae, Q. 74, A. 3 ad 2.

An even more important difference is that Protestants—including Milton—tended to regard Adam's original perfection as wholly natural rather than the result of supernatural grace.[9] The consequence of this doctrine of "pure nature" is that the Fall results in the total depravity of man's nature, not merely in his being deprived of supernatural gifts, as in Aquinas. Thus for Calvin fallen man's "nature is not only destitute of all good, but is so fertile in all evils that it cannot remain inactive." He warns us not to listen to the philosophers who tell us that the "reason of the human understanding is sufficient for its proper government; that the will, being subject to it, is indeed solicited by sense to evil objects, but, as it has a free choice, there can be no impediment to its following reason as its guide in all things." Actually, says Calvin, the reason, though not totally destroyed by the Fall, "exhibits nothing but deformity and ruin," and the will is "fettered by depraved and inordinate desires, so that it cannot aspire after anything that is good." We ought to add, however, that Calvin is not so pessimistic as he sounds in these passages. He distinguishes between one understanding for terrestrial things and another for celestial. In divine things "our reason is totally blind and stupid," but in the earthly sciences of mathematics, logic, etc., human reason, "fallen as it is, and corrupted from its integrity, is yet invested and adorned by God with excellent talents."[1] To judge from the dismal recital of human history in the last two books of *Paradise Lost*, Milton undoubtedly agreed with this estimate of unregenerate fallen human nature.[2]

Another consequence of the Protestant doctrine of pure nature is that it enabled extremists to assert that regeneration by Christian baptism resulted in the restoration of the believer to the state of natural perfection in which Adam first existed. Such a belief led to a sharp dichotomy between the secular and the spiritual and to the excesses of millenarianism and antinomianism.[3] Milton himself adopted this theory of restoration, though not of course in its extreme form. Arthur Barker, who has written definitively on this subject in his *Milton and the Puritan Dilemma*, tells us that Milton, like other Protestants of the day, dis-

9. Weemes, *Pourtraiture*, pp. 291-9; Miller, *The New England Mind*, p. 183; Battenhouse, "The Doctrine of Man in Calvin and in Renaissance Platonism," *JHI*, 9, 454.

1. *Institutes*, II. i. viii, II. ii. iii, II. ii. xii, II. ii. xix, and II. ii. xv.

2. In Barker's judgment Milton accepted "without substantial variations, the Calvinistic doctrine of man's original corruption. . . . His opinion of the powers of fallen and unregenerate man was no whit higher than Calvin's." *Milton and the Puritan Dilemma*, p. 305.

3. See Woodhouse, "Milton, Puritanism, and Liberty," *University of Toronto Quarterly*, 4 (1935), 483 ff.

tinguished between the primary and the secondary laws of nature, a distinction basically foreign to the thought of Aquinas. The primary law of nature is that which was engraven on the heart of Adam; the secondary law of nature is the law of fallen human nature. In the *Christian Doctrine* Milton asserts that the primary law of nature " in the regenerate, under the influence of the Holy Spirit, is daily tending towards a renewal of its primitive brightness." [4] It is only the truly regenerate who can claim full Christian liberty under the primary law of nature, and for them the entire Mosaic Law is abrogated. [5]

Against this background of speculation the answer to the question raised by Woodhouse and Barker, [6] whether Milton succeeded in integrating the orders of nature and grace, becomes largely a matter of definition. If by " nature " is meant the nature of fallen man, it is obvious that Milton, with his Calvinistic view of the potentialities of fallen human nature, saw nothing but irreconcilable conflict between nature and grace, " supernal Grace contending / With sinfulness of Men " (*P. L.*, XI, 359-60). If by " nature " is meant the so-called natural virtues, Milton certainly did not repudiate nature, but he recognized that it is insufficient without the Christian virtues of faith, hope, love, patience, and obedience—the fruits of grace. Christ in *Paradise Regained* admits that in some pagan writers " moral virtue is express'd/ By light of Nature not in all quite lost " (IV, 351-2). But even this knowledge is obscured, and of man's supernatural destiny they have no knowledge at all:

> Ignorant of themselves, of God much more,
> And how the world began, and how man fell
> Degraded by himself, on grace depending.
>
> (*P. R.*, IV, 310-12)

If by " nature," however, is meant nature in its primitive integrity, then Milton envisages no conflict between nature and grace, since in the regenerate, under the influence of grace, the primary law of nature " is daily tending towards a renewal of its primitive brightness." What complicates the question is that while theoretically Milton's doctrine of pure nature and the regeneration of the Elect aligned him with the more extreme Protestants, in practice his humanistic definition of pure nature aligned him with the Catholic tradition of Aquinas and Hooker. He

4. II. xxvi, in Patterson, p. 1024. See Barker, *Dilemma*, pp. 116-18, 176-7.

5. Woodhouse, *UTQ*, 4, 487.

6. Barker considers the question of the integration of nature and grace the central concern of Milton's artistic life. He feels that in *Comus* this integration is not achieved because the Lady's doctrine of virginity is a negative one, a denial of nature. *Dilemma*, pp. 8-11. See above, pp. 205-13.

is therefore able to incorporate in his idea of regenerate nature many elements that the more extreme Puritans regarded as works of fallen human nature, such as human art and learning and even the pleasures of the flesh.

In one respect, however, Milton carried his doctrine of pure nature to its logical conclusion by demanding with other Puritans a clean sweep of those institutions and customs that representatives of the Catholic tradition like Hooker had defended in the name of Nature. In the central classical-Christian tradition, the institutions, laws, conventions, and customs that have developed in the course of centuries are themselves "natural" insofar as they are expressions of man's attempt to participate in the eternal law by the exercise of reason. " The love of things ancient doth argue stayedness," says Hooker, " but levity and want of experience maketh apt unto innovations. . . . antiquity, custom, and consent in the Church of God, making with that which law doth establish, are themselves most sufficient reasons to uphold the same, unless some notable public inconvenience enforce the contrary." [7] Hooker does not deny that there may be " lewd and wicked " and " corrupt and unreasonable " customs,[8] but custom and experience are not to be outweighed by the reason of any one man: " Sharp and subtile discourses of wit procure many times very great applause, but being laid in the balance with that which the habit of sound experience plainly delivereth, they are overweighted." [9] And in the Dedicatory Epistle to Archbishop Whitgift Hooker derides those who give " too much credit . . . to their own wits, for which cause they are seldom free from error."

Now Milton, in spite of the many similarities between his thought and that of Hooker, has an entirely different conception of the relationship between nature, reason, and custom. For him, as for Puritans in general, custom and " fallen " reason are a corruption of pure nature:

> But let them chant while they will of prerogatives, we shall tell them of scripture; of custom, we of scripture; of acts and statutes, still of scripture; till the quick and piercing word enter to the dividing of their souls, and the mighty weakness of the gospel throw down the weak mightiness of man's reasoning.[1]

In this passage Scripture is opposed to custom; in the following passage from *The Tenure of Kings and Magistrates* reason is opposed to custom:

---

7. *Ecclesiastical Polity*, V. vii. 3.

8. Ibid., I. viii. 11, and I. x. 10.

9. Ibid., V. vii. 1.

1. *The Reason of Church Government Urged against Prelaty*, II. ii., in Patterson, p. 528.

If men within themselves would be governed by reason, and not generally give up their understanding to a double tyranny of custom from without, and blind affections within, they would discern better what it is to favor and uphold the tyrant of a nation.[2]

Milton is not referring to the reason of fallen man but to the reason of those who have been deputized by God:

Hence it is, that error supports custom, custom countenances error; and these two between them would persecute and chase away all truth and solid wisdom out of human life, were it not that God, rather than man, once in many ages calls together the prudent and religious counsels of men, deputed to repress the incroachments, and to work off the inveterate blots and obscurities wrought upon our minds by the subtle insinuating of error and custom.[3]

Similarly, in his note on the verse of *Paradise Lost* Milton defends his use of blank verse by saying that those modern poets who have adopted rhyme have been "carried away by Custom, but much to their own vexation, hindrance, and constraint to express many things otherwise, and for the most part worse than else they would have exprest them." Daniel, it will be recalled, had defended rhyme precisely because it was customary and hence in a sense natural:

Custome that is before all Law, Nature that is aboue all Arte. Euery language hath her proper number or measure fitted to vse and delight, which Custome, intertaininge by the allowance of the Eare, doth indenize and make naturall.

The Generall Custome and vse of Ryme in this kingdome, Noble Lord, hauing beene so long (as if from a Graunt of Nature) held vnquestionable, made me to imagine that it lay altogither out of the way of contradiction, and was become so natural, as we should neuer haue had a thought to cast it off into reproch, or be made to thinke that it ill-became our language.[4]

In spite of his frequent diatribes against religious, political, and literary "custom," however, Milton is no enemy to art. In the well-known passage from *The Reason of Church Government* in which he speaks of his poetic plans, he says that he had resolved to "fix all the industry and art I could unite to the adorning of my native tongue."

---

2. *The Tenure of Kings and Magistrates*, in Patterson, p. 754.

3. *The Doctrine and Discipline of Divorce*, in Patterson, p. 573.

4. Samuel Daniel, *A Defence of Ryme*, in *Elizabethan Critical Essays*, ed. G. Gregory Smith (London, Oxford University Press, 1904), 2, 359, 357.

> Time serves not now, and perhaps I might seem too profuse to
> give any certain account of what the mind at home, in the spacious
> circuits of her musing, hath liberty to propose to herself . . .
> whether the rules of Aristotle herein are strictly to be kept, or
> nature to be followed, which in them that know art, and use judg-
> ment, is no transgression, but an enriching of art. . . .[5]

But true art, like true reason, belongs only to the regenerate:

> For doubtless that indeed according to art is most eloquent, which
> returns and approaches nearest to nature, from whence it came;
> and they express nature best, who in their lives least wander from
> her safe leading, which may be called regenerate reason.[6]

There is thus a theoretical distinction between Hooker's and Milton's
conceptions of reason. Hooker, conscious of the fallibility of the individual, appeals to the historical reason of mankind; Milton, conscious
of his own sense of election, says that ". . . reason is the gift of God
in one man as well as in a thousand."[7] Actually, however, Milton's
reason was nourished by the same tradition of Christian humanism as
Hooker's, and it is not surprising that there should be many points of
contact between them. Nevertheless, they differ in the role each would
assign to "custom," and there seems to be no question that Milton's
conception of regenerate reason represents a movement away from the
rationalism of Hooker toward the Rationalism of the Enlightenment.
The difference, of course, is that in the classical Enlightenment reason
is regenerated by nature; in the Christian Milton it is regenerated by
grace.

The Poetic Vision

Not to define Milton's idea of Nature in the abstract, however, but
to explore his poetic use of the idea of Nature has been the principal
object of this study. Though Milton certainly was not averse to
abstract definition, he was usually able to incorporate it in the larger
poetic unity. Even in *Comus* the Lady wins her argument not so much
in the intellectual debate with the Tempter as in the imagery of nature
so skilfully employed by Milton, in the two opposing visions of nature
perverted by Comus and elevated and irradiated by Divine Grace. In
Paradise Lost also, the idea of Nature is central to both the intellectual
and poetic structures. Physical nature and human nature alike are

5. Patterson, p. 525.
6. *Apology for Smectymnuus*, in Patterson, p. 543. See above, pp. 264-5
for a discussion of this theme as it appears in *Paradise Lost*.
7. *Animadversions*, in Patterson, p. 485.

shown to be inadequate without God. In the description of Chaos we
see the blind, purposeless activity of Epicurean matter, a universe without meaning; and in the account of the activities of fallen angel and
fallen man we see the horror of human nature left to its own devices.
Over against these visions of disorder and aimlessness stand the two
great creative acts of God: the creation of the physical universe and the
re-creation of the spiritual Paradise with its metaphorical fruits in the
mind of regenerate man. But Milton's symbolic use of the idea of
Nature is more complex than this. In itself, outer nature as created
by God is good, but in *Paradise Lost* as in *Comus* Milton frequently
uses outer nature to reflect the inner natures of the men who inhabit it.
The most obvious example of this is the descent of Adam from the
Garden of Essences to the Wilderness of Existence. A more subtle
example is the description of the " nether Flood,"

> Which from his darksome passage now appears,
> And now divided into four main Streams,
> Runs diverse, wand'ring many a famous Realm
> And Country whereof here needs no account,
> But rather to tell how, if Art could tell,
> How from that Sapphire Fount the crisped Brooks,
> Rolling on Orient Pearl and sands of Gold,
> With mazy error under pendant shades
> Ran Nectar . . .   (IV, 232-40)

" Darksome," " wand'ring," and " mazy error " do not imply that
Nature is already fallen; they speak, paradoxically, of a Nature that is
innocent but capable of falling, of a Nature in which, as Arnold Stein
has said, there is " rightness of wandering—before the concept of error
is introduced into man's world and comes to signify wrong wandering." [8] This dangerous ambivalence in nature—or rather in man's attitude toward nature—is even more strikingly revealed in the following
passage, where the mining of gold is implicitly compared to the creation
of Eve from Adam's rib:

> Soon had his crew
> Op'n'd into the Hill a spacious wound
> And digg'd out ribs of Gold. Let none admire
> That riches grow in Hell; that soil may best
> Deserve the precious bane.   (I, 688-92)

" Precious bane " precisely describes not only Eve but the whole of
created nature for which she stands. The proper attitude toward

8. *Answerable Style* (Minneapolis, University of Minnesota Press, 1953),
pp. 66-7.

nature, as Adam himself says, is to see it as the scale " whereon / In contemplation of created things / By steps we may ascend to God " (V, 510-12), and his love for Eve, Raphael tells him, " is the scale / By which to heav'nly Love thou may'st ascend" (VIII, 591-2). But instead of ascending from the literal to the metaphoric, " From shadowy Types to Truth, from Flesh to Spirit " (XII, 303), Adam, like Solomon, " Beguil'd by fair Idolatresses, fell / To Idols foul " (I, 445-6). The sequence *fair-fell-foul*, with its alliteration and its artful regression from front to back vowels, sums up for us the fall of Adam from the Garden to the Wilderness. At the crucial moment Adam seems to forget that " beauty is excell'd by manly grace / And wisdom, which alone is truly fair " (IV, 490-1).

But there is another vision: the vision of fallen human nature regenerated and raised to a supernatural level. When Adam and Eve " prostrate fell " before God and watered the ground with their tears (X, 1099-1102), the " first fruits " of God's " implanted Grace in Man " sprang up on earth (XI, 22-3). Though the literal Paradise is destroyed by the Flood, a " paradise within . . . happier far " (XII, 587) will be " rais'd in the waste Wilderness" (*P. R.*, I, 7). Christ will join man's nature to His own and sit incarnate on the Throne of God (*P. L.*, III, 282, 314-15). The nature of this union between man and Christ, between human nature and divine nature, is defined in *Paradise Regained*, where the rudiments of our warfare with " Satanic strength / And all the world, and mass of sinful flesh " (*P. R.*, I, 161-2) are laid down by the Great Exemplar. But this vision, like those of Raphael and Michael, is too abstract, too " angelic." It needs to be completed by *Samson Agonistes*, where we see in the figure of Samson existential man, blind, groping, agonized, enslaved. Only to a chosen few in each age is given the inward vision of pure nature enjoyed by the blind Poet-Priest; the rest of us, like Samson, " see through a glass darkly," " groaning and travailing in pain," waiting with St. Paul for the redemption of created nature.